# GEORGE FREDERICK BRISTOW

## AMERICAN

## *Composers*

A list of books in the series appears
at the end of this book.

# George
# Frederick
# Bristow

*Katherine K. Preston*

UNIVERSITY OF
ILLINOIS PRESS
Urbana, Chicago, and Springfield

Publication supported by a grant from the
Henry and Edna Binkele Classical Music Fund.

Library of Congress Cataloging-in-Publication Data
Names: Preston, Katherine K., author.
Title: George Frederick Bristow / Katherine K. Preston.
Description: Urbana : University of Illinois Press, 2020. |
    Series: American composers | Includes bibliographical
    references and index.
Identifiers: LCCN 2020020082 (print) | LCCN 2020020083
    (ebook) | ISBN 9780252043420 (cloth) | ISBN
    9780252085321 (paperback) | ISBN 9780252052309
    (ebook)
Subjects: LCSH: Bristow, George Frederick, 1825–1898. |
    Composers—United States—Biography.
Classification: LCC ML410.B8523 P74 2020 (print) |
    LCC ML410.B8523 (ebook) | DDC 780.92 [B]—dc23
LC record available at https://lccn.loc.gov/2020020082
LC ebook record available at https://lccn.loc.gov/
2020020083

# CONTENTS

# ACKNOWLEDGMENTS

THIS PROJECT STARTED MANY YEARS AGO, with my edition of George Bristow's Symphony No. 2 in D Minor, op. 24 ("Jullien"), published in the Music of the United States of America series (2011). I wrote a lengthy introduction for that edition to make up for the lack of a published biography of Bristow. It did not occur to me that I would be the person to write the biography until several years later, when I had a conversation with Laurie Matheson, director of the University of Illinois Press, in which I pointed out that the very useful American Composers Series published by UIP was heavily weighted toward twentieth-century composers (to the neglect of those from the nineteenth). I suggested that I might be willing to write a volume on Bristow, and she took me up on the offer.

I started the research for this book during my final sabbatical from the College of William & Mary (2017–2018). As the David N. and Margaret C. Bottoms Professor of Music, I had access to some valuable research funds, for which I am very grateful. I was also fortunate enough to be awarded a short-term fellowship from the New York Public Library (NYPL), which allowed me to spend valuable time during summer 2018 carefully examining materials in the Bristow Collection in the Music Division of the Performing Arts Library (PAL). Most of the archival work for this book was conducted there, and I thank the staff of the PAL, especially Jessica Wood, assistant curator for Music and Recorded Sound, and George Boziwick, former chief of the Music Division, who before his retirement was responsible for acquiring from Mrs. Louis T. (Marion) Edwards, niece of Bristow's granddaughter Violet Dearborn Latham, the family letters, photographs, and miscellaneous materials (Bristow Collection, Additions) that have been invaluable for this book. The Swem Library of the College of William & Mary was also important for my research. I thank Kathleen DeLaurenti (then the arts librarian) and, in particular, the invaluable staff of the Interlibrary Loan Department, especially Cynthia Mack (now retired) and Carol Frieden. Several scholars have been particularly helpful in providing advice and in some cases copies of useful primary and secondary source materials. These include Barbara Haws (then archivist of the New York Philharmonic), James Armstrong, Brian Bailey, Douglas Bomberger, Amy Camus, David Crean, John Graziano, Brandon Moss, Barbara Owen, and Joanne Swenson-Eldridge. Douglas Shadle generously shared copies of primary documents from his work on Bristow's symphonies, and N. Lee Orr was an invaluable source of information and advice in the realm of sacred music. Many thanks to the folks with whom I worked at the University of Illinois Press, especially Julie Laut, Tad Ringo, and copyeditor Jill Hughes. And warm thanks to my longtime friend Laurie Mattheson, director of the U of I Press, who made writing and producing this book into a real pleasure. I thank the National Portrait Gallery of the Smithsonian Institution for permission to reprint a portrait of Bristow, and my friends Tony Anemone and Carolyn Holmes for putting me up in New York while I was doing research there at different times. I also thank Jalal Gohari of Queens for answering many questions related to the research done by his late wife, Carol Elaine Gohari, on the Bristow family, and for turning over to me some of her files and notes. Carol's diligent research informs parts of this book. Finally (as always), thank you and much love to my family: my husband, Daniel, and son, William, both of whom are accomplished writers.

# Introduction

$\downarrow$

GEORGE FREDERICK BRISTOW (1825–1898) is best remembered today by scholars of American music for his passionate support for the musicians and music of his native country, primarily through his outspoken participation (along with William Henry Fry) in a journalistic battle in early 1854 with the music critics Richard Storrs Willis (1819–1900) and John Sullivan Dwight (1813–1893). The subject of this battle was the lack of support for American composers by the New York musical establishment in general and the Philharmonic Society of New York in particular. As music historian Vera Lawrence has observed, "Bristow's special significance as an ardent champion and practitioner of American music during the earlier stages of its struggle for recognition can scarcely be overestimated."[1] But his angry denunciations in that very public contretemps helped to create a historical reputation as a hotheaded individual who might even have been sympathetic to the anti-immigrant Know Nothing movement. (See chapter 2.) This image, coupled with a lamentable paucity of personal information and the rather stodgy and somber mien communicated by the few surviving contemporary portraits, has contributed to a characterization of George Bristow as a one-dimensional individual who was serious and conservative (even reactionary), old-fashioned, painfully reticent, and decidedly dull.

Contemporary commentary from letters and the print media, however, reveal a man who was a hardworking and extraordinarily productive composer, a skilled performer, a champion of early nineteenth-century European music, a businessman, an educator, and an ardent proselytizer not just for American composers but also for the transformative power of music in general. He was kind and generous, patient (especially with students), had a droll sense of humor, and was devoted to his family. Perhaps more important than these personal characteristics, however, is his undeniable ability as a composer and a performer, which resulted in a solid reputation among his contemporaries as one of the leading representative musicians in America. He was, in fact, a "highly esteemed composer and musician" who had a profound impact on musical culture in nineteenth-century New York City.[2] His *Oratorio of Daniel*, op. 42 (1866) was admired as "unquestionably the most important composition in this form yet produced by an American composer"; his opera *Rip Van Winkle* (1855) was regularly described as the first grand opera by an American on an American subject; and his orchestral works (overtures and five symphonies) were praised for formal clarity, melodic abundance, and strong orchestration—especially for winds.[3] He also wrote chamber music, songs, piano pieces, secular choral works, and a large number of compositions for church services.[4]

In addition to his enviable record of successful compositions, Bristow was also a skilled violinist, pianist, organist, and conductor. His wide-ranging experience as a performer—in regularly scheduled concerts as well as benefit or miscellaneous events, as a member of supporting ensembles, as an instrumental soloist or member of chamber ensembles, and as a church organist and choir director—provided him with a thorough grounding in the various genres of Western European music. This probably instilled in him an interest in composition, but it also marked him as a typical journeyman musician of the period: a man who taught music (privately and in schools), served as a church organist, performed in or conducted concerts, and in general contributed mightily to the development of musical culture in his hometown. This rich variety of professional activity marks George Bristow as a perfect prototype of an urban journeyman musician, for his career represents, in microcosm, a compendium of the kind of work typically available to nineteenth-century performers, whether American or Western European. Furthermore, the totality of his professional activities illustrates an entire swath of musical culture in mid- and late-century New York City that usually goes unmentioned in studies of music history. This biography, then, is a portrait of both an important American musician whose historical image is seriously in need of correction and of the musical culture that he helped to create.

| I | # "The Life of a Musician" |

*"Troubles and Trials, &c";*
*Emergence as a Composer*

## Childhood and Early Training

George Bristow was the son of William Richard Bristow (1803–1867), who immigrated to the United States from Kent, England, sometime before July 1823, and his wife, Mary Ann (Tapp) Bristow (1805–1880), also a native of England. They married in Brooklyn, New York, in February 1825, and their first child was born there on December 19, 1825.[1] William was well known in both Brooklyn and Manhattan as an organist, clarinetist, conductor, church musician (at St. Patrick's Cathedral in Manhattan and at St. Paul's Church in Brooklyn), theater musician, concert organizer, teacher, general freelance performer, and—according to his son—a prolific composer.[2] The elder Bristow introduced his son to the piano when the latter was but five years old, for according to an unpublished autobiographical sketch that the composer later wrote, his father's greatest hope was that "he might have a son who should also become a musician and a great one."[3] The next big event in young George's life was a trip with his family in 1832, when he was six years old, to the United Kingdom, perhaps to visit other family members; this would be the composer's only known travel outside the United States.[4] During these early years the Bristow family relocated to Manhattan, living at various locations in the Tenth and Seventeenth wards.[5]

The young musician's first public appearance at the keyboard was when he was nine; shortly thereafter he began his professional career in the orchestra of the Park Theatre (where his father worked), first playing cymbals and side drum, later graduating to the violin, with his father as teacher.[6] Bristow's portrayal of his father's expectations and tutelage is enlightening although not particularly sympathetic. For example, writing about himself in the third person and as a member of the "Apollo family," he explains that when he started to play violin in this orchestra, he was "not sufficiently advanced to play all the music that was put before him." This jeopardized his new position, which, according to George, infuriated his father, who "did not stop to think that his son was having the very life crushed out of him" as a result of these expectations.[7]

In 1838 the young violinist and his clarinetist father moved to the National Theatre, and from there to the Olympic Theatre in Manhattan (in 1839).[8] By this time young George had advanced significantly in his violin playing as the result of a constant diet of "scales, and exercises, and nothing else." But although the thirteen-year-old musician could play the music "well enough," he was "not a good reader." This presented a problem, for the musicians of this ensemble were "expected to do everything, sometimes to play without having either seen or heard the music." Happily for young George, however, he was befriended by an older and more patient musician in the orchestra, one William Musgrif (or Musgriff), apparently an accomplished cellist active in New York. Because of the cellist's help, Bristow remembered, he "was able to get on a little better," although he admitted that he still "hated music" and resented having to pursue the career that his father had chosen for him.[9]

The repertoire of the Olympic was both "entirely different" from what he was used to and more challenging in ways that eventually would be beneficial. "The plays," he wrote, "were of the Burlesque, and Extravaganza kind . . . [with] occasionally an Opera, or pieces with operatic selections, all of which was certainly new to the boy." There was, in fact, a particular operatic selection that brought about a "somewhat sudden change, a conversion to the belief that there was something good and beautiful in music," which occurred when the young violinist was thirteen or fourteen (during his second year at the Olympic). The stirring "Liberty Duett from Puritani," as he described it ("Suoni la tromba" from Vincenzo Bellini's opera), was interpolated into one of the plays mounted at the theater. The melody, he wrote, "was so different from anything he had heard before, so striking &c [that] he thought there was a fire in it which would stir up anybody, and from this period did our young violinist take a start. Yes, a veritable jump!" By this time Musgrif was both George's mentor and his teacher, and with the cellist's advice and encouragement, young Apollo "began to think it *was* possible for him to do something in music, to play well, to even compose." As a result, the boy "made up his mind" to succeed at music—despite his father—and "he went to work with a right good will," practicing "early and late, never flagging." George quickly mastered both violin and piano as the result of tenacious, self-imposed ← work; Musgrif clearly had a profound impact on the future composer.[10]

Bristow's account of his childhood experiences is illuminating, both for the information it provides about the early training of a child musician in New York and for the rare glimpses into his personality. He provides copious details about his ambitious father, whom he portrays as a relentless tyrant who used as incentive "the oil of strap," which "had a very lubricating effect, for without it, little or nothing would have been done [by the boy] in the way of Music." He refers to himself as a "poor wretch" who "was compelled to scrape, scrape, scrape until he was able to take his place in a minor theatre as second violin" and resented the fact that his father pocketed all of his earnings. In essence, his description is of a stolen childhood, for he was expected to be "up early and late" and experienced "no pleasure, no nothing, but the same old hum-drum life, and all before he was 12 years old." It is remarkable, however, that Bristow's account—although vivid and horrifying from a modern point of view—is not bitter but rather almost dispassionate. He tacitly implies, in fact, that his father had made it possible for him to take the "veritable jump" when, with the help of a more patient and understanding mentor, he discovered fire in music and became determined to feed it. George Bristow, however, eventually decided to follow the example of his mentor rather than that of his father; as we shall see, he later became an effective but patient and gentle teacher. As he observed in his essay, "Encouragement is a good thing for children, and at the proper time is of incalculable benefit." It also probably helped that, as the result of his hard work, Bristow soon outstripped his father as a performer, which he indicates was deeply satisfying.[11]

After working at the Olympic Theatre for some time, Bristow noted "a great change." The leader had resigned and a new conductor, whom he described as a "vain, good hearted, fat, fussy, little Englishman" and "the leader of the [Philharmonic] Society," took over. This was the British composer and conductor George Loder (1816–1868), who started at the theater in 1840.[12] It took "some time" for Bristow and this new leader "to understand each other," but he explained that eventually they "became fine, firm friends." This was a crucial relationship because it led to an invitation to the young violinist to join the orchestra of the newly formed Philharmonic Society, apparently in 1842. This made the young violinist "supremely happy," until he learned that because "nearly every member" of the seven-person Olympic Theatre orchestra had also joined the Philharmonic Society, Loder decided that some of the musicians had to hold down the fort at the theater. (The other musicians could hire substitutes, as was the custom.)[13] Loder informed the two Bristows (perhaps because William had not been invited) that they had to perform at the Olympic when theater performances conflicted with Philharmonic Society concerts. George relates that he was allowed to attend the society's rehearsals but not to perform in concerts for his entire first year as a member. If this account is true, then he was one of the charter members of the society, although (because he was not performing) his name is not included on any reconstructed lists of orchestra members during 1842–1843.[14]

George was chagrined at be "stuck in a theatre to fiddle" instead of playing the "sublime strains" performed by the Philharmonic Society. As revenge, he decided to play pranks on the substitute musicians. He describes his tomfoolery in his autobiography: pouring water into an unattended trombone, with easily imagined results; surreptitiously oiling the bow of the cellist, who, when he started to draw "a strong bow . . . with the dignity of a Spanish Grandee . . . nearly wheeled himself off the stool . . . onto the Double Bass player who was standing next to him"; adding lamp oil to the snuff that orchestra members (including his father) used after intermission, which resulted in "such sneezings and coughings" that the musicians could hardly play the *entre-act* music. Such acts, of course, were childish but were undertaken by a "young scamp" (as Bristow referred to himself) who may have been a prodigy but was nevertheless still a young and immature boy—and one with a sense of humor.[15]

As Bristow points out, he eventually grew older and wiser and "left off playing tricks." He did not, however, "leave off" his musical study, which "was always faithfully attended to." During the society's second year (1843–1844), Loder allowed George to become a performing member of the orchestra's first violin section. He already knew Musgrif, Loder, and others from the Olympic Theatre ensemble and, if he had been attending rehearsals during 1842–1843, must have felt right at home during his first performing year.[16] This move meant another dramatically increased set of performance expectations for a violinist who was not yet seventeen years old but who later would be described by the *Message Bird: A Literary and Musical Journal* as "having grown up in an orchestra." By this point he had begun "to think that he could take a higher place in the world, than that of playing the violin in the theatre," and welcomed the challenge of mastering "the Great Orchestral works of the Old Masters."[17] (The recollections and terminology, of course, are of a man who was probably in his forties.)

## A Career Starts to Blossom

Bristow's status after 1843 as a full-fledged performing member of the city's only permanent orchestra helped to satiate his hunger for the "masterworks"; it also provided him entrée into important New York music circles. His first appearance as a conductor had occurred in 1842, but his activities as a performer started to accelerate in the middle of the decade. In 1846, for example, Ureli Corelli Hill (1802–1875) and four other Philharmonic Society members invited him to join them as pianist in a performance of Henri Bertini's Piano Sextet No. 3 in E Major, op. 90. A year later he directed the Philharmonic Society's premiere performance of his first published orchestral piece, the Concert Overture in E-flat Major, op. 3, and in the same year made his keyboard debut with the orchestra in Johann Nepomuk Hummel's (1778–1837) Piano Concerto in A-flat, performing with a pickup ensemble under George Loder, primarily of Philharmonic Society members. Two years later he conducted the premiere performance of the cantata *Eleutheria: A Hymn to Liberty* by his friend George Henry Curtis (1821–1895), which he had orchestrated.[18]

As Bristow later recalled, the performance of the Hummel concerto, when he was sixteen, was seminal. He recounted the audience reaction in his memoirs: the performance elicited "such a storm of applause, as would cheer the heart of Liszt himself. [Young Apollo] is called, and re-called, he bears his success modestly; receives compliments in showers, various are the remarks made on this occasion,—such as who is this young Apollo? How well he plays! I have never heard of him before! And how should they, when he was cooped up in a theatre all his life!" This event, he wrote, marked the beginning of his musical career. Now he "was much sought after" as a performer. "Many were the invitations he received to attend parties, soirées, &c" but not "from any particular regard . . . for him as a man [but rather] because he played well." Suddenly, "if any religious, or charitable association required any assistance, young Apollo was immediately requested, either to give a concert or [to] play at one."[19] These insights illustrate both the important role of music in the social lives of New Yorkers in the 1840s and an undeniably upward arc to young Bristow's career. But there was a negative side to all of this activity: Bristow "acceded to these requests" regularly because he was young, naïve, and "totally unacquainted with the ways of the world." Unfortunately, however, the engagements were "*always without remuneration.*" He was still supporting himself by working in the theater, but eventually the number of times he absented himself from his regular job in order "to attend to the many concerts, parties, &c, for which he received *no pay*" led to his dismissal. Although he was still a member of the Philharmonic Society, that organization gave only four concerts per year and was not at all the source of a living wage. He also was an organist in a small unnamed church, but the salary, he reports, was only $125 per year (about $4,350 purchasing power in 2019 dollars). After some sober reflection, young Bristow attempted to get his theater job back, but his place had already been filled; as he wryly observed, "Fiddlers [were] as plentiful as blackberries in July." Faced with few options for supporting himself, he eventually turned to teaching music, at the suggestion of an older musical colleague.[20] (See Interlude A.)

During this period, Bristow assiduously worked at his musical skills and continued to mature and improve, in part by taking advantage of the rich musical culture available in the city. As he wrote, "young Apollo" "had heard the great players, both on the violin and Piano, who had visited the city," and he had been inspired by them, especially as he considered himself (in comparison) a "nobody." But he "sought their acquaintance . . . [and] took lessons of them . . . and to their credit . . . they rendered him every assistance in their power." One of these visiting musicians was the pianist Henri Herz (1803–1888). According to critic and editor Travis Quigg (ca. 1830–1893), while that virtuoso was visiting New York in early 1847, young Bristow—who "had become quite an accomplished pianist"— visited Herz's boardinghouse every morning to play "duets with him." Another visitor was the English composer George Alexander Macfarren (1813–1887), who lived in New York briefly (1847 through most of 1848). Quigg reports that "Mr. Macfarren took a great liking for and an interest in young Bristow, who was not only an apt pupil, but an insatiable searcher after musical knowledge." The young American was grateful for all of this support and encouragement and later wrote in his sketch that this willingness to help others was a characteristic of "all true musicians, who are ever ready to help a brother artist, when they see he is willing to help himself," which suggests that the musical community in New York during this period was close-knit. Bristow clearly wanted to be a contributing member of this group, and his own "determination to be great was now stronger than ever." Over time Bristow studied violin with both C. W. Meyrer (another founding member of the Philharmonic Society) and the Norwegian virtuoso Ole Bull (1810–1880); composition and orchestration with the organist, pianist, and trombonist Henry Christian Timm (1811–1892, also a charter member of the Philharmonic); and composition with Macfarren.[21] His musical tutelage, although mostly from European immigrants, was conducted entirely in New York.

Eventually Bristow was sufficiently skilled and well known as a violinist and pianist that he could resume (or continue) his work as a freelance musician—but now for remuneration. Like most other rank-and-file performing musicians of the time, he played regularly in the usual assortment of concerts that were a normal part of the urban cultural landscape. For example, during the 1840s he spent several summers (when theaters were typically dark) playing in small orchestras assembled for regular summer concert series. He also performed in concerts as a member of the Euterpean Club, appeared as a pianist in a complimentary event for journalist Richard Storrs Willis, participated in vocal concerts as an accompanist or ensemble director, and performed in private entertainments.[22] Activities of this nature set the stage for a burgeoning career as a working musician, which would expand during the 1850s and 1860s.

## Cultural Life in New York at Mid-Century

The musicians with whom young George Bristow studied in New York—and the "great players" whose performances inspired him—were mostly Europeans. They were among a large cadre of instrumentalists, singers, ensemble members, soloists, composers, and teachers who either immigrated outright to the United States or visited the country, organized performance tours, and subsequently either went back to Europe or decided to stay in America. These immigrants, who spread out all over the country, contributed mightily to an emerging musical culture in the United States.

The late 1840s were the foundational period for the performance culture that was developing in North America. The year 1847, for example, served as a threshold for the performance of English- and Italian-language opera mounted by itinerant companies, in part because of the arrival in 1848 of two important impresarios, Max Maretzek (1821–1897) and Maurice Strakosch (1825–1887). Both would use New York as the base for their touring companies and would have a profound impact on the performance of opera in America for decades to come.[23] The increased number of opera companies, combined with the ever improving caliber of the troupes, also had a positive impact on the performance of instrumental music, as opera companies needed good instrumental performers for adequate accompaniment. As Frédéric Louis Ritter (1834–1891) remembered in 1883, "Since the musical forms of opera rest upon fine instrumental accompaniments, efficient orchestral bands become necessary in order to do justice to such accompaniments."[24]

In fact, there were countless European vocalists, singing families, pianists, violinists, double bassists, and other instrumentalists active on the American stage during the 1840s, 1850s, and later. Some of them conducted high-profile concert tours; others relocated to the New World and began to teach, organize concerts, compose, and perform. The itinerant instrumental ensembles that visited from

Europe in the 1840s included the Styrian (or Steyermarkische) Orchestra (1846) as well as three groups that arrived in 1848: the Gung'l and Saxonian orchestras and the Germania Musical Society.[25] This greatly increased the number of trained singers and instrumentalists living in the United States, thereby adding to and improving both the performance and audience pools for concerts.[26] This continuous influx of European musicians not only contributed to the development of a rich musical culture in New York and elsewhere but also encouraged the creation of vocal and instrumental ensembles in cities all over the country. Some of the groundwork for the upsurge in local musical activity was laid in the 1830s with the establishment of many "standing" performance organizations (including musical fund and sacred music societies) in various places, mostly on the eastern seaboard.[27] The 1840s also saw an increase in the number of instrumental organizations (such as wind bands and philharmonic societies) in places like Milwaukee, Boston, St. Louis, and New Orleans.[28]

New York, however, was the largest urban area in the United States in the 1840s and 1850s; it was three times larger than second-place Baltimore in both decades. As a result, New York had more established ensembles than any other urban area during the period of young Bristow's musical coming of age. The first important choral society established in Bristow's hometown was the New York Sacred Music Society (1823–1849); in the latter year it merged with a rival, the American Musical Institute (founded in 1846), to become the New York Harmonic Society, an organization that Bristow would later direct. German singing societies also emerged in the late 1840s and early 1850s. The Philharmonic Society of New York, as mentioned, was founded in 1842, the third organization of that name in the city and the only one to endure into the twenty-first century (now the New York Philharmonic Orchestra). In 1851 the German immigrant conductor Theodore Eisfeld (1816–1882) organized a series of string quartet concerts, and several years later William Mason (1829–1908) and Theodore Thomas (1835–1905) founded the Mason and Thomas Chamber Music Soirées (1855–1868). New York could also boast of numerous local wind bands, including the National Brass Band founded by Allen Dodworth (1817–1896) in 1835. Other wind ensembles organized by the Dodworths, Claudio Grafulla, and Patrick Gilmore (1829–1892) proliferated during the 1840s, 1850s, and later. In 1855, for example, newspaper advertisements mention numerous active wind bands, including the New York Brass Band, the American Brass Band, the German Cotillion Band, and others. And in 1857 another orchestra emerged in the greater New York area—the Philharmonic Society of Brooklyn (which was still separate from Manhattan), which Bristow immediately joined as a violinist.[29]

Adding bulk to this rich musical stew were hundreds of local musicians (like the Bristows) who played in the ensembles that accompanied the most popular and ubiquitous forms of public entertainment at the time: theatrical productions and dances. In general, musical performances were a regular and expected part of all sorts of public and private events, such as commencements, festivals, benefit performances, musical evenings, "monster" concerts, picnics, soirées, promenade concerts, informal entertainments, and charity affairs. The variety of musical styles represented in these events illustrates well the richness of musical life in New York during the mid-century period, for the repertoires performed by these musicians included symphonic works; music for marching and concert bands; solo compositions (sonatas, potpourris, dances, variations) for piano, violin, and other instruments; chamber music; theatrical music; operas; oratorios; cantatas; dances; glees; and various kinds of popular songs.

George Bristow, who turned twenty-four in late 1850, was by that time completely engaged in the New York musical scene as an accomplished and recognized performer. In the mid to late 1840s, he participated regularly in informal chamber music sessions at the home of double bassist James Pirsson. The group included pianists Henry Timm and William Scharfenberg; violinists William Vincent Wallace, Michele Rapetti, Joseph Noll, and Louis Wiegers; cellist Alfred Boucher; flutist Jullian Siede; oboist Señor de Ribas, and others. Bristow later remembered that these musicians would rendezvous at Pirsson's home to play chamber works by Beethoven, Mozart, Haydn, Louis Spohr (1784–1859), and others, "almost without intermission from 8 o'clock in the evening to midnight." In fact, he reported, sometimes he would play "until I have seen the day break on my way home, which was only a short distance from Pirsson's house." The participants, Bristow reported, were all associated with the Philharmonic Society, "and there was a genuine feeling of brotherly affection between musicians—an artist feeling which must be felt to be appreciated."[30]

By the late 1840s and early 1850s, George Bristow was increasingly sought out for concert performances as a solo or chamber music performer on both violin and piano. He publicly performed string trios (by William Sterndale Bennett and Hummel) with George Loder and Alfred Boucher (1846); violin and piano duos (by Herz, Charles Philippe Lafont, George Osborne, and Charles-Auguste de Bériot) with his friend Curtis on piano (1850); and an unidentified double quartet by Spohr (probably his Double String Quartet No. 4, in G Minor, op. 136), with William Vincent Wallace and others, mostly from the Philharmonic (1851). During that year he was quite active as a chamber artist, especially in several concert series; the chamber works included arrangements for septet of two of

Beethoven's overtures (with many of the musicians he had played chamber music with informally). In 1852 he performed in Spohr's Quintet in C Minor, op. 52, and sextets by Friedrich Ernst Fesca and Bertini. [31]

Bristow also appeared regularly during these years as a featured pianist, performing a piano sextet by Bertini (with four string players from the Philharmonic, 1846), Herz's *Grand Nocturne* and *Polka de Concert* (1850), and duos for piano and violin (by Julius Benedict and de Bériot) with Theodore Thomas on violin (1853). [32] He was likewise featured as a soloist with the Philharmonic Society in 1850 and 1851, performing Johann Kalliwoda's *Grand Duo for Two Violins and Orchestra* (April 1850), Ludwig Maurer's *Concertante for Four Violins and Orchestra* (May 1850), and a repeat performance (from 1847) of the Hummel concerto (1851). [33]

During this time there were also numerous opportunities for young Bristow to perform in large ensembles and expand his conducting experience. In September 1850 (and again in May 1851), for example, he served in the first violin section of the orchestra that accompanied the soprano Jenny Lind (1820–1887) in her spectacularly successful series of New York concerts under conductor Julius Benedict (1804–1885). [34] Later in 1851 he replaced Theodore Eisfeld as conductor of the New York Sacred Harmonic Society (later the New York Harmonic Society), a position he would hold for over a decade. (See chapters 3–4.) In late 1852 William Henry Fry hired him to conduct the musical illustrations for his series of eleven lectures on the "History and Esthetics of Music" (from November 1852 through February 1853), which gave Bristow the opportunity to conduct operatic arias, symphonic works, excerpts from oratorios, "Medieval" and "Oriental" selections, and both choral and solo sacred compositions. (See chapter 2.) In 1853 Bristow was one of the many Philharmonic Society members who joined the Jullien Orchestra, under the direction of the virtuoso French conductor Louis Antoine Jullien (1812–1860), for its extensive concert seasons in New York in autumn 1853 and spring 1854. And in spring 1855 he performed as accompanist for the stars of the Pyne and Harrison English Opera Company on their concert tour, after which he was named musical director of the troupe during its summer season at Niblo's Garden Theatre, where he conducted the premiere performance of his opera *Rip Van Winkle*. [35]

## George Bristow: Emerging Composer

The increasing amount of freelance work in which Bristow engaged as a performer, coupled with the repertoire he played with the Philharmonic Society, significantly expanded his musical horizons in the 1840s and early 1850s; this exposed him to a wide range of contemporary (and older) European compositions. This solid grounding in various types of European musical styles also undoubtedly influenced his budding voice as a composer. Composition, in fact, was something in which he was very interested. The already mentioned epiphany he had experienced as a member of the Olympic Theatre orchestra inspired the young musician "to think it was possible . . . to do something in music, to play well, to even compose." In fact, his first published work—a set of waltzes for piano—dates from 1840, the year he turned fourteen.[36]

As might be expected, most of the compositions that Bristow wrote as a fledgling composer during the 1840s are for voice or piano. He wrote at least five songs (there are also undated songs, some perhaps from this period), including several sentimental tunes and an adaptation of a minstrel show work. His earliest published song, "The Rum-Seller's Farewell," is clearly aimed at a particular market, as it was "Respectfully dedicated to the Cold Spring Temperance Society of New York." But he also wrote serious works for voice: William Treat Upton described Bristow's 1846 song "Thine Eye Hath Seen the Spot" as "simple and genuine" and "quite unusually rich and effective, a distinctly new note in American music of the day."[37] The young composer's sixteen works for the piano from this period, however, are clearly aimed at the popular market. They are mostly duets, dances (waltzes, quicksteps, a march), and arrangements (such as "Dream of the Ocean," an 1849 arrangement of a melody by Joseph Gung'l). He also used tunes from the minstrel stage as the basis for piano compositions, including variation sets on pieces like "Dandy Jim from Caroline," "Miss Lucy Long," and "The Boatman's Dance," as well as a quickstep inspired by "Old Dan Tucker" (and written by "F. G. Wotsirb," another example of the composer's quirky sense of humor).[38] That ten of these piano pieces were published indicates the popularity of such works.

Bristow was also very interested in chamber music at this point in his life—aided, no doubt, by his frequent performances of this style of music (both private and public) during the 1840s and early 1850s. The vast majority of such works, in fact, date from the period 1844 to 1849. They include two duos for violin and viola (one in G major, the other in G minor, both from 1845); two string quartets (op. 1 in F major and op. 2 in G minor), and the Violin Sonata in G, op. 12, the latter three all from around 1849. He also wrote three chamber works for violin and piano, including the *Duo concertante* (1844, revised in 1850 as *La cracovian pour le Violon*, op.13); *Fantasia Zampa*, op. 17 (1844); and *Friendship: Morceau for the Violin*, op. 25 (1855). Although these works are almost entirely unknown today, Rogers asserts that they are the "most important" of Bristow's instrumental compositions, perhaps in part because of that scholar's tendency to dismiss the orchestral works. Nevertheless, the chamber compositions deserve to be better known.[39]

Apparently only the Quartet No. 2, op. 2, has been performed since the nineteenth century.[40] It is in four movements, all in the home key of G minor except for the second. The first violin dominates the quartet, although Bristow also provides the cello with occasional solos. The first movement, Allegro moderato, is a good example. In sonata form, it commences with a yearning theme for the first violin, followed by a more optimistic secondary theme in the dominant major that is introduced by the cello. This leads to a brief dialogue between the two instruments. The development features solos by both cello and first violin and explores the dotted rhythms introduced in the exposition. It is somewhat harmonically adventurous, modulating to C minor and B major before returning to the home key of G minor. The second movement, Andante, in D major, consists of a lilting rounded-binary theme followed by five variations (mostly elaborations on the theme) that provide some solo passages to each of the instruments. The third movement, titled Menuetto, has more of the character of a fast-paced and upbeat scherzo and features a contrasting trio. The quartet concludes with a dance-like finale (marked *Presto*) that moves like the wind. In modified sonata form, it features both numerous virtuosic passages for the first violin and contrasting slower, more lyrical sections.

Bristow's chamber compositions—and his conducting—clearly suggest the overlap between his performance and compositional activities. This was certainly the case with his appearance at the Tabernacle in New York on April 11, 1849, when he conducted the premiere of Curtis's *Eleutheria*. Bristow, in fact, had orchestrated this work, apparently quite skillfully. Vera Lawrence commented that his contribution "was by far the best thing about the work—not only was the scoring generally good, but in some places [it was] even brilliant."[41] The performers were members of the Sacred Harmonic Society, accompanied by instrumentalists from the Philharmonic Society "and other bands"; the cantata itself (subtitled "A Hymn to Liberty") was intended to illustrate the career of Freedom, "including its Religious as well as Political elements."[42] The reaction of one critic to this work suggests the appeal of cantatas to Americans; he described the genre as "of a similar character to the Oratorio, but to our mind very pleasingly superior, inasmuch as the choruses were of less duration. The solos, recitatives and duett [*sic*] portions were constantly coming to the relief of the more massive portions of the music."[43] *Eleutheria* had an almost immediate repeat performance on April 20 and additional performances in 1850 at Plymouth Church in Brooklyn (Henry Ward Beecher's congregation) and in 1851 at the Apollo Rooms in Manhattan.[44]

Bristow's orchestration success with *Eleutheria* perhaps encouraged him to make his first forays into composing for large ensembles, for shortly thereafter he produced the previously mentioned Concert Overture, op. 3 (1845) and his Symphony No. 1, op. 10 (*Sinfonia*, 1848), both in E-flat major, as well as three dances, two of them for a Columbia College commencement. The former were the most important of these works; both were performed by the Philharmonic Society—the first in a regular subscription concert on January 9, 1847, the other at a public rehearsal on May 25, 1850.[45] The *Sinfonia* was heard in a second public concert but never in the regular season.[46]

The Concert Overture is scored for a standard early Romantic period orchestra (strings, pairs of flutes, oboes, clarinets, bassoons, trumpets, horns, and timpani) plus a piccolo, two additional horns, and one trombone. Rogers considers it the best of Bristow's early orchestral works and singles out the second theme as an early example of the composer's "sensitivity to orchestral color." But he also suggests that Bristow might have had orchestration help on this piece, for he describes it as superior to that of his next five orchestral works, including the *Sinfonia*.[47] Several critics, including Henry Coad Watson (1818–1875) and Richard Grant White (1822–1885), were encouraging. Watson's assessments (in the *Albion* and the *Mirror*) were mixed, for he noted on one hand "much talent and promise" but on the other pointed out many "reminiscences of the Italian, German, and French schools." He then offered the type of contradictory advice that Bristow (and other American composers) would subsequently hear on a regular basis: that he should go to Europe to study, presumably to learn how composition was really done.[48] White was kinder. Despite some similarities to musical styles of European composers, he noted, Bristow was "no servile imitator." He also wrote that the work was well received by "the audience and the band," with "long and hearty applause." The Concert Overture enjoyed repeat performances several months later and in the 1850s.[49]

Neither the concert program for the premiere performance nor the critics mentioned that this was the first work by a native-born American composer to be performed by the Philharmonic Society, an ensemble that featured mostly European music.[50] In fact, despite the Concert Overture's generally positive reception, another two full years would pass before the orchestra played another American work, Bristow's *Sinfonia*, performed (as mentioned) in a public rehearsal, along with another "American" work—an overture by German conductor and composer Theodore Eisfeld, who had just arrived in New York.[51]

The *Sinfonia* is in four movements, marked [*Andante*] *Allegro vivace*; *Adagio*; *Minuet/Trio*; and *Allegro vivace*. Like the Concert Overture, it is scored for the usual complement of strings and paired winds, supplemented by two horns (four in the final movement), two trumpets, and a trombone.[52] Douglas Shadle suggests that Bristow had tried to follow Watson's advice from two years earlier, specifically "to model himself upon Mozart's instrumental work," and notes a similarity between the opening of Bristow's first movement and the slow introduction of Mozart's Symphony No. 39.[53] After this opening gesture, however, Bristow switched gears. Herrman Saroni (1824–1900) criticized this approach in a scathing review, describing the movement as "a musical chessboard, with a field for each composer from the time of Haydn to Mendelssohn-Bartholdy" (this from one of several critics who regularly advised Americans to study at the feet of the European masters). He also grumbled that the composition was both overlong and monotonous, a criticism that was perhaps justified, as three of the four movements are in the same key. Furthermore, as Shadle points out, Bristow tended to repeat his phrases by reorchestrating them.[54]

But this was the composer's first attempt at a symphony (he was twenty-three years old), and others found much to praise. Julius Schuberth (1804–1875), writing in the *Staats-Zeitung* after a later performance, described it as "full of melody [and] touching and genial passages" and remarked in particular on the "beautiful elaborated motive for the wind instruments at the beginning of the piece." The critic for the *Daily Tribune* (probably Alexander Wheelock Thayer [1817–1897]) was likewise impressed; he noted that Bristow "has shown himself a skillful instrumental composer" and expressed interest in hearing "more of his works."[55] Frederick Nicholls Crouch (1808–1896), the *Message Bird*'s presumed critic, was enthusiastic, calling the symphony "a musical achievement, withal so respectable, and of so much higher grade, we believe, than anything heretofore attempted in this country [that] something more than a passing notice is justly due, both the author and the work." Crouch subsequently wrote a two-part essay in which, among other issues, he pointed out the difficulties faced by fledgling composers in a young country like the United States. He observed, "When the lack of facilities under which a musical student labors in this country—especially if he is poor—is duly considered . . . the attainment of sufficient knowledge and skill to construct a *Grand Symphony* under such circumstances really becomes a matter of wonder and surprise."[56] In this context, Bristow's *Sinfonia*, although admittedly the product of a young and inexperienced composer, was a major accomplishment.

But Crouch's list of impediments (which included the "rarity of suitable books and models, the want of sympathy," and the necessity of devoting time to "the minor drudgeries of the art for subsistence") was incomplete, for he also should have included the difficulties that any mid-century American orchestral composer experienced when attempting to have his large works performed. This was a crucial component in the learning process, and composers active in New York during this period (and later) had limited opportunities in this realm. They could either organize (and pay for) a pickup orchestra or try to convince the Philharmonic Society to program their compositions. The former option was too costly for most composers; the latter presented its own difficulties, for by as early as the mid-1840s, New York composers were fighting an uphill (and usually unsuccessful) battle with their local orchestra for any kind of support. Bristow, of course, seemed to enjoy a (somewhat) favored-composer status, for the orchestra performed two of his early works. But hindsight suggests that it should have been completely unexceptional for the only standing orchestra in the country to perform an overture and symphony by a promising young native composer who also was a member of the ensemble itself. But this was not the case, and in that context, Bristow's relative success in the late 1840s and early 1850s was extraordinary. He was, however, the exception that proved the rule, for in reality the general situation was not auspicious. In the late 1840s, in fact, there was serious and growing tension between American composers living in New York and the country's only established orchestra—in marked contrast to the 1840s culture of collegiality that Bristow later remembered about chamber music sessions in which he had participated. In the context of this growing tension, the young composer's orchestral music helped to propel him into the limelight.

## Background to the Conflict

According to its first prospectus, one of the Philharmonic Society's principal goals was the improvement of musical taste and the elevation of art in America, accomplished "by performing the Grand Symphonies and Overtures of Beethoven, Mozart, Haydn, Spohr, Mendelssohn, and other great Masters." But Harvey Dodworth (1822–1891), who was one of the founding members of the society, later remembered that the orchestra also intended to promote "if possible, . . . an American school of musical composition."[57] In 1843 this goal was added to the society's constitution as a bylaw that required the ensemble to perform every season at least one work written in the United States, as long as it was deemed of adequate caliber.[58]

It is telling that it took another four years after adoption of this bylaw for the orchestra to play its first work by a native-born composer—Bristow's Concert Overture. But New York musicians had been patient during those years, and once the ice was broken in 1847, many believed that at long last the local orchestra would finally begin more assiduously to adhere to its own stated goals. As is well known, however, that did not happen. When the orchestra failed to program any American-written compositions in the 1847–1848 or 1848–1849 seasons, composers and critics began to complain.[59] One such reproach was penned by Anthony Philip Heinrich (1781–1861), who had helped to found the Philharmonic Society in 1842. In December 1848 he sent an open letter to the *Herald* that chastised the society, noting that on several occasions he had written to the orchestra requesting its consideration of one of his compositions for possible performance. But he had been completely ignored, without even the courtesy of a response.[60] Almost a year later, the *Message Bird* took up the call. In its brief notice of the first concert of the Philharmonic's 1849–1850 season (again devoid of an American composition), the editor noted that since the performance of his Concert Overture, Bristow had completed his first symphony, and he suggested that this work should be considered. He also reminded the orchestra of its pledge: "Bye-the-bye," he wrote, "what has become of a certain symphony which cost a talented member [of the society], and one of the original founders, some four years of hard study in order to [bring about] the production of a creditable *native* performance by this society? When shall we have the pleasure of hearing this interesting production? Our patriotism is becoming a little pricked in anticipation of this event."[61] After the conclusion of this season, Herrman Saroni also weighed in, reminding the orchestra of its pledge "to arouse and stimulate the latent creative powers of native or resident musicians, by placing in their hands the means to have their works performed." He granted that the other goal of the Philharmonic Society was to cultivate American taste for the "great masters," but pointed out that the ensemble had readily agreed in the previous several years to program works by perfectly capable, but "non-master," composers (such as Peter Josef von Lindpaintner, Jan Ladislav Dussek, and Heinrich August Marschner). Even in that context, the ensemble still "refused to perform any domestic compositions at their concerts." It is "needless to comment," Saroni concluded, "upon the narrow-mindedness of such proceedings."[62] Perhaps as a result of the chorus of criticism, Saroni surmised, the orchestra had agreed to perform two "American" works in a June public rehearsal (Bristow's *Sinfonia* and Eisfeld's Concert Overture). This was a good start, the editor suggested, but not enough.

The Philharmonic Society evidently never even considered any American works (the board, according to Bristow, either failed to establish a committee tasked with examining such submissions or established a committee that never met), and this contributed to a growing belief among composers and critics in New York and elsewhere that compositions by Americans were automatically dismissed as inferior to works by any European.[63] This, in turn, fed a growing belief that the orchestra was deliberately marginalizing American composers' efforts, which put George Bristow into a difficult position. Although still only in his mid-twenties, the young musician was growing in stature as a composer, building on his reputation as a skilled performer, and carving out an increasingly prominent place in the New York musical community. But he was also a long-term (possibly charter) member of the orchestra and the only American-born composer whose works had been performed by the ensemble. A number of events that occurred in late 1853 and early 1854 would function as significant catalysts for a public fight between the orchestra and American composers, and Bristow, who would emerge as a defender of American musicians, would find himself in the middle of the fight. It would have an important impact on both his subsequent career and historical reputation.

| Interlude A | **Pedagogy I** |
|---|---|

*Private Teaching*

GEORGE BRISTOW WAS A MUSIC EDUCATOR for his entire professional life, both privately and in New York schools and conservatories. (For the latter, see Interlude C.) He turned to teaching—as an instructor of both piano and violin—in the mid-1840s, when he was in his early twenties, around the same time that he was beginning to build a reputation as a performer and a composer. He could have spent his career pursuing the prestige and public acclaim associated with the latter two activities, as did many musicians who are better known historically. But he also firmly believed in music's power to enrich the lives of ordinary people. As he later pointed out in his autobiographical sketch, after "composing symphonies, cantatas, &c, &c," he decided to "come down from [the] high Pedestal of Musical Thought, to the level of ordinary human beings." He acknowledged that "every body cannot appreciate and be great in music" but believed that "there are a great many who love and encourage it." As a result, he decided that his lifelong quest to "do all [that] I can for art" could best be achieved by the laudable (although undervalued) task of teaching music to both adults and children.[1] This occupation also had the benefit of providing him with a steady income so that he could continue to compose, since those symphonies or cantatas, despite being "successful musically," resulted in negligible hard cash.

## Early Endeavors

The first concrete evidence of Bristow's activities as a private teacher is from May 1847, with an announcement that the American Musical Institute, headquartered at 446 Broadway, would soon start to offer a class for beginning violinists taught by the twenty-one-year-old G. F. Bristow. The AMI, as it was known, had been founded the previous September by George Loder, with significant financial help from the music-loving entrepreneur Henry Meiggs. Its dual goals were "to encourage musical taste in this city" through performances and to spread musical knowledge by founding "an American school where music shall be taught thoroughly at a merely nominal expense to the public."[2] The AMI offered classes in voice, piano, flute, and violin for modest fees, apparently the result of generous subsidies by Meiggs. How long Bristow worked in this capacity—or even if his advertised class attracted enough students to be viable—is unknown. By March 1848, however, the beginning violin classes were taught by Ureli Corelli Hill, and later that year the AMI itself ceased operations.[3]

Information about when Bristow started to teach music privately is more elusive, although he does mention this endeavor in his autobiographical sketch. As noted in chapter 1, the young musician increasingly chafed at playing in theater orchestras; such employment, he wrote, "had lost its charm," for he was no longer content to play "the same thing over and over."[4] He continued to perform for soirées and benefits, but the theater job was financially crucial (he reports being paid eight dollars per week, the modern equivalent of around $280). A friend encouraged him to give up all the gratis performances and take up teaching instead. It was, the colleague pointed out, "far more respectable than wasting your time, in the way you have. Take my advice," he continued, "teach and be a gentleman." Bristow reports that he took this advice, although "not immediately."[5]

His eventual decision to turn to pedagogy probably coincided with a decision (around 1847) by William Bristow to move his family from Manhattan (on Forsyth Street, south of Grand) to "the suburbs of an adjoining city" in order to find "a cheaper abode." As George explained, "The elder Apollo [found that] expenses of his family exceed[ed] the incomes of himself and son." Indeed, the family had grown: by 1850 George (the eldest and still living with his parents) now had five sisters and two brothers. The family relocated to the Bushwick area of Brooklyn, which, George lamented, was "a great distance from his business," as the travel time to and from Manhattan was significant. (This was well before subways, elevated railroads, streetcars, or even a bridge across the East River.)

Evidently George moved to Brooklyn with the family, but doing so provided incentive for him to leave home. The friend who had advised him to teach, in fact, offered to put him up until he had secured a sufficient number of students to support himself, and he accepted the offer, if somewhat reluctantly. George may have eventually maintained a residence in a Manhattan boardinghouse.[6] Locating a place to live, however, was not the only problem, for he confessed to his friend that he had no idea how to find students to teach. As a result, his more worldly comrade took him to a party where he was asked to play the piano. His impromptu performance, as intended, charmed everyone present—so much so, he remembered, that both the "lady of the house" and two additional women signed up to take lessons. One of the latter was young; the other was a "maiden lady of some considerable maturity"; both, however, were wealthy, sensible, and studied the piano "*not for fashions sake*" but because they loved music.[7]

The launch of his teaching career took time, effort, and some mental adjustments on the part of the young musician. After some months, he realized that his total number of pupils was stalled. This was discouraging, for he saw "others with not the 30th part of his knowledge" flourish as music teachers. In fact, "their time [was] more than taken up," he wrote, and they were "making money and comparatively living at their ease and comfort" while he "was barely able to get enough [students] to keep body and soul together." This changed, however, when his "maiden lady" pupil realized that her teacher was "downcast" about his inability to attract additional students. She contacted some of her friends and very quickly recruited a large number of new pupils, some of them from "the crème de la crème families." Bristow was ecstatic. "To this maiden lady," he later remembered, "Apollo owed everything for his success as a music teacher."[8]

But this success also required a change in his attitude toward some of his students. As he pointed out later, he "lacked . . . business tact" and "did not understand the science of humbug." The latter required the application of at least some degree of flattery to students who were either lazy or unskilled. He realized that some of the more prosperous teachers had no difficulty telling a student that "he or she was playing well" when this was false, or to tell someone with no ability that they possessed it in abundance. A good teacher, of course, cannot simply resort to such insincere blandishments, but Bristow eventually realized that "there was a . . . difference between himself and his pupils" in that he "had made music a profession" while "they [considered it] an amusement." He enjoyed playing waltzes by Chopin; some of his students, in contrast, preferred to learn such pieces to accompany actual dances. At one soirée he played an ambitious program that included a popular fantasia by Sigismund Thalberg (1812–1871), only to be asked afterward to play "any of the fashionable music of the day," meaning not Thalberg but "Carry Me Back to Old Virginny." But instead of continuing to dismiss these people as lamentably ignorant, he resolved to "overcome the feeling of disgust he had hitherto entertained for people without musical talents and be more liberal in his views," which made a marked difference in his teaching. He discovered that "he [could] give a lesson in a more amiable mood . . . and so endear a pupil to him"; furthermore, he "left off scolding, so his pupils loved him."[9] This pedagogical philosophy—combined with what he had conversely learned about effective teaching methods from his father—helped him to become a kind and patient teacher, characteristics that would serve him well when he began to teach elementary school children.

Eventually "young Apollo" filled up his schedule with as many pupils as he could accommodate. They were all from "the best families," he wrote, and represented a "gold mine." We do not know where these families lived, or whether he maintained a studio or went to students' homes, but his memory of this period was positive. "Now all was happiness," he wrote, for he was "in the full tide of prosperity."[10] As a result, by the late 1840s or early 1850s, Bristow was supporting himself primarily through teaching piano, which resulted in a schedule that was much more flexible than was possible with theater work, thus allowing him the luxury of participating in the chamber-music jam sessions mentioned in chapter 1. Furthermore, the resumption of his freelance musical activity worked to his advantage as a teacher because of its exposure of his abilities. It is unclear if his teaching was in Manhattan, but by 1854 George was living on Broome Street on the Lower East Side.[11]

Most of Bristow's pupils were young women, and by the early 1850s he fell in love with one of them. He could not yet support a wife (besides, the object of his affections was already engaged), so instead of asking her to marry him, he did what he called "the next best thing": he wrote a nocturne, titled "La belle Amerique" (1850). This became a pattern in what must have been an emotionally tumultuous several-year period for the young man, as he fell in and out of love with a succession of women. During these early years of the 1850s, he later wrote, "It is not on record how many times Mr. Apollo fell in love," but since he composed "six or eight nocturnes, the probability is that he fell in love six or eight times." In fact, Bristow wrote seven piano nocturnes, all but one during the period 1850–1852 and most with French titles. Apparently only two of them were published and are extant: the aforementioned "La belle Amerique" (op. 4, dedicated to Mlle

Fanny Miller, 1850) and "L'etoile du Soir" (op. 7, which suggests a composition date during this period despite its publication date of 1884).[12] If these two works are representative, then George Bristow was a serious pianist, with large hands. "La belle Amerique," for example, is in roughly ternary form, with the undulating accompaniment and cantabile melody associated with nocturnes. But stretches of a tenth are regularly required for both right and left hands; in addition, the melody is an inner voice in the right hand, *within* a tenth interval that has a sustained upper voice and a lower voice that participates in the accompaniment pattern. "L'etoile du Soir," in 12/8 meter, is a more interesting piece, with a cantabile melody (*sempre legato*) that floats atop right-hand chords (frequently tenths) to an undulating broken-chord left-hand accompaniment. Also in ternary form, the work is in G-flat major with a middle section in the dominant; the restatements of the themes in each section are separated by 16th- and 32nd-note flourishes. Neither of these nocturnes is a simple parlor piece, nor would either have been appropriate for a student, but they nevertheless suggest an overlap between pedagogy, composition, performance, and Bristow's personal life.

According to Delmer Rogers, Bristow continued to teach privately for almost his entire career. Advertisements in the *American Art Journal* from 1879 and onward indicate that he gave private lessons in piano, organ, singing, and theory at his Steinway Hall studio until he retired from such activity in 1888.[13] He continued to teach in the public schools, however, until his death in 1898. (See Interlude C.)

## Teaching through Composition

In 1851 Bristow published *Ferdinand Beyer's School for the Piano-Forte* (New York: Firth, 1851, 1866), which he had translated and adapted for the American market.[14] This publication marks his first venture into the realm of pedagogical publishing, a relatively minor activity in which he engaged occasionally throughout his career. In the 1860s he compiled a vocal collection titled *The Cantilena: A Collection of Songs, Duets, Trios, and Quartettes* (New York: Abbey & Abbott, 1861) and (with fellow teacher Francis Nash), the vocal textbooks *Cantara I* and *Cantara II* (1866 and 1868). (See Interlude C.) Later, in the late 1880s, he assembled and edited *George F. Bristow's New and Improved Method for the Reed or Cabinet Organ* (New York: R. A. Saalfield, ca. 1887), an anthology that includes a pedagogical section and a large and varied collection of compositions. Bristow described his choices in the book's preface as "all kinds of music, from the grave to the gay, from the

Psalm-tune to the waltz"; he further noted (with tongue firmly in cheek) that "the person who cannot find something interesting here, must be indeed hard to please."[15] His final pedagogical collection, *Bristow's Two-Part Vocal Exercises* (op. 75) appeared in 1890.[16] Whether or not these pedagogical works were successful financially is unknown, but such efforts were completely unexceptional both for an educator and a journeyman musician who regularly had his fingers in a wide variety of musical pies. Bristow was clearly both a teacher and an entrepreneurial musician throughout his professional career.

## 2 | Fry, Willis, and Jullien

### *Bristow Becomes an Americanist*

**ON NOVEMBER 11, 1852,** the critic and composer William Henry Fry (1813–1864), a youthful-looking man with a thin face, a tall forehead, and an unruly explosion of hair, arrived in New York to start a position as music critic for the *New York Daily Tribune*.[1] He had spent the previous six years in Europe, serving since December 1849 as the *Tribune*'s Parisian correspondent. Journalist Beman Brockway later wrote that Fry was "one of the brightest men ever upon the Tribune" and "one of the best-informed . . . [and] most caustic writers" at the paper. Even before leaving France, Fry had already decided to present a series of ten lectures in New York on the "History and Esthetics of Music," an undertaking that had been heavily publicized in the city since April. The series covered a dizzying range of topics, including musical genres, modern composers, and "curious and rare music of all ages and cultures." It ended with an extra eleventh lecture in which he covered, in addition to various other subjects, the topic of "American music."[2] The musicians who performed the examples in this series included soloists from Max Maretzek's struggling Italian opera troupe, a chorus of more than one hundred singers (mostly from the Harmonic Society), an orchestra of eighty performers (many from the Philharmonic Society and probably, as Fry claimed, the largest orchestra ever to play in the United States up to that point), and a military band of fifty (from Dodworth's and the Tenth

Regiment Bands). Fry hired Ureli Corelli Hill as concertmaster and Bristow as conductor, surely a feather in the cap of the twenty-six-year-old musician.[3]

How Fry came to hire Bristow is not known. Before his arrival, the critic had not been a resident of New York; furthermore, he had left Philadelphia for Europe when Bristow was only twenty. It is possible that Fry knew of Bristow's work with both the New York Harmonic Society and the orchestra of the Philharmonic Society, for in December 1851 Bristow had taken over directorship of the choral society and in March 1852 had been considered as a replacement for George Loder, who had resigned as the orchestra's conductor. Despite being passed over for the latter position, Bristow was still clearly a rising star in New York.[4] Conversely, Bristow at best knew of Fry only by reputation—perhaps he had heard of his opera *Leonora* (which would not be performed in New York until later in the 1850s). More likely, however, he had read Fry's essays in the *Tribune*.[5] It is unlikely that Bristow had ever heard any of Fry's music before he started to rehearse various of those works for performance in this series.

The chance to conduct the musical examples for this series provided Bristow with enormous exposure, for thousands attended the lectures given at Metropolitan Hall over a span of ten and a half weeks (November 20, 1852, to February 8, 1853). It also gave Bristow the opportunity to conduct a wide variety of musical styles and genres, including operatic arias, symphonic works, excerpts from oratorios, secular choral and solo compositions, and examples of "curious and rare music" (that is, Fry's interpretations of such historical and non-Western musical styles as Medieval, Greek, Egyptian, Siamese, Persian, and others). Of even more importance historically, however, is the probability that this sustained and intense encounter with the outspoken and opinionated older musician (Fry was twelve years Bristow's senior)—especially his views on American music—made a strong and lasting impression on Bristow.

The most influential lecture was certainly the final one, delivered on February 8, 1853. Fry enlisted the services of over three hundred performers, and the event attracted, according to Alexander Wheelock Thayer of the *Tribune*, "not less than three thousand auditors, filling the house to the second gallery and the ceiling."[6] Fry tackled a large variety of subjects in his "grand finale," including the nature of the symphony, for which he chose as his example the Allegro vivace finale of Bristow's *Sinfonia*, another endorsement for the young composer. During the final thirty minutes of the lecture, however, Fry turned his attention to a topic about which he was clearly passionate: the "artistic duties and relations . . . the interests of society in art, and the shortcoming of the American mind in that regard." His statements included, in Vera Lawrence's words, both "a cultural Declaration of Independence from all foreign models and influences" and a ringing proclamation on the need for Americans to adopt an attitude of independence so that American artists could "discard their foreign liveries, and found an American School in Painting, Sculpture, and Music." He also demanded that American ensembles (surely a swipe at the Philharmonic Society) should "devote rehearsal time to reading American works" and that such compositions deserved the same attention as what was being bestowed on works by Europeans. Although undeniably verbose, the wiry Fry was passionate about his topic and could be persuasive.[7] There is no concrete evidence to suggest the impact that Fry's convictions had on Bristow's emerging concepts about nationalistic music, but this event—occurring as it did during a period of growing tension in New York between musicians and the Philharmonic Society—clearly either planted seeds or provided significant fertilizer and water for seeds that were already beginning to sprout.

Later that same year, there was a second event that would also have a seminal impact on Bristow's emerging Americanist identity: the arrival in New York (August 7, 1853) of the virtuoso French composer and conductor Louis-Antoine Jullien and the twenty-seven European virtuosi who were to function as the core of his ensemble. Jullien quickly recruited enough musicians (many, including Bristow, from the Philharmonic Society) to create an unparalleled orchestra of slightly over one hundred. His goal was twofold: to entertain and educate American audiences, which he accomplished by blending "the most sublime works" (by Beethoven, Mozart, Mendelssohn, and others) "with those of a lighter school" (quadrilles, waltzes, polkas, schottisches, and the like).[8] The Frenchman was a charismatic and flamboyant showman but also a superb conductor—better than any who had yet appeared in the United States. Audiences and critics alike were astounded by the performances given by his orchestra, which completely outstripped the Philharmonic Society in terms of concerts given (six per week, in comparison with the Philharmonic's four per year) and sheer performing excellence. During its nine months in America, the ensemble undertook some 223 concerts: 90 in New York City (fall 1853 and spring 1854) and over 130 elsewhere in the country, the result of two tours that introduced tens of thousands of Americans to the concept and sounds of orchestral concerts. The orchestra, and its charismatic conductor, had a significant impact on the development of musical culture in mid-nineteenth-century America.[9]

Even more important, however, was the conductor's influence on American composers, for he commissioned orchestral works by Americans and programmed them frequently. The most obvious beneficiaries of this support were William Fry and George Bristow, but he also championed other Americans as well as some European composers then living in New York. The native-born musicians must have regarded endorsement by this celebrated European conductor as a shot in the arm, for they were (to use Lawrence's expression) "performance-starved." The support was particularly beneficial to Bristow; as Delmer Rogers points out, Jullien's actions represented one of the few times that Bristow had "received unsolicited encouragement as a composer."[10] In addition, the chance to hear their works performed by such a *good* orchestra—an ensemble undoubtedly superior to that of the Philharmonic Society—must have been a heady experience for both Fry and Bristow. And such performances occurred repeatedly between late September 1853 and January 2, 1854, in New York, Boston, Baltimore, and Philadelphia. Fry's works included his symphonies (or tone poems) *A Day in the Country* (1853) and *The Breaking Heart* (1852), which were heard (either in individual movements or in their entirety) more than thirty times during this period; Bristow was represented by the Minuet from his *Sinfonia*, which the ensemble played seven times, in New York, Boston, and Philadelphia. Toward the end of the orchestra's December season in New York, audiences also heard two new works that Jullien had commissioned: Fry's new programmatic *Santa Claus (Christmas) Symphony* (five times) and the first movement of Bristow's Symphony No. 2 in D minor, op. 24 (twice).

## The "Jullien" Symphony

The "Jullien" Symphony was one of Bristow's two major compositions from the 1850s (the other was *Rip Van Winkle*); Jullien premiered its first movement on December 29 in a "Grand American Night" and performed it again two days later. Whether or not Bristow had already started the composition before its commission is unknown but likely, as it was ready for performance by late December. The amount of the commission was reportedly two hundred dollars (roughly $6,800 in 2019 currency), and the grateful composer named the symphony for his benefactor.[11]

A substantial work in four movements (marked Allegro appassionato, Allegretto, Adagio, and Allegro agitato—*Grandioso*—*L'istesso tempo*), the symphony, like his first, is scored for the standard orchestra of Beethoven, Schubert, Carl Maria von Weber, and Mendelssohn: strings, pairs of winds (flutes, oboes, clarinets, bassoons), brasses (horns and trumpets), and timpani, to which he added two horns (for a total of four) and three trombones.[12] All four horns are used in the first and last movements and all three trombones only in the finale, although there are prominent trombone solos in the first and third movements. Like the instrumentation, Bristow's compositional style is that of the nineteenth-century Germanic composers whose works he knew as a performer with the Philharmonic Society. Particularly influential were Beethoven and Mendelssohn. As a result, although there are some hints of nationalistic writing, the symphony is essentially a piece of absolute music.[13] Fry recognized this, calling Bristow's style "strictly classical, modeled on the forms of the great masters"; this contrasted clearly with his own more programmatic approach (or that of Anthony Heinrich, Louis Moreau Gottschalk [1829–1869], Elsworth Phelps [1827–1913], and other American composers). But as the older composer put it, Bristow had "chosen his school [and] is satisfied with determined forms" (what Fry regarded as the old-fashioned "classical" or "formalist" approach).[14]

The Allegro appassionato, in D minor, is in sonata-allegro form. It opens with a stormy, passionate, and *fortissimo* introduction that leads to an ominous and brooding first theme, played by celli and bassoons. The contrasting second theme—in the relative major, introduced by the strings, and repeated with the addition of winds—is somewhat wistful and evocative. The exposition ends with a resolute closing theme. In the development, Bristow wrote a striking trombone solo as an effective foil to the brooding first theme; this returns in the recapitulation as a countermelody to that string-and-bassoon-dominated motive. The second movement, in the parallel major, is a scherzo with two trios. It is the most obvious example of "Americanism" in the symphony, for it is a polka or a schottische—two dances (with shared rhythmic patterns) that were immensely popular in America. It is also slightly more adventurous harmonically: the first trio (in G major) modulates to A-flat major; the second is in B-flat major, with a brief nod to G minor. The third movement Adagio, which Richard Storrs Willis described as "the best of the movements" and James William Davison (1813–1885) of *The Times* (London) as "melodious and extremely well written," is a bipartite exploration of three different melodies that either contrast with or are outgrowths of each other. It illustrates well both Bristow's gift for varied melody and the effective extension and development of his tunes.[15] In B-flat major, the movement is laid out in two parallel sections, followed by a brief coda. One of its most striking features is another prominent solo for the trombone: a yearning, cantabile melody supported by gentle accompaniment in the strings. The finale, in the compound duple meter of 6/4, and beginning in the home key of D minor, provides a fitting conclusion. Scored for the entire orchestra, including four French horns and all three trombones, the movement is a rondo with an intense driving rhythmic energy that moves like the wind. The symphony ends with a coda in the form of a grand march (marked *Grandioso: L'istesso tempo*, in the parallel major, and in aaba form) that is based on an unidentified anthem-like tune.

Bristow's melodic materials in this work are straightforward and tuneful, somewhat reminiscent of Mozart or Schubert. His texture (especially in the second movement) occasionally exhibits the "elfinish" quality sometimes heard in Mendelssohn's orchestral compositions. His obvious model overall, however, was Beethoven. His skillful motivic development, the expansiveness of his sonata forms, use of syncopation and dynamics to build drama, and sudden shifts between segments that are in turn placid and turbulent indicate that Bristow had thoroughly assimilated many of the stylistic techniques used by the Bonn composer. The overall musical impression conveyed by Bristow's Second Symphony, however, is that of a contemporary cosmopolitan work, an effect that is created by a harmonic language that relies on third relations, rich and abundant melodies, skillful orchestration, a sense of drama, and thorough grounding in early nineteenth-century symphonic style. But there are also several elements that personalize the work and that could be considered a means by which Bristow responded to Fry's call for an American musical "Declaration of Independence." His use of a polka as his dance movement was one way to do this. Another was his exploitation of brass instruments in general and of the trombone in particular as an atmospheric reference to the United States, since most New Yorkers of the period associated that timbre with brass bands, which were ubiquitous at mid-century and that many considered to be quintessentially American. Bristow also skillfully exploited cyclic techniques in this work. He subtly links several of the movements, for example, by using the trombone's unusual sonority, in part by writing several gorgeous lyrical themes and countermelodies for the instrument. Furthermore, as Douglas Shadle points out, the principal themes of three of the four movements share a gesture of syncopation followed by a downward melodic motion. Both techniques are sophisticated and contribute to the overall sense that the composer was attempting to integrate the various movements.[16]

The performance history of this work is a bit more complicated than that of Bristow's other symphonies (except the *Niagara*) because the Jullien Orchestra played parts of it in New York (during winter and spring 1854) and later in the United Kingdom. There were, rather strangely, only a handful of reviews of the first two performances. Willis wrote a strong and positive assessment of the premiere performance, calling the symphony "a good specimen of the musical abilities of this gentleman." He also noted that the orchestration of the new work was "somewhat different" from that of the Minuet from the *Sinfonia* (also played that night); perhaps he considered the increased prominence of brass—the only difference in orchestration—as suggesting an American voice; this, he wrote, was "easy to perceive." Bristow's "classic" approach clearly fit into Willis's musical universe. "A clever thing is this composition," he concluded, "reflecting much credit upon Mr. Bristow."[17] William Fry, in the *Tribune*, also wrote generally positive comments. Although the symphony was more conservative than he preferred, he predicted that Jullien would take it abroad, where it would "help to show that Americans can afford to send something worthy back for what she has received from Europe." This, in fact, did happen, for the Jullien Orchestra later performed movements of the symphony in England, where, according to the ensemble's concertmaster Henry Weist Hill (1828–1891), it was well received. All of Jullien's American performances of the work were in New York; the premiere of the complete symphony would not occur until 1856. (See chapter 3.)[18]

## The Musical Battle

Late 1853 to early 1854 was clearly a triumphant period for both Fry and Bristow. Ironically, however, this situation quickly turned sour in January, when Fry overreacted to Willis's criticism of his *Santa Claus Symphony*. Jullien's support had emboldened both of the American stars of the "Grand American Night," and the review—and Fry's initial reaction to it—served as a spark that ignited the simmering resentment shared by many New York musicians who had endured what they considered years of condescension from the German immigrants who were now in control of the Philharmonic Society orchestra.

This latter issue was an important and complicated one, for a growing number of immigrant musicians, especially those who arrived in America during the late 1840s, were Germans, and concomitant with complaints about the unbalanced programming of the orchestra was a growing sense of unease and displeasure at the increasing domination of New York musical life in general—and the Philharmonic Society orchestra in particular—by these immigrants. Not only did the percentage of Germans in the orchestra grow from 42 percent in its founding year to nearly 80 percent by the mid-1850s, but American critics and composers began to mention a sense of "clannishness" among the German musicians with whom they worked. This perception was in stark contrast with Bristow's later (but telling) recollections of the "genuine feeling of brotherly affection between musicians" of the 1840s who "were all philharmonic, not only in name but in spirit as well."[19]

A further complicating factor that directly involved Bristow was the 1852 selection (by the orchestra's board of directors) of the German immigrant Theodore Eisfeld as its first permanent conductor. The board had been deadlocked about a successor to George Loder, whose final concert on the podium was in January; Bristow, who was then concertmaster, had decided to throw his hat into the ring. But when he received three yea and three nay votes, the board decided to appoint Eisfeld, who was admittedly an older and more experienced candidate. Nevertheless, some New Yorkers viewed this decision not only as a further solidification of Teutonic control of the orchestra but also as a snub to the young American.[20] The smoldering (but growing) unhappiness with this situation set the stage, in January 1854, for what would become a bitter and very public argument that involved Fry, Bristow, and the critic Richard Storrs Willis; it was played out in the pages of that editor's *New York Musical World* (and, to a lesser extent, *Dwight's Journal of Music* in Boston). Bristow would have a seminal and very public role in this "musical battle of the century," a participation that eventually colored his historical reputation.[21]

The contretemps, which Gilbert Chase dubbed "one of the most extraordinary public correspondences in the annals of American music," erupted in early January 1854 with Willis's review of the "Grand American Night" concert on December 29, 1853. The program included two works by Fry (his symphony *A Day in the Country*, described on the program as "a descriptive overture," and the Adagio from *The Breaking Heart*) and two by Bristow (as noted, the Minuet from the *Sinfonia* and the first movement of his "New Symphony, composed expressly for this occasion"). (See fig. 1.)[22] Willis commented on Fry's two pieces but added a paragraph about his "New Grand Christmas Symphony, entitled 'Santa Claus,'" which the Jullien Orchestra had performed on December 28. His observations were generally positive, but he declared that the composer's programmatic approach did not represent true "musical unity" and reproached Fry for misusing the term "symphony." He also dismissed "Santa Claus" as a mere "Christmas piece" and "hardly . . . an earnest work of Art."[23]

In hindsight, this seems like an innocent enough remark, especially from a critic who was well known in New York's musical community. But Fry took serious offense. He believed (and had stated in his final lecture the previous February) that American critics should support American composers, especially since, as he put it, "the Philharmonic Society of this city is consecrated to foreign music." And his response, which was a lengthy, rambling, and self-serving—but essentially civil—statement, reflected the pent-up frustration and indignation that

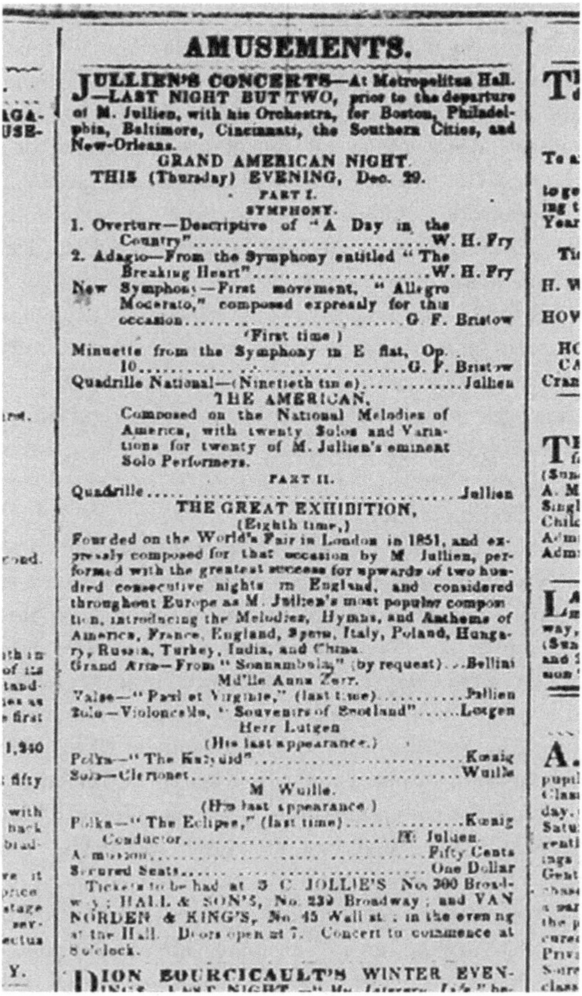

**AMUSEMENTS.**

JULLIEN'S CONCERTS—At Metropolitan Hall.—LAST NIGHT BUT TWO, prior to the departure of M. Jullien, with his Orchestra, for Boston, Philadelphia, Baltimore, Cincinnati, the Southern Cities, and New-Orleans.

GRAND AMERICAN NIGHT.
THIS (Thursday) EVENING, Dec. 29.

PART I.
SYMPHONY.

1. Overture—Descriptive of "A Day in the Country" .......... W. H. Fry
2. Adagio—From the Symphony entitled "The Breaking Heart" .......... W. H. Fry

New Symphony—First movement, "Allegro Moderato," composed expressly for this occasion .......... G. F. Bristow
(First time.)
Minuette from the Symphony in E flat, Op. 10 .......... G. F. Bristow
Quadrille National—(Ninetieth time) .......... Jullien
THE AMERICAN,
Composed on the National Melodies of America, with twenty Solos and Variations for twenty of M. Jullien's eminent Solo Performers.

PART II.

Quadrille .......... Jullien
THE GREAT EXHIBITION,
(Eighth time.)
Founded on the World's Fair in London in 1851, and expressly composed for that occasion by M. Jullien, performed with the greatest success for upwards of two hundred consecutive nights in England, and considered throughout Europe as M. Jullien's most popular composition, introducing the Melodies, Hymns, and Anthems of America, France, England, Spain, Italy, Poland, Hungary, Russia, Turkey, India, and China.
Grand Aria—From "Sonnambula" (by request) .......... Bellini
Md'lle Anna Zerr.
Valse—"Paul et Virginie," (last time) .......... Jullien
Solo—Violoncello, "Souvenirs of Scotland" .......... Lutgen
Herr Lutgen
(His last appearance.)
Polka—"The Katydid" .......... Koenig
Solo—Clarionet .......... Wuille
M. Wuille.
(His last appearance.)
Polka—"The Eclipse," (last time) .......... Koenig
Conductor .......... M. Jullien.
Admission .......... Fifty Cents
Secured Seats .......... One Dollar

Tickets to be had at S. C. JOLLIE'S No. 300 Broadway; HALL & SON'S, No. 239 Broadway; and VAN NORDEN & KING'S, No. 45 Wall st.; in the evening at the Hall. Doors open at 7. Concert to commence at 8 o'clock.

DION BOURCICAULT'S WINTER EVEN-

**FIGURE 1.** Program of the "Grand American Night" concert on December 29, 1853, by Jullien's orchestra. Willis's review of this concert precipitated the "musical battle of the century." (New York *Tribune*, December 29, 1853, 1.)

had been building for years among New York composers.[24] The original point of disagreement was between Fry and Willis. The composer, who had recently returned from Europe, believed that programmatic music was new and progressive and that the Philharmonic Society's dismissal of such music was inexcusable, old-fashioned, and insulting to forward-looking (American) composers. Willis, who had a tendency to lecture the few local composers whose works he reviewed, countered that Fry did not understand "musical unity," by which he apparently meant absolute music and clear-cut musical forms. In his second letter, Fry wrote a point-by-point rebuttal of Willis but then turned to Dwight (who had reprinted part of Fry's original letter in his journal) and broadened the argument to American music in general, again reflecting the views he had voiced so stridently in his eleventh lecture. "It is my firm belief," he wrote, "that if there were not some one like myself, determined that American Musical Art should not be beaten down and extinguished, it would be."[25]

By now the topic of the entire disagreement had shifted to the festering issue of the Philharmonic Society and its lack of support for American composers. Dwight inadvertently threw fuel on the fire by reprinting parts of the correspondence and adding comments that he intended to be lighthearted. Unfortunately, the levity indicated that he did not understand the serious underlying tension between New York musicians and their orchestra, an issue that was an inescapable context for local musicians. His poorly chosen words, then, were a miscalculation that infuriated Fry and, increasingly, Bristow, who had not yet joined the fray. The Boston critic's contention, for example, that the music of these two composers "was sure to be accepted . . . just as soon as their audiences shall feel that there is genius, inspiration, beauty [and] poetry of music in their symphonies, at all proportioned to the audacity and oddness of their designs," betrayed his unfamiliarity with Bristow's more "classic" compositions. The comment also completely ignored the basic point that Fry had been attempting to make: that audiences needed to *hear* the music of American composers if they were ever to "feel the genius, inspiration, beauty [and] poetry" of their compositions. "How are American [composers] to win their way in compositions," he challenged Dwight, "unless their compositions are played?"[26]

Willis likewise committed a serious faux pas. In one of his responses to Fry, he denied the composer's denunciation of the Philharmonic Society as anti-American by pointing out that the officers of the society—including George Bristow, whom he mentioned by name—were "men quite above any narrow prejudices of nation." The fury of Bristow's response (this was his entry into the quarrel) suggests that the younger composer had been paying close attention to the altercation and regarded Willis's evocation of his name as an affront. He indignantly informed Willis that Fry's claim about the Philharmonic's lack of support for American composers was "perfectly accurate" and pointed out that in the eleven years of the orchestra's existence it had performed "one whole American overture [and] and one whole rehearsal of one whole American symphony" (both by himself).

Warming to his subject, he continued (with comments that have frequently been quoted):

> Now, in the name of the nine Muses, what is the Philharmonic Society . . . in this country? Is it to play exclusively the works of German masters, especially if they be Dead, in order that our critics may translate their ready-made praises from German? Or is it to stimulate original Art on the spot? Is there a Philharmonic Society in Germany for the encouragement solely of American music? Then why should there be a society here for the encouragement solely of German music, to the exclusion of American, unless, as Mr. Fry says, the object be to render us a Hessian Colony, which we most incontestably are?

He continued at some length in this vein, accusing the German members of the New York musical community of "little short of a conspiracy against the Art of a country to which they come for a living." As further evidence of their anti-American bias, he pointed out that Jullien's Orchestra—an ensemble with which the Philharmonic Society "cannot compete"—had been regularly performing American works since its inaugural concerts in New York the previous August. "Mr. Jullien, a stranger [and] traveler," he wrote, "finds during a short visit to this country American instrumental compositions that he adapts [*sic*] in his symphonic repertory . . . although . . . the Philharmonic Society have never been able to discover any such works during eleven years."[27] This, he believed, undermined the claim by both Willis and Dwight that the Philharmonic Society orchestra refused to play American compositions because they were not yet of a high enough caliber. Bristow then turned to Dwight, with whom he was justifiably angry, for the critic had breezily dismissed his music, only to admit in a later issue that "of Mr. Bristow's music we have never heard a note." But instead of apologizing, Dwight defended his "too thoughtlessly" written comment by claiming he had paired Bristow's music with Fry's "simply because we found the two names coupled" in Fry's first letter.[28] Bristow finished his missive with a final parting shot by "respectfully" requesting that Dwight reproduce the letter in his *Journal of Music* and "let America have one word to say in his paper where Germany has had ten thousand."

Willis responded more temperately to Bristow than he had to Fry. He admitted that he knew "nothing of the *interior* state of the Philharmonic" and agreed that "it would be [a] nobler thing on the part of the Philharmonic to have *one* of the four [yearly] concerts devoted to the production of American compositions."[29] Meanwhile, however, he had published three letters from representatives of the Philharmonic Society, all of whom unequivocally dismissed Bristow's "unjustifiable" charges of anti-American bias; one of them included a list of eleven works by "American" composers that he claimed *had* been performed by the orchestra.[30]

Bristow handily refuted this assertion by pointing out that of the eleven composers named, only two (besides himself) were Americans, and their works had
been performed by concert soloists, who traditionally chose what they played.
The remaining compositions were by Europeans. Most of the works, in any case,
had been performed at public rehearsals, not in subscription concerts, which, in
Bristow's mind, did not really count.[31]

Bristow's second and third (final) letters, although still angry and unyielding,
were both civil, rational, and characterized by none of the ethnic slurs that had
marred his first missive. As already mentioned (in chapter 1), in the former letter
he confirmed the suspicion that no appointed committee of the Philharmonic
had ever met to review possible American compositions, thus neatly circumvent-
ing the orchestra's own bylaw requiring performance of American compositions
that were deemed fit by such a body. He also announced his resignation from the ⬉
Philharmonic—both from the board and the orchestra itself—which apparently
surprised his fellow performers in the ensemble. But the resignation (temporar-
ily, it turns out) was necessary, he wrote, "to my own dignity, and the dignity of
my country." His third letter (April 22) was mostly a refutation of a claim made
by a correspondent known as "Pegan" that the Philharmonic Society had been
formed by German immigrants.[32] This was Bristow's final contribution to the
contretemps, but the quarrel lingered on for several months even in the popular
monthlies.[33]

From the vantage point of the twenty-first century, Bristow's anger at the
Philharmonic Society in 1854 seems somewhat puzzling. He had been a member
of the ensemble from the start and a performing member since its second year.
The previous fall he had been elected to the board of directors and enjoyed something akin to favored-composer status, as the only native American to have had *any*
orchestral compositions performed by the orchestra. But as he pointed out in his
second letter, the performance of his Concert Overture had occurred seven years
earlier, "before the Germans had obtained complete sway over the direction" of
the ensemble, and even then its performance "*was due to the influence of Mr. Hill,*"
so this could not be used to refute his charge of a current anti-American bias. He
apparently was also seriously upset by his inability to convince the orchestra to
perform his first symphony. The fact that the ensemble had played it in a public
rehearsal had made the situation even more untenable, for Bristow declared in
the same letter that "there could hardly be any greater insult offered to any composer than to rehearse his piece and not perform it,—the inference being that the
piece so rehearsed is unworthy to be performed."[34] In addition, he may still have
been smarting from the public snub that had occurred in 1852 when he had been

passed over in his bid to become the first permanent conductor of the ensemble. All of this, in combination with the public fight, led to his resignation.

But Bristow and Fry were not the only local musicians to express unhappiness over the increasingly Teutonic mien of the orchestra, as suggested by comments mentioned in chapter 1 from the editor of the *Message Bird* and by the indignant letter in the *Herald* from Anthony Heinrich. Moreover, at least according to Bristow, Ureli Corelli Hill, vice president of the Philharmonic Society, was also unhappy, for the composer reported that Hill had confided "in conversation with me and others" that the society, which had originally been "founded by himself and others, Americans, or men with liberal American views," had "fallen under the control of German cliques" and that these musicians "still retain control, and [their] acts have uniformly showed their disposition to crush and extinguish everything American." This comment, admittedly shared by a biased Bristow (but not publicly denied by Hill), suggests that the reaction from the community of non-German New York musicians was a cri de coeur from individuals who, after almost a half decade of complaints, had reached a crisis point.[35] Not only was their livelihood threatened by what they viewed as a collective blockage of their efforts, but so was their attempt to join their literary and artistic brothers in creating a national cultural identity that was not, as Fry had put it, a Hessian colony. Several decades later William Thoms (1852–1913), editor of the *American Art Journal*, would articulate similar sentiments in reference to Theodore Thomas's refusal to have the American (or National) Opera Company, of which he was artistic director, perform any operas by American composers. According to Thoms, the conductor was "effectually opposing the advent of American music and working against the success" of American composers and "an honorable place for [the United States] among the musical nations of the civilized world." As such, Thoms asserted, the conductor (who was German-born) was part of a clique of German musicians active in the United States who had gained control of musical institutions in the country during its musical infancy (the 1830s and 1840s) but who refused to relinquish control to "*native intruders*," even though American musicians and composers could, by the 1880s, direct their own destiny.[36] Clearly, New York musicians in the early 1850s had recognized a potentially serious problem that, unchecked, eventually became a fait accompli with an adverse impact on attempts to develop an American musical voice well into the twentieth century.

Some scholars, however, have characterized the frequently quoted anti-German comments in Bristow's first letter as evidence that the composer was petulant and quarrelsome or perhaps even supported the xenophobic Know-Nothing movement, descriptions that have unfairly colored his historical reputation. As early as 1884, for example, Frédéric Louis Ritter labeled Bristow as "nativistic" and claimed that he was "blinded by his antipathy towards German musicians"; twenty years later Louis Elson described Bristow's communications with Willis as "an anti-German crusade which was an exhibition of ill-judged partisanship." Gilbert Chase, in 1987, called the composer's comments "intemperate," and Vera Lawrence (1995) wrote of his "hot tempered combativeness."[37] Henry Krehbiel (1854–1923), in his obituary of Bristow, wrote that his "assaults" on the Philharmonic were "singularly bitter" and, by implication, suggested that Bristow was in sympathy with "Knownothingism." More recently, Douglas Shadle followed Krehbiel's lead and characterized Bristow's "missives" (in the plural) as "filled with anti-immigrant invective characterizing Germans as conniving, cliquish, and, worst of all, abusers of American political independence," language that "reflected the broader nativist sentiment called 'Know-Nothingism' that was sweeping the country."[38]

That the first letter (which *was* filled with invective) reflected serious anger is undeniable. But it also can be read as an incensed statement from a frustrated and still young musician (he had just turned twenty-eight) who for five weeks had silently watched the fight between Willis and Fry, the latter a colleague whose strongly stated opinions on the current state of American music Bristow apparently found persuasive. His pent-up anger had clearly been growing before he responded to the gauntlet that Willis had thrown down, for the critic had used Bristow's name to counter accusations by Fry that the younger musician supported. But it is significant that for the rest of his professional career, George Bristow regularly worked with German immigrant musicians in New York, many of whom were both colleagues and friends. (He later called Carl Bergmann [1821–1876] "an intimate friend.")[39] He also taught German immigrant children in the New York public schools and regularly and habitually programmed compositions by the standard-bearers of the German musical canon (Handel, Haydn, Mendelssohn, and, in particular, Beethoven). Furthermore, he was an outspoken devotee of Beethoven's music to the end of his days. He clearly was not at root anti-German; rather, he was opposed to the activities of a particular group of German immigrants in New York in the late 1840s and early 1850s whose activities he correctly understood to be injurious to both an emerging American musical culture and the musicians who were struggling to create it.

## After the Fight

The whole contentious experience, however, had a silver lining for the young composer and his colleagues, for Jullien's support had been inspiring. The conductor's steady and continued encouragement for four months had convinced Bristow, Fry, and other American composers that their works *were* worth hearing, *could* stand on their own, and were *not* inherently inferior to anything and everything from the other side of the Atlantic. Jullien's actions had clearly emboldened both Fry and Bristow to take their public stand. Moreover, the conductor's support continued throughout the spring, even though he was absent for most of the acrimonious journalistic exchange, for he had taken a pared-down version of his orchestra (thirty-five members, including most of the virtuoso performers he had brought from Europe) on tours to the American South and East (January–May). During these tours the ensemble continued to perform American works, including Bristow's Minuet in Boston, Philadelphia, Louisville, and New Orleans. After completion of the second tour, by which time everything had calmed down on the journalistic front, the Jullien Orchestra returned to New York for a farewell engagement at Castle Garden that commenced on May 15. Although advertised to last ten nights, the ensemble actually performed until June 5 (twenty-three concerts) and featured works by Fry, the Irish composer William Vincent Wallace (1812–1865) (who was living in New York), and Bristow, including his Minuet (May 18) and the Andante (probably the third-movement Adagio) from his "Jullien" Symphony (May 24, 26, and 31).[40]

After the echoes of the "final" concert died away, the president and directors of the Association for the Exhibition of the Industry of All Nations announced that they had persuaded Jullien to preside over a "Grand Musical Congress," a ten-performance extravaganza. Held at the Crystal Palace, this major cultural event—a perfect example of the giganticism that infected the Western musical world at mid-century—was billed as similar to "those great choral and orchestral meetings" that had become annual celebrations in England, Germany, and France; it was designed as an opportunity to unite "in one gigantic ensemble the elite of the instrumental celebrities of Europe with those of America." The "colossal orchestra" included Jullien's (which probably also numbered in its ranks many members of the Philharmonic Society), the Germania Musical Society orchestra, members of the Philharmonic Society of Philadelphia, Dodworth's military band, the United States Military Band, the Italian Opera orchestra, and many other "orchestral artists and amateurs" from around the country. Nineteen named choral societies (from New York, Boston, Philadelphia, Baltimore, and elsewhere), as well as numerous church choir groups were included, as was a cast of twenty-six vocal and instrumental soloists. George Bristow was the only American listed as a "leader," although Carl Bergmann, H. B. Dodworth, and W. L. Bloomfield (of the US Military Band) were among the conductors. Performances during the

"Congress" lasted ten nights, and the lengthy program of concert fare included "some of [the] latest works" by "the distinguished American Composers, Mr. Wm H. Fry and Mr. G. F. Bristow."[41]

The Grand Farewell Concert of this Musical Congress (the Jullien Orchestra's 105th concert in New York) marked the end of Jullien's ten-month visit. Bristow was tapped to conduct the "combined chorus of 600 voices" performing "The Heavens Are Telling" from Haydn's *The Creation*, in front of a crowd that was reported to number between twenty thousand and forty-five thousand, an experience that surely was thrilling for the twenty-eight-year-old musician despite the fact that most critics agreed that the acoustics in the hall were awful. During the intermission, Fry presented Jullien with a gold laurel wreath and a gold tablet as tokens of esteem from "his warmest friends and admirers." Jullien, who was "evidently and unaffectedly embarrassed by the compliment," responded at first "with some hesitation." He subsequently warmed to his subject, however, and "spoke fluently and to the point."[42] He confessed that he had not expected to succeed in America during his first year, but instead had arrived thinking he would need five years to accomplish his goals. He effusively praised American concert-giving organizations for preparing the way for his orchestra, and finally turned his attention to American composers. He fulsomely praised William Fry "as a composer of music for the orchestra, in the romantic school of grandeur," and continued, "'then there is Mr. BRISTOW' (turning to that gentleman, who was on the platform) 'who in classic music, in the symphony, or the quartet, will compare in purity with the classic masters, and hold his place of honor.'"[43] This was high praise indeed from a European musical superstar. Unfortunately, there is no record of a reaction from the normally reticent Bristow.

The French conductor left America two days later, and in the aftermath of the Jullien tornado, Bristow was faced with salvaging his damaged personal relationships with former colleagues in the Philharmonic Society. When he had resigned in March, members of the board had lamented that "he may have alienated from himself sympathies, which hitherto have always been cordially rendered him."[44] On the other hand, his parting shot in his second letter had shown that there were bruised feelings on both sides, for he wrote, "I will neither see my country nor myself, continually kept in the background, by those who should cherish its best efforts in Art."[45] But the composer's experiences over the previous eighteen months—starting with his close association with William Fry in January and February 1853, continuing with his validation as a composer by Jullien, and culminating in the French conductor's public approbation of his compositional abilities—had helped the New York musician to sort out his own feelings as an

American composer. From this time forward, in fact, he was solidly dedicated to the idea of supporting American composers in general as well as writing music that reflected an American national identity.

This latter goal is illustrated most clearly in his compositional activity immediately following Jullien's departure. Early in 1854 Bristow apparently had started to compose a third symphony (which, like his second, is nonprogrammatic) and had made sufficient progress to show the French musician what he had written before Jullien departed. The following December, Bristow received a letter from the conductor (via his secretary) in which he reminded the composer that he was "waiting for your Symphony in F♯ minor."[46] Despite this encouragement—and the implication that his new work would be performed—Bristow had put this partially completed instrumental composition on hold and turned instead to *Rip Van Winkle*. The opera, which is based on Washington Irving's 1819 short story (set in colonial and Federal-period America), is much more overtly nationalistic than his nonprogrammatic third symphony. It was completed in 1855. Later that same year he wrote another nationalistic composition: *Ode*, op. 29, a secular choral setting of a patriotic text by poet Augustine Duganne (1813–1884). (See chapter 3 for discussion of both works.) It was not until 1858 that he returned to and finished his Symphony No. 3.

In the performance realm, Bristow's mid-1850s activities were less overtly nationalistic. Although he had announced in his second letter to Willis his intention to form an American Philharmonic Orchestra to "promote and cultivate" music regardless of any *national* prejudices," he never followed through on this pledge—possibly because he had become overextended, in part for personal reasons. (See chapter 3.) He did, however, support the efforts of Charles Jerome Hopkins (1836–1898), who in June 1855 proposed establishment of the New York American Musical Union (later the New York American-Music Association), an organization designed to encourage "the efforts of young American composers" by providing them with a means to perform "their productions . . . in a suitable manner."[47] During the organization's second season, Bristow (and Richard Willis and George Henry Curtis) agreed to serve on the board of consultants; according to Shadle, Bristow worked behind the scenes to help Hopkins organize the endeavor.[48] But his enthusiasm cooled dramatically when the association moved away from its original pledge to perform "nothing but American compositions" and started to include works by Europeans. Others must have shared Bristow's reservations, for although the organization mounted three concert series (1855–1856 to 1857–1858), by June 1857 it had become a one-man show. As Willis pointed out (perhaps facetiously), by that point Hopkins was president, vice president, treasurer, and director of the organization, which suggests a lack of engagement by other members of the New York musical community.[49]

It is also entirely possible that Bristow pulled back from Hopkins's endeavor not because of a lack of true support for an organization designed to perform American compositions but because he felt that his time was better spent elsewhere. Hopkins was a self-taught musician from Brunswick, Maine, who was barely nineteen when he founded the organization, and perhaps Bristow considered him naïve and inexperienced. The New Yorker, in contrast, although only twenty-nine years old himself (in 1855), was worlds away from Hopkins in terms of both experience and accomplishment. By the time the American Musical Union was in its first season (1855–1856), Bristow's opera had opened to good reviews (summer 1855), his "Jullien" Symphony was scheduled for performance by the Philharmonic Society (March 1856), and several of his orchestral works were being performed in London and elsewhere in the United Kingdom. The previous March, in fact, Jullien's concertmaster, Henry Weist Hill, had written a chatty letter to Bristow, noting he had "just returned to London having been on a Tour with Jullien," during which "we have played the slow movement of your Symphony nearly every night." He reported that it "made a great impression on the Orchestra and the public. Also the Times newspaper (the terror of all composers) gave you what is considered here a first rate notice." He continued, "You are known as <u>the American</u> Composer."[50]

Other evidence likewise attests to Bristow's consistent and strong support for American composers, despite his lack of enthusiasm for Hopkins's association. As artistic director for the Harmonic Society, for example, he programed both small and large works by native, immigrant, and even visiting composers much more regularly than was the norm during the 1850s and into the early 1860s. (See chapter 3.) By the middle of the decade, in fact, Bristow's goals, which he had articulated clearly in the letters he wrote to Willis in early 1854, were unambiguous: he supported American composers, advocated for the development of American musical culture, and promoted the creation of an environment that would provide native composers the opportunity to have their music performed. His star was continuing to rise in many arenas. At this point in his career, he had every reason to think that the doors were beginning to open—for him and for other American musicians.

# 3 | The 1850s

## *During Which Young Apollo Becomes a Jack-of-All-Trades and a Renowned Musician*

**THE EARLY 1850S,** which culminated in the "musical battle" in early 1854, were clearly a pivotal time in George Bristow's expanding professional career. This period was also, however, an important time for him personally; as he later remembered, "The world is full of changes and our musician, being human . . . had to submit to them."[1] But while there is sufficient information from print sources to construct a portrait of his public identity, there is little to shed light on his personal life, for he left behind only a handful of letters and no papers beyond the autobiographical sketch from the 1860s. Any real sense of Bristow as a man in the 1850s, then, has to be pieced together from bits of evidence.

Bristow's description of his physical appearance during this period is rather self-conscious but also somewhat sardonic. Young Apollo, he wrote, was "tall, not well proportioned, angular," balding even in his twenties (as he put it, "he had but little '*where the wool ought to grow*'"), and in general "not what might be called handsome." However, he continued, "neither was he bad looking." Furthermore, the help of a good barber (who "made the most" of what was there) and a new suit of clothes went a long way "towards supplying nature's deficiencies," with the result of making Bristow (or, as he put it, "Mr. Apollo") "decidedly pleasant to look upon."[2] During the 1840s and into the 1850s, as we saw in Interlude A, young

Apollo gradually moved away from theater work and increasingly into teaching for his livelihood. He also, as already mentioned, fell into and out of love with a succession of his female students. Eventually, his teaching and work as a church organist (see Interlude B) became sufficiently stable that he could consider marriage. And on September 14, 1853, he took this step, marrying Harriet Newell Crane of Newark, New Jersey. Delmer Rogers suggests that she was a singer and that the two had met at a concert at the Brooklyn Female Academy in 1851; indeed, her vocation is confirmed by a later description of her as "a teacher of music, and an experienced choir singer."[3] Little else is known about Crane beyond her nativity in Newark and adulterous behavior in the 1850s and 1860s as detailed in Victor Yellin's account of Bristow's 1863 divorce. But that unhappiness would be in the future. At the time of his marriage, Bristow was thoroughly occupied on all fronts, for this coincided with the arrival in New York of Jullien and his orchestra, Bristow's subsequent performances with that ensemble, the commissioning and completion of his Symphony No. 2, and the performance by Jullien's Orchestra of his *Sinfonia* and parts of the new symphony. As a result, the period just before the unsettling 1854 journalistic storm was probably a happy and very productive time for George Bristow as a person and a musician, as well as a period during which he was astonishingly busy. The fight was clearly a threshold event in the young musician's life, but it was also undoubtedly an unhappy and infuriating interruption to a period of tremendous productivity and happiness.

## Freelance Activities

After Jullien left the United States in June 1854, musical life in the metropolis returned to normal. The type of freelance activities in which Bristow had been engaged prior to the French conductor's whirlwind visit continued and increased, as could be expected in a city that was growing rapidly. Over the decade of the 1840s, the population of Manhattan had increased by 65 percent (from about 313,000 to nearly 516,000); the 1850s would see an increase of 57 percent (to nearly 814,000 by 1860). This population growth was fueled in large part by European immigrants. By 1850, 45 percent of Manhattan's residents (about 236,000) were foreign-born (56 percent of them from Ireland); by 1860, the percentage was even higher, at 47 percent (about 384,000 out of 814,000). Apparently such statistics are not available from the 1840 census, but in 1830 only 8 percent (18,000) of Manhattan's 202,500 residents were foreign-born.[4] This population explosion, coupled with the increasing role of New York as a major transportation center—and hence the home base for many foreign musicians who toured the United States—meant that opportunities for freelance musicians like Bristow grew more numerous throughout the 1850s.

As a consequence, during the period 1854–1860, Bristow appeared in a wide variety of concerts as pianist, organist, or other type of assisting artist. Later in the decade his performance activity was increasingly in the realm of conducting rather than solo or ensemble performances as a pianist or violinist (the exception was his continued orchestral work). The events in which he participated included special performances that featured artists who were either local or visiting (e.g., Louis Gottschalk, Christine Nilsson [1843–1921], Sigismund Thalberg, Elizabeth Greenfield (ca. 1819–1876]), benefit concerts, occasional extra engagements that included the standing ensembles of which he was a member, concerts given by his public school students, and performances that marked special occasions (Washington's Birthday, floral festivals, anniversary concerts). (See table 1.) Longer-term engagements included his work as accompanist on a concert tour given by the principal singers of the Pyne and Harrison Opera Company (spring 1855) and as musical director and conductor of the opera company during its season at Niblo's (May to November 1855). Table 1 represents a sample of the types of short-term performance work in which Bristow engaged. But it is not comprehensive (there were many more benefit concerts), nor does it take into consideration the non-trivial amount of time devoted to rehearsals. Presumably many of the events listed—especially those with large numbers of performers—required at least some rehearsal, as did Bristow's various church choirs. The table does suggest, however, the significant amount of time needed to make a living as a performing musician in mid-nineteenth-century America; it also reveals the wide variety of musical entertainments that were a regular part of urban American culture at the time.

During the mid to late 1850s, Bristow also enjoyed performances of his own music; these numbers would increase in frequency during the 1860s. After numerous performances of movements from his first and second symphonies by the Jullien Orchestra and the premiere (and subsequent performances) of *Rip Van Winkle* by the Pyne and Harrison Opera Company in late 1855, the most commonly programmed works were arias or fantasias from the opera. Harvey Dodworth, for example, regularly programmed a "Fantasia" and a "Quickstep," based on tunes from *Rip Van Winkle* (in 1856 and 1857), and several arias from the opera were performed during the second season of Jerome Hopkins's New York American-Music Association.[5] And, as discussed below, Bristow's orchestral music likewise enjoyed some high-profile exposure: both his second and third symphonies were given their premiere performances by the Philharmonic Society (in March 1856

**TABLE 1.** *Select Sample of Bristow's Performance Engagements, 1854–1860*

| GFB's Role | Date | Event | Location | Other Artists | Source |
|---|---|---|---|---|---|
| pianist (acct) | Apr. 26, 1854 | Testimonial concert | Niblo's | Dodworth concert band, full orchestra | NYT, Apr. 25, 1854, 5 |
| conductor | Nov. 13, 1854 | Concert | Church of Divine Unity | Harmonic Society | NYT, Nov. 13, 1854, 4 |
| conductor | Dec. 25, 1854 | Concert | AM | Harmonic Society, Maria Brainerd | NYT, Dec. 25, 1854, 8 |
| pianist | Feb. 24, 1855 | Grand Concert | Niblo's | Dodworth band and grand orchestra | NYT, Feb. 23, 1855, 5 |
| conductor | Mar. 14, 1855 | Sacred & Misc. music concert | RI | Georgiana Stuart | NYDTrib, Mar. 14, 1855, 7 |
| conductor | Apr. 2, 1855 | Vocal & Instrumental concert | DA | Georgiana Stuart | NYT, Apr. 30, 1855, 7 |
| pianist | Feb. 23, 1855 | Grand Concert | Niblo's | Dodworth Band and Orchestra | NYT, Feb. 23 1855, 5 |
| conductor | Mar. 14, 1855 | Sacred & Music Concert | RI | Georgiana Stuart | NYDTrib, Mar. 14, 1855 |
| pianist | Mar. 31, 1855 | Grand Concert | Niblo's | Pyne & Harrison Opera Company | NYT, Mar. 31, 1855, 5 |
| pianist, conductor | Feb.–May 1855 | Concert tour | Various cities | Pyne & Harrison Company soloists | Lawrence II: 622; Quigg AM V: 7 |
| pianist | May 1, 1855 | Concert | BA | Caroline Lehmann | NYT, May 11, 1855, 5 |
| conductor, mus. director. | May–Nov. 1855 | Opera Company season | Niblo's | Pyne & Harrison Opera Company | See chapter 3 |
| conductor | Jan. 30, 1856 | Grand Vocal Concert | BT | Students of Grammar School No. 42 | NYT, Jan. 29, 1856, 5 |
| pianist (acct) | Feb. 1, 1856 | Complimentary Concert | CAR | John Kyle (flute) | NYT, Jan. 29, 1856, 5 |
| pianist | May 6, 1856 | Second Concert | BA | Kate V. Comstock, others | NYH, May 6, 1856, 7 |
| conductor | May 21, 1856 | Grand Concert | BT | 600 students of 5th ward school No. 44 | NYH, May 20, 1856, 7 |
| pianist (acct) | June 4, 1856 | Benefit, Signor La Manna | Wallack's | Various artists | NYT, June 4, 1856, 7 |
| organist | Oct. 22, 1856 | Organ exhibition | Church of All Souls | Exhibition of new organ at church | NYT, Oct. 22, 1856, 3 |
| conductor | Dec. 5, 1856 | Concert | BT | Students of Grammar School No. 42 | NYH, Dec. 3, 1856, 3 |
| assisting artist | Dec. 12, 1856 | Performance of *The Flower Queen* | AM | Pupils of Grammar School No. 11 | NYH, Dec. 9, 1856, 7 |
| conductor | Jan. 28, 1857 | Grand Concert | BT | Misses Snow, Wm. Oakley (Alleghenians) | NYH, Jan. 28, 1857, 3 |
| conductor | Feb. 20, 1857 | Benefit Concert | Niblo's | Harmonic Society | NYH, Feb. 17, 1857, 7 |
| conductor | Mar. 10, 1857 | Concert (*Stabat Mater*) | Niblo's | Thalberg, Harmonic Society | NYT, Feb. 10, 1857, 3 |
| conductor | Mar. 12, 1857 | Concert | AM | Thalberg (last concert), Harmonic Society, Parodi, D'Angri, others | NYH, Mar. 12, 1857, 7 |

**TABLE 1.** *Continued*

| GFB's Role | Date | Event | Location | Other Artists | Source |
|---|---|---|---|---|---|
| pianist | Mar. 20, 1857 | Benefit Concert | Niblo's | For the stage manager at Niblo's | NYH, Mar. 18, 1857, 7 |
| pianist (acct) | Apr. 11, 1857 | Benefit concert, Mr. Horncastle | BA | Louisa and Susan Pyne, Georgiana Leach, others | NYH, Apr. 11, 1857, np |
| conductor | Apr. 28, 1857 | Benefit Concert for Brooklyn YMCA | PC | Orchestra | NYT, Apr. 21, 1857, 2 |
| conductor | Feb. 16, 1858 | Grand Concert | MH | Hattie Adem, other performers | NYT, Feb. 11, 1858, 5 |
| conductor | Feb. 22, 1858 | Washington's Birthday concert | AM | Portion of Harmonic Society; performance of *Ode*, op. 29 | NYH, Feb. 16, 1858, 7 |
| conductor | Apr. 19, 1858 | Oratorio (*Elijah*) | AM | Harmonic Society | NYT, Apr. 28, 1858, 2 |
| conductor | Apr.– May 1858 | "Musard Concerts" oratorios | AM | Harmonic Society, other performers | NYT, Apr. 27, 1858, 2; other advertisements |
| conductor | June 27, 1858 | Monster Concert and Pic Nic | MM Jones' Wood | Maretzek, Bergmann, Anschütz | NYH, June 8, 1858 |
| pianist (accompanist) | Aug. 5, 1858 | Reading and musical entertainment | New Rochelle | Members of the Harmonic Society | NYH, Aug. 9, 1858, 5 |
| conductor | Sept. 1, 1858 | Atlantic Cable Celebration | CP | Various choruses and orchestras, including Harmonic Society | BDE, Sept. 2, 1858, 2 |
| conductor | Sept. 9, 1858 | Grand Musical Entertainment | CP | Harmonic Society | NYT, Sept. 9, 1858, 3 |
| pianist (acct) | Jan. 27, 1859; Feb. 2, 1859 | Second annual vocal concert | MH | Miss Dingley | NYDTrib, Jan. 7, 1859; NYT, Feb. 2, 1859, 4 |
| pianist | Mar. 11, 1859 | Testimonial Concert for J. B. Brown | AM | Some student performers | NYT, Mar. 11, 1859, 3 |
| conductor | Apr. 26, 1859 | 40th anniversary: Odd Fellows | Madison Square | Unidentified choir | NYDTrib, Apr. 27, 1859 |
| conductor | May 17, 1859 | Musical Soirée | AM | Metropolitan Musical Society | NYDTrib, May 16, 1859, 2 |
| conductor | June 7, 1859 | Floral Festival | PC | orchestra of Phil Soc members | BDE, June 6, 1859, 11 |
| conductor | June 21, 1859 | Promenade Concerts | PG&H | Metropolitan Musical Society | NYT, June 22, 1859, 7 |
| conductor | July 18, 1859 | Festivals of Music | Jones' Woods | Maretzek, Anschütz, Grill | NYH, July 11, 1859, 5 |
| conductor | Nov. 11, 1859 | Oratorio (*Elijah*) | AM | Harmonic Society | NYH, Nov. 8, 1859, 7 |

Key: AM  Academy of Music    CAR  City Assembly Rooms    MH  Mozart Hall    RI  Rutger's Institute
BA  Brooklyn Athenaeum    CP  Crystal Palace    PC  Plymouth Church (Brooklyn)
BT  Broadway Tabernacle    DA  Dodworth's Academy    PG&H  Palace Garden and Hall

and March 1859, respectively), and his *Winter's Tale Overture* was performed regularly in conjunction with a new production of the play (in 1856 and 1857).

## Regular Performing: Church Job and Choral Societies

Bristow's two most important steady conducting and performing engagements during the 1850s were his positions as church organist and choirmaster and as conductor and music director of the New York Harmonic Society, which Vera Lawrence called "New York's foremost and largest singing group."[6] His work for the church was an activity in which he was engaged throughout his entire career; that part of his professional life is dealt with in Interlude B. But his very public position as conductor and musical director of the Harmonic Society was a significant professional activity, primarily during the 1850s, and it is dealt with here.

During this mid-century period, Americans were enamored of music performed by massed choirs of mostly amateur singers, not unlike what was happening in England and elsewhere in Western Europe. In the United States, especially in larger towns and cities, the new availability of affordable music abetted this burgeoning craze for choral music performances. By the 1850s, amateur singers could readily purchase many popular European works in the new, cheaper octavo editions published by the British firm Novello and made available in the United States through Oliver Ditson and Company of Boston, which in 1852 became Novello's American distributor.[7] The term "octavo" is from the innovative practice of printing eight pages per sheet (rather than the traditional four of quarto size); this resulted in smaller but significantly cheaper editions of choral music. Novello also adopted the newer technique of typesetting rather than engraving music, which allowed for large print runs.[8] The two techniques reduced the cost of the company's publications, which helped to fuel the amateur choral craze on both sides of the Atlantic. In addition, many members of church choirs also joined larger choral societies, which helped to link sacred and secular choral music in the minds of many Americans. These developments made this style of amateur music-making not just an important part of the American soundscape but also, as musicologist Lee Orr puts it, "the most ubiquitous type of formal music-making in the United States."[9]

## New York Society Choirs

The longest-lived and most important choral society for Bristow was the New York Harmonic Society (also briefly known as the New York Sacred Harmonic

Society), which he led for most of twelve years. His first concert at the helm was December 11, 1851, at Tripler Hall; the chosen work was Haydn's *The Creation*. Bristow took over after the resignation of Theodore Eisfeld, who had conducted during the organization's debut season (1850–1851), and served in this capacity throughout the entire decade, with one brief hiatus, finally stepping down from the helm in 1863.[10] Later he would conduct the New York Mendelssohn Union (1867–1871) and the Harlem (also known as the Morrisiana) Mendelssohn Union (1871–1873). (See chapter 4.) The experience gained from conducting these large ensembles was obviously more significant than what he learned from his church choir work, for the Harmonic Society was large enough to tackle serious choral masterpieces, and the caliber of performance was also undoubtedly superior. By 1856 the ensemble numbered 130 male and 147 female singers.[11] But Bristow's work with such choral societies bled over into his activities as a church musician, for many church choir members also sang with one or more of the city's larger ensembles. (See Interlude B.) Membership in the various societies themselves also sometimes overlapped: as Frédéric Louis Ritter observed, there were not enough skilled singers in New York in the 1850s to support two large ensembles (not to mention the Männerchor or Liederkranz ensembles in the German community), which meant that some singers belonged to both the Harmonic Society and the Mendelssohn Union (founded in 1854) during their overlapping years. As a result, the two ensembles frequently competed with each other for the city's amateur singers, which sometimes created friction.[12]

According to Ritter, it was the Harmonic Society that started the popular practice of performing the *Messiah* in New York on Christmas Eve. Other compositions favored by the organization during this decade (which Bristow chose) included standard mid-century choral works (*The Seasons, Israel in Egypt, Judas Maccabaeus, Elijah, Lobgesang*), some lesser-known pieces (Carl Loewe's *The Seven Sleepers* [*Die sieben Schläfer*], *Le Désert* by Félicien David, *Stabat Mater* by Gioachino Rossini, and Sigismund von Neukomm's *David*), as well as numerous works by native or immigrant Americans, including Bristow's first oratorio, *Praise to God*; Ritter's *Forty-Sixth Psalm*; *The Waldenses* by New Englander Asahel Abbot (1805–1888); and George Curtis's *Eleutheria*.[13] The reliance on works by European composers was absolutely typical; as Orr points out, "American choral societies and festival choruses relied almost exclusively on European works by Handel, Haydn, Mendelssohn, Beethoven, and Mozart" and only later added American compositions. The New York Harmonic Society, however, was apparently ahead of the curve, for during the 1850s and early 1860s the ensemble also performed—over and above the American works already noted—various shorter works by American-born, immigrant, or visiting composers, including William Fry, George Loder, William Howard Glover (1819–1875), and William Wallace. That they did so during Bristow's tenure as music director illustrates his continued support for his fellow composers, although apparently he did not program enough of these latter works to satisfy Jerome Hopkins, who complained bitterly in 1861 about the society's "blind Pagan adoration of old things because they are old."[14] But such choral works, especially those by Handel, continued to appeal to the Harmonic Society's audiences; this also contradicts the claim by some scholars that Bristow was adamantly opposed to Germans and German music.

The Harmonic Society presented a regular season, although the number of concerts fluctuated from year to year. The organization generally gave performances in both fall and spring, as well as its annual Christmas production of the *Messiah*. The society, however, also regularly participated in special events—sometimes as the entire ensemble and sometimes only as a smaller group of singers. A sample of such performances is illustrative: the organization participated in Fry's 1852–1853 series of lectures, appeared in a complimentary concert for that critic/composer at Metropolitan Hall in the latter year, participated in both the grandiose opening of the Crystal Palace Exhibition of Industry in July 1853 and in the Grand Re-Dedication of the same hall in May 1854 (the latter organized by P. T. Barnum), and appeared in the already mentioned Musical Congress with Louis Jullien in June 1854.[15] (Other examples are included in table 1.) The ensemble also participated in innumerable large and small benefit concerts—to help churches, humanitarian organizations, individuals, and needy groups (such as "indigent veterans of the War of 1812"). In fact, as Vera Lawrence points out, in 1854 the society "largely dominated the miscellaneous and sacred benefit concerts given for and at the various churches," and during the following year "the givers of independent sacred concerts were apt to lean on members of the Harmonic Society" for their events.[16] George Bristow participated in most, if not all, of these events—conducting the choral society and frequently also the accompanying ensemble, or conducting and accompanying the ensemble himself on piano or organ. Another demand on Bristow's time was the society's rehearsals, held regularly every Monday evening during the season.[17]

Commentary about Bristow's conducting ability is fairly elusive, but as the conductor of the Harmonic Society he was generally regarded as skilled. In July 1852, for example, Richard Storrs Willis observed that Bristow "did all that one could expect of any conductor. Patient, attentive, and persevering as ever was this valuable ally in our musical undertakings." Several years later a contributor to *Dwight's* wrote, "Never have choruses been rendered by any society in this City with the same aplomb [as those] under the direction of Mr. Bristow," and in 1858 a notice in the *Times* described him as having "perhaps no equal as a conductor of oratorio on this side of the Atlantic."[18] A number of journalists (including Charles Bailey Seymour [1829–1869], then critic for the *Times*) agreed that Bristow had greatly improved both the caliber of the society's performances and its appeal to audiences. In 1854, for example, Seymour—writing about a performance of *The Seasons*—noted that "the only fault we can find with this Society is, that the performances are too much like Angels' visits—few and very far between."[19] Bristow's ability as a conductor was also praised in connection with his work as a church organist and choir director, a different type of activity but one that overlapped significantly with his work with the Harmonic Society.

## CHORAL COMPOSITION

Bristow's significant work with the Harmonic Society undoubtedly whetted his appetite for writing choral music, but this interest would blossom primarily in the next decade. During the 1850s he did write one large choral composition, but it was secular (and nationalistic) in orientation. The *Ode* for soprano, SSA chorus, and orchestra (op. 29) dates from 1856 and is a strictly utilitarian setting of an overtly patriotic text by poet and dime novelist Augustine Duganne (1823–1884). Composed to mark the fifty-fifth anniversary of Andrew Jackson's 1815 military victory in New Orleans, it had one semi-staged performance, by female choristers from the Harmonic and Mendelssohn societies. Bristow conducted the singers and an accompanying orchestra, the performance was deemed "generally satisfactory," and the work was subsequently shelved.[20]

## Work in the Theater

One of Bristow's most prominent short-term engagements at mid-century was his appointment as artistic director of the Pyne and Harrison English Opera Company during its 1855 New York season. This was the only time that Bristow ever served as the artistic director or conductor of an opera troupe, but he undertook this assignment soon after completion of *Rip Van Winkle*, which perhaps made him feel more comfortable working within that genre. William Fry welcomed this development: "Mr. George Bristow led the orchestra," he wrote in a review, "which we were glad to see, as there is no reason why New-York may not supply a capable operatic orchestral chief."[21] Bristow had served as piano accompanist for the company singers during a concert tour they mounted between the conclusion of their run at the Broadway Theatre (in mid-February 1855) and the beginning of their summer season.[22] His appointment as artistic director started with the commencement of the company's season at Niblo's (May 23) and lasted until November 3—twenty-three and a half weeks, or 125 performances, the longest engagement during the London troupe's very successful thirty-two-month visit to the United States (October 1854–May 1857). According to Travis Quigg, Bristow was "urged to continue as conductor" when the company left New York in November on what would be the first of two triumphant American tours (November 1855–May 1856 and August 1856–May 1857), but financial obligations in New York precluded acceptance of the position. (See Interlude D.) Instead, he recommended the fifteen-year-old Anthony Reiff Jr. (1830–1916), son of "his old and esteemed friend" Anthony Reiff Sr. (1803–1880). [23]

Under Bristow's direction, the company mounted many of the "standard" operas that English-language troupes performed in America and Great Britain at mid-century, including adaptations/translations of bel canto and *opéra comique* favorites (*Cinderella, Daughter of the Regiment, Barber of Seville, La Sonnambula,* and *Fra Diavolo*) and works originally written in English (Michael Balfe's *Bohemian Girl* and *Daughter of St. Mark* and William Vincent Wallace's *Maritana*). They also presented some less "standard" English-language works (including Bristow's *Rip Van Winkle*). The company enjoyed what Lawrence called a "hitherto unparalleled run" in Manhattan, and as late as mid-September Willis commented on the troupe's "usual success," by which he meant "good houses" and "exquisite singing on the part of Miss [Louisa] Pyne."[24]

### RIP VAN WINKLE, OP. 22

In late August the company began to rehearse Bristow's opera, which Delmer Rogers claims he had started to write around 1852.[25] Although titled a "grand romantic opera," the work (with spoken dialogue) is actually a comic opera—an adaptation by John Howard Wainwright (1829–1871) of Washington Irving's famous story, originally published in 1819 in *The Sketch Book of Geoffrey Crayon, Gent.* (with exquisite engravings by F.O.C. Darley). By mid-century the work was considered an American folktale.[26] It was the perfect subject for a composer who, by early 1853, had become increasingly interested in musical nationalism and who apparently considered opera to be a superior medium for communicating such ideas. The opera company, and William Niblo, pulled out all the stops for this production; the costumes were described as "uncommonly good" and the scenery was "a marvel of artistic skill and completeness." The entire mise-en-scène, in fact, was inspired by Darley's illustrations; some were reproduced on stage as *tableaux vivants*.[27]

Audiences clearly enjoyed the opera. Fry's lengthy and laudatory review of opening night (September 27) reported that Niblo's Theatre—which he rather smugly observed "holds more people than the Paris opera house"—was "densely filled" for the event. The opera was presented nightly through October 6, then additional times over the next three weeks, for a total of eighteen performances. The public response was "decidedly successful."[28] Critics were mostly generous and congratulatory, although several observed that Bristow had produced "a popular, and not a classical work." This assessment was based on the fact that his music had "simple and graceful themes, set in stirring, strongly marked rhythms [which] keep the public feet in motion and the public heart bounding with delight" and that it "wins upon and thoroughly seizes hold of the ear and heart of an audience, and . . . leaves . . . a lasting impression." To some, the fact that the music resonated with audiences was not a positive attribute; Seymour of the *Times*, for example, complained that the "light and cheerful music" was not "strikingly original."[29] But while opera (as a genre) would eventually be regarded in America as a means for cultural uplift, in the 1850s it was still popular entertainment, and New Yorkers enthusiastically attended performances in large numbers.

Bristow drew on various sources for his musical inspiration, including continental composers. Steven Ledbetter, for example, describes Alice's act 2 aria "Yes, I'll Follow the Battle" (sung by Louisa Pyne) as "straight out of the Italian mold," and Fry wrote that the spirited and upbeat "Soldier's Chorus" in act 2, scene 3, was "Auberish."[30] But Bristow also relied on American popular song, hymnody, and ballads, which created an eclectic mixture of European and American influences. Several affective arias and duets illustrate his gift for melody; there are also stirring choruses, a drinking song, tuneful duets, a Morris dance, an *Allegro pastorale* chorus with a hurdy-gurdy bass, and a song for *vivandière*. The mixture of styles (especially the tuneful "American" sound) explains the opera's resonance with New York audiences and its genial dismissal by some critics as a "non-classic" work. But refreshingly few critics complained that they heard echoes of European composers; as Edward Wilkins (1829–1861) of the *Herald* wrote, the music of the opera "is full of beauties, entirely the author's own."[31]

Some reviewers criticized the orchestration, but others called it "excellent"; Fry particularly praised the "fine musical writing" in "the supernatural bits" where Rip encounters Henrick Hudson and his crew.[32] The major criticism of the opera was its libretto. Not only is Irving's story a two-part tale that is separated by the protagonist's twenty-year nap, but also there is no love interest. To solve these problems, Wainwright created as act 2 a new love story between Rip's grown daughter and a Continental Army captain set during the Revolutionary War (while

Rip was sleeping). Some critics enjoyed this; others thought it tedious. Several suggested that it could be fixed with some tweaking, and Wilkins reported that "a great deal of dreary recitation" had been cut after the premiere and that "more piquancy [was] infused into the comic parts" in subsequent performances. Others, however, were less forgiving; Seymour, for example, wrote curtly, "The least said about the libretto, the better."[33] The inferior libretto undoubtedly contributed to the most common complaint about Bristow's music: that it lacked drama. Willis described the "easy flow of melody" in the opera but pointed out that attributes needed in a dramatic composition were lacking. Seymour likewise commented that "Mr. Bristow does not identify himself with the emotional requirements of the drama; he is never passionate nor dramatic."[34]

Nevertheless, the general assessment was quite positive. One anonymous correspondent to *Dwight's* (an unidentified recent German immigrant) concluded that "the work really does an American composer credit; it is the first one of the kind which has inspired me with respect." Willis agreed. Writing genially about "Our George" (evidently the two men had buried their hatchets), he noted that Bristow "has every cause of congratulations on his success." He urged the composer to "make this first opera a great study to improve upon," a sentiment that was echoed by Seymour.[35] The composer must have enjoyed the positive response and the pleasure that audiences took in the work, especially on the heels of the acrimonious events of early 1854. Bristow, who was not yet thirty, was clearly on a roll.

### WINTER'S TALE OVERTURE

Almost immediately after relinquishing the baton for Pyne and Harrison, the composer threw himself into another theater-related endeavor: an overture designed as the curtain-raiser of a new production of Shakespeare's *Winter's Tale* at Burton's Theatre. This was his third overture (of six), preceded by his Concert Overture and the overture from *Rip Van Winkle*; it was his second for a theatrical work.[36] He would eventually write three more, all of which would be performed as stand-alone orchestral works.

All of Bristow's overtures (except the first) are programmatic and, as such, overtly contrast with his other large instrumental works up to that point, especially his first two (and, to a certain extent, his third) symphonies. Bristow perhaps discovered that it was easier to write one-movement overtures in a programmatic style (or, conversely, to write program music as one-movement overtures). Working in a theatrical context might also have pushed him in this direction. But it is also possible that he was influenced by the repertoire that he played as a member of the Philharmonic Society orchestra: absolute (or quasi-absolute) symphonies by Beethoven, Haydn, Mendelssohn, Mozart, Schubert, and Schumann, and programmatic overtures by Berlioz, William Sterndale Bennett, Peter Josef von Lindpaintner, Étienne Méhul, Mendelssohn, Weber, and others. He also clearly used his programmatic overtures to address his growing interest in nationalistic instrumental music, for all of his programmatic overtures, except *Winter's Tale*, are Americanist in orientation.

*Winter's Tale Overture* dates from late 1855. Marked *Allegro pomposo*, it is scored for strings (including contrabass), pairs of winds (plus piccolo), pairs of brass (horns in E and G, trumpets, and trombones), and percussion (timpani and side drum). It is sectional in format, with clear musical allusions to different parts of the play: there is a dance, a storm, a rustic melody in the oboe and a birdlike tune in the flute (alluding to rural life), and a fife-and-drum melody (piccolo and side drum) to represent the military. The overture was performed with the play in both 1856 and 1857. When it was featured in 1859 as part of a concert, it was apparently the hit of the evening, for it was "received with great favor, and the composer was called out several times."[37] Whether or not Bristow conducted the overture—and the rest of the music that accompanied the play—during either theatrical run is unknown. But it is plausible, since he had plenty of theater-orchestra experience. Moreover, such an engagement would have been perfectly unexceptional for a musician who habitually assumed the many and diverse roles expected in the musical world of mid-century New York.

## Symphonies

Shortly after his triumph with *Rip Van Winkle* and his achievement as music director of a successful opera company, Bristow rejoined the Philharmonic Society orchestra. His return to the ranks in November 1855 meant that he had essentially taken an unpaid leave of absence from the ensemble for eighteen months.[38] Perhaps as a peace offering to the newly reinstated violinist (and its most prominent native composer), the orchestra agreed to perform the complete "Jullien" Symphony on March 1, 1856, under Carl Bergmann. Although this was the premiere performance of the symphony, neither the orchestra (on the program) nor any of the critics mentioned this, although the program does use the symphony's nickname, "Jullien," for the first time.[39] Several critics, however—in marked contrast to their reception of the opera—quickly sharpened their knives and started hacking away at this new work. American critics (including Fry) regularly applauded the programming of American compositions, but their responses to the actual works (especially instrumental compositions), as Lawrence observed, "were usually a mass of reservations, if not downright disdain."[40]

In the case of Bristow's Symphony No. 2, critics followed the well-established pattern of demonstrating their own musical sophistication by disparaging the work being reviewed. The unnamed New York critic for *Dwight's*, for example, acknowledged the symphony's "richness of instrumentation, its wealth of pleasing melodies, and numerous other merits" but then claimed that "Weber, Mendelssohn, Spohr, Haydn, Mozart, and I know not what others, seem to be playing ball with snatches of their melodies, and tossing them to and fro in merry confusion." Henry Watson, writing in *Leslie's*, offered lukewarm praise but then denounced the work's lack of "individuality, [and] any evidence of an original train of thought.[41] Willis also noted that the symphony was a "very cleverly instrumented and credible work," written by a "skillful and practiced instrumentalist"; the Adagio (incorrectly identified as Andante) was "the best of the movements," and the Scherzo (which he compared to a schottische), was "neatly and cleverly worked and of pleasing effect." He also again heard hints of a personal voice but could not resist lecturing Bristow about his ignorance of compositional technique, including the "proper place for free modulation" in "what is called *die freie Fantasie*, which is the commencement of the second part of any first movement" (the development section). His final assessment was that the work "suffers from excess of modulation and . . . lack of harmonic unity" and that it "needs scissoring."[42]

The most damning review, however, was from Theodore Hagen (1823–1871), critic for the *Musical Review & Gazette*, former contributor to Robert Schumann's *Neue Zeitschrift für Musik*, and recent immigrant, who could find nothing to praise. He dismissed Bristow's instrumentation as lackluster and his musical motives as "quite common, lacking entirely in nobility of expression." The melodic similarities he heard were not to great masters but rather to music that was played by amateur bands in "garden-concerts." He also dismissed the "only originality" he found in the symphony: the second-movement Scherzo, which he identified as a polka. He argued that to replace an "aristocratic" minuet with a mere "popular dance" was absolutely inappropriate for a symphony and scornfully dismissed this attempt by Bristow to stamp his symphony with original ideas. He lamented that a Philharmonic concert, the only place "where the purest taste and the greatest finish in our art ought to prevail," had been given over to a "second- or third-rate" composition and recommended that a work like Bristow's symphony should be relegated to "our theatres between the acts," a sneer that must have burned.[43]

None of the critics, who seemed quite self-satisfied with their hatchet jobs, noticed the skillful writing for winds, the clever instrumentation and developmental techniques, or the tuneful "earworm" melodies that abound in the symphony. Nor did they seem to recognize either the innovative proto-cyclic style of composition or the deliberate use of instrumentation and sonority, both of which were elements of the composer's nascent personal voice.

Buried in this avalanche of negative reviews, however, were words of praise from several quarters. Fry noted that Jullien had taken the symphony to the United Kingdom, where it had been well received, and chided the Philharmonic because Bristow's work was being produced "in his own country" only after it "had been successfully heard in London." He also called the innovative Scherzo the "best hit" of the symphony, praised the final movement, and concluded that the whole work "was well received, and constituted an era in the annals of the Society."[44] And Émile Girac (d. 1869) a French critic who recently had started writing for the *Albion*, thanked the Philharmonic Society for playing Bristow's work, commented that "native art can never receive too much encouragement," recommended that the orchestra devote one concert per year to composers living in the United States, and suggested that Bristow's success should inspire the ensemble to be much "less exclusive for the future, and renounce all small and parsimonious proceedings."[45] He then turned to Bristow, a man with "delightful personal qualities" whose "talent we have long loved." He pointed out that Jullien had demonstrated to the public that Bristow "was capable of composing long and valuable works" and that the young American was now returning the favor by naming his new symphony for his "musical god-father." Girac, who as a composer had had his own differences of opinion about Jullien, cleverly suggested that Bristow's symphony was a symbol of the mark that the French conductor had made on American music. "Do you know how much is expressed by those two little words, the *Jullien Symphony*?" he asked rhetorically.

> They mean simply that Jullien did more for Concert music in three months, than the Philharmonic Society has accomplished since Mr. U. C. Hill created it and brought it before the world. [Jullien] gave us Mozart, Beethoven, and Mendelssohn, as we have never heard them interpreted in New York. He taught us the art of shades and effects in music. . . . He revealed to us the powers of Bristow, Fry, and Eisfeld, and did far more for their reputation than was ever done by the Society, which owed so much at least to the first and last of these noble and courageous musicians.

"This," he concluded, "is the true meaning of Bristow's symphony."[46] But most New York critics, and certainly the Philharmonic Society itself, were interested neither in valorizing Jullien nor encouraging promising American composers. The orchestra shelved the piece and never played it again. Bristow, the "stalwart composer" (as described by both Thurston Dox and Douglas Shadle), was somehow able to put the discouraging and callous comments aside and resume composing.[47]

## SYMPHONY NO. 3

We do not know when Bristow began to work on his Symphony No. 3 in F-sharp Minor, op. 26, but, as already mentioned, we know that it was partially completed by June 1854. Although Jullien strongly encouraged Bristow to complete the work and send it to him, the composer was fiendishly active in the several years after the French conductor's departure and apparently did not return to the work until 1856. From that point until the end of the decade, however, he published little, which suggests that he was devoting most of his compositional attention to it.

The work was premiered by the Philharmonic Society orchestra on March 26, 1859, under Carl Bergmann—the fourth of Bristow's works to be played by the ensemble and the third in a subscription concert. It is scored for pairs of winds, four horns, two trumpets, three trombones, timpani, strings, and harp. It is in four movements (Allegro, Scherzo, Nocturno, and Finale: Allegro con fuoco), each of which was assigned a poem (or portion of one) as an epigraph.[48] They are listed on the third page of the Philharmonic Society program:

### 1. ALLEGRO

My soul is dark—Oh! quickly string
The harp I yet can brook to hear;
And let thy gentle fingers fling
Its melting murmurs o'er mine ear.
If in his heart a hope be dear,
That sound shall charm it forth again:
If in these eyes there lurk a tear,
'Twill flow, and cease to burn my brain.

But bid the strain be wild and deep,
Nor let thy notes of joy be first;
I tell thee, minstrel, I must weep,
Or else this heavy heart will burst;
For it hath been by sorrow nursed,
And ached in sleepless silence, long;
And now 'tis doomed to know the worst,
And break at once—or yield to song.

### 2. *SCHERZO*—"THE BUTTERFLY"

Gay being, born to flutter thro' the day;
Sport in the sunshine of the present hour;
On the sweet rose thy painted wings display,
And cull the fragrance of the opening flow'r.

### 3. *NOCTURNO*—CALM

Pure was the temp'rate air, and even calm
Perpetual reign'd, save what the zephyrs bland
Breathed o'er the blue expanse.

### 4. FINALE: *ALLEGRO CON FUOCO*—ANGER

Next anger rushed, his eyes on fire,
In lightnings own'd his secret stings,
In one rude clash he struck the lyre.
And swept with hurried hand the strings.

The first poem is Lord Byron's "My Soul Is Dark" (1815); the second is the text to a duet by British composer John Bernard Sale (1779–1856). The epigraphs for the third and fourth movements are both from larger works: the third is from *The Seasons: Spring* by the Scottish poet James Thomson (1700–1748); the fourth from "The Passions: An Ode for Music," written in 1746 by the English poet William Collins (1721–1759). All of the poems were in print during the nineteenth century.[49]

Both Gregory Fried and Shadle suggest that Bristow was inspired to add poetic epigraphs to this symphony by Louis Spohr's Symphony No. 4 (*Die Weihe der Töne*), which Bristow knew well, since the orchestra had performed it six times since 1846, including most recently in November 1857. But Spohr's symphony is an overtly programmatic piece, clearly based on a poem by Carl Pfeiffer. Bristow's symphony, in contrast, is still very much absolute music, and although the imagery and emotional content of each epigraph is portrayed musically (more or less) in its movement, there is no narrative component nor any discernable connection between the poetic samples. As Trovator (pseud.), the New York correspondent to *Dwight's*, pointed out, "I must confess that I could neither find any connection of ideas between [the poetic mottos] nor discover their interpretation in the music, so I preferred to listen to the latter only for itself." Theodore Hagen made a similar comment, noting that he could not see any programmatic connection between the "dark soul" of Byron's poem and the butterfly of the Scherzo.[50] In fact, it is not clear if Bristow used the poems as inspiration or found poetic imagery that, after the fact, worked with his already composed music. The latter, however, seems probable, for he had started to write the symphony earlier in the 1850s, when he was still committed to his "classic style." By the time he resumed work on it later in the decade, however, he was clearly moving in the direction of program music.

The first movement, in sonata-allegro form, commences with a somber and brooding unison theme in the low strings (basses and celli), similar to the beginning of the "Jullien" Symphony; the contrasting theme in the dominant, an upbeat scalar melody with a gentle dance-like rhythm, is given to first violins and clarinets, with accompaniment by the harp. All of these musical gestures—the somber ("dark") start and the introduction of the harp ("lyre")—fit with the epigraph; furthermore, the overall sense of the movement (alternation between melancholy and happiness) also works with the poetic imagery ("heavy heart" vs. "notes of joy"). Bristow skillfully used material introduced in the exposition—including the primary theme treated fugally—in the development. The movement builds to a climax at the end, at which point the somber opening theme reenters, almost like an echo, before the work ends with a cadence in the major, followed by harp arpeggios. Hagen, apparently in search of a more programmatic treatment, commented that the final line of the poem ("And break at once—or yield to song") led him to expect that "in the second part of the work something or somebody will either break or sing."[51] Neither happens, which supports the idea that the work is absolute music overlaid with poetic imagery.

The second movement Scherzo works quite well as an illustration of the epigraph (and as an excellent example of Bristow's skill at orchestration); most critics pointed out the obvious influence of Mendelssohn's "elfinish" style. Willis wrote that "the most prominent beauties" of the movement were the "delicate contrasts of shading, skillful alternations of string, brass, and wood instruments, sharp, crispy phrasing, all subdued, producing a soft, fluttering, airy gaiety," and Trovator praised this movement as "exceedingly fresh and lively, and finely worked up." He continued, "the *motif* of the first part, it is true, partakes somewhat of the nature of a polka and a jig, but the melody of the trio is lovely and flowing and *caressing* enough to reconcile me to anything." The movement, he noted, was encored.[52] The Nocturno is calm and melodious and features variations achieved through skillful orchestration. Most of the critics, however, found it monotonous, although Willis conceded that perhaps a second hearing would convince him of its value. The symphony ends with an Allegro con fuoco movement, once again in the home key of F-sharp minor. Starting with a stormy, tense, and urgent theme over a restless accompaniment (again like the "Jullien"), the movement also has a contrasting secondary theme that is more lilting. Bristow skillfully tosses both themes around and frequently builds to interim climaxes; he also utilizes the trombones very effectively in a countermelody to the first theme in the recapitulation, also like the "Jullien." Jerome Hopkins, writing in the *Burlington (VT) Free Press*, pointed out that Bristow was one of only a handful of composers who knew how to write for brass instruments, surely a compliment, coming from a fellow composer, albeit one who was young and fairly inexperienced.[53] After the performance, according to Trovator, the composer "was called forth with vehement applause."

Most of the critics, somewhat surprisingly, wrote positive assessments of this work.[54] The exception was Seymour of the *Times*, who wrote a remarkably snarky review in which he noted that although the symphony exhibited "meritorious execution in a technical point of view," it nevertheless was "frequently weak and ill-sustained." He took the composer to task for writing dance-like melodies, pointing out that "the writer of a symphony should have a musical intelligence superior to the temptation of ordinary dance themes" (inexplicably overlooking the dance movements that were a normal part of many symphonies), and groused that "Mr. Bristow frequently surrenders himself to these pleasant inspirations and mars, we think, the happiness and value of his work as a classical composition." He ended with a patronizing (and ironic) observation that "with more opportunities to have his works performed," the composer "would do much better than he has done with this work."[55] Hopkins, who called the symphony "certainly a great Composition" and praised Bristow's linkage of musical expression with poetry, took great exception to Seymour's comments, calling the critic a "grandiloquent, verbose, pretentious and condemnatory ignoramus!" In fact, most critics were graciously complimentary; Trovator wrote that Bristow's "work has the happy quality of being popular enough to please the multitude, and yet possessing sufficient depth and intrinsic worth to preserve it from being trivial," and even Hagen conceded that "Mr. Bristow's Symphony was well received, and deservedly so."[56]

It is significant that the critics did not resort to their usual carping about the similarity of some of Bristow's melodies to works by particular European composers (and the accusation that such "echoes" made American composers' works derivative). Even the observation that the Scherzo was Mendelssohnian was broached in a noncritical manner; as Hagen pointed out, the movement was "entirely Mendelssohn, but quite effective."[57] It is possible, in fact, that the critics had finally begun to recognize that Bristow was a composer of some merit, with a style that—while it incorporated elements of the Western European musical language—was nevertheless personal and valid. This is perhaps reflected in Willis's conclusion about the symphony: the fact that it was "a creditable composition, in classic proportions, by a native composer was, of itself a good and commendable feature . . . not simply because the composition was good, nor because it was of American origin, but because it was American and good."[58]

## Other Activities and Accolades

The positive reception of Bristow's Symphony No. 3 can be read as a solid indication of his increased prominence as a member of the New York music community. His stature as a composer had clearly risen during the decade, and his position as conductor and music director of one of the city's most prestigious choral societies likewise indicates his rank as one of the more important musicians (and arguably the most prominent native one) in New York and possibly in the country. Another indication is his participation, in 1859, in the creation of an ambitious new organization, the Metropolitan Musical Society, to mount a series of monthly concerts at the Academy of Music. The goal was to offer concerts of both popular and serious music at moderate prices (à la both Jullien and Philippe Musard) and to "encourage and patronize . . . the meritorious native and resident composers who have heretofore had but rare opportunities of placing their compositions before the public." Its "first musical soirée" was held on May 17, under the musical leadership of Bristow, Harvey Dodworth, and Maurice Strakosch. The performing forces included a large orchestra, a military band, and the Harmonic Society. Another event—a "monster promenade concert," which was also "in the style of Jullien and Musard"—was held at the Palace Garden and Hall in June; this time the conductors were Bristow (sans the Harmonic Society), Dodworth, and Bergmann.[59] Although the organization was short-lived, its goals illustrate again Bristow's interest in providing performance opportunities for American composers. Moreover, the fact that he was working as a team with some of the most prominent conductors in the city clearly indicates that by the end of the 1850s he had become one of the city's music leaders—as a conductor as well as a composer.

In addition to all of the activity already described in this chapter, Bristow was engaged in numerous other endeavors during the decade, which suggests that he continued to wear numerous musical hats. In 1854, for example, he launched a piano and melodeon business (see Interlude D) and began to teach music in the New York Public Schools (Interlude C). In 1852 he became an officer of the American Musical Fund Society and six years later replaced Theodore Eisfeld on the Philharmonic Society's board of directors.[60]

Two more examples illustrate the increasing esteem in which Bristow was held. The first, which attests to his reputation in New York, was a "Grand Testimonial Concert" sponsored by the Harmonic Society and held on March 7, 1859, at the Academy of Music. The advertisement for the event reads like a press release and mentions Bristow's position as "among the highest in his profession," his recognition in Europe, his "untiring and indomitable perseverance, as well as his disinterested zeal and earnest devotion to the advancement of his art," all of which contributed to "the respect and esteem of all with whom he has been associated, both as a man and an artist."[61] The artists who agreed to participate in the event included a large number of prominent local singers, as well as violinist Joseph Burke (1817–1902); pianists Richard Hoffman (1831–1909), Henry C. Timm, and William Mason; harpist Thomas Aptommas (1829–1913); and the Harmonic and Philharmonic societies.[62] Henry Watson, still writing for *Leslie's*, joined in the accolades but also provided some insight into the composer's personality. He explained that although the testimonial was long overdue, Bristow was "one of those modest men who are content to work silently and steadily, and do not seek to blazon the world [with] the greatness of their merits." But, he argued, the composer "was born among us [and] has studied here, gaining knowledge by slow and painful experience [always] sustained by that active and earnest love of the art which gives hope to the true musician." As a result, he now "stands at the head of the musicians of his native country."[63] The event was a lengthy concert that included only a handful of Bristow's compositions: an unidentified movement from the "Jullien" Symphony, a song from *Rip Van Winkle* (sung by Louise Holder, his future wife), and the *Winter's Tale Overture*, which, as we have seen, was greeted with great enthusiasm. Seymour called the event a "success in every sense of the word. The house was handsomely filled and the performances went off with rare precision."[64] It must have been a heady, but perhaps uncomfortable, experience for the unassuming Bristow.

The second example attests to the composer's increasing renown elsewhere in the country. In March 1858 he received a long letter from the French-born Leopold Meignen (1793–1873), a Philadelphia composer, conductor, and publisher; William Fry's teacher; and a member of both the Musical Fund Society of Philadelphia and the unknown Harmonia Sacred Music Society.[65] The letter, addressed familiarly to "Dear George," explained in detail an enclosed document from the secretary of the latter organization, which had just conferred on Bristow the honorary degree of Doctor of Music. Meignen explained that in 1857 the society (founded in 1850) had petitioned the Pennsylvania legislature for permission to create an Academy for the Diffusion of Knowledge in Music, along with the "power to confer the degrees of Bachelor and Doctor of Music to such persons who, by their proficiency in the Art, may be entitled to such a distinction."

That the petition had been approved for a music society, Meignen pointed out, was "without a precedent in this country."[66] He observed that some state universities had the power to confer degrees, but none (by 1858) had any music faculty qualified to make such decisions, which meant that such degrees represented "a deception practiced upon the public." These decisions, he argued, should be left to musicians with the requisite expertise and practical experience.

The society had already conferred doctorates to Carl Hohnstock (1828–1889), William Henry Westray Darley (1810–1872, composer and president of the Sacred Music Society), and Meignen and had instructed them to recommend three more honorees, "in order to form a definitive Faculty of Six Doctors of Music." They nominated Fry, Charles Hommann (1803–after 1866), and Bristow. The plan was for these six individuals to prepare a "programme of the course of studies" for the degree of Bachelor of Music and to determine the requisite achievements that might warrant award of the Doctorate of Music. There was no mention of establishing a teaching institution; rather, the plan was for the six faculty members to examine manuscripts submitted by candidates, confer with one another, and decide if they should award what were essentially degrees of the professional practice. Whether Bristow ever participated in such deliberations, or if the organization actually conferred any additional degrees, is unknown. But the honor—coupled with Meignen's request that he be allowed to dedicate his new Double Quartet (Vocal) to Bristow—surely attests to the New York composer's growing reputation as an important native composer in the United States.

| # Sacred Music

## *Church Music Director and Sacred Music Composer*

CHURCH MUSIC COMMITTEES, according to George Bristow, "are always chosen with the perfect understanding that they shall be totally ignorant of everything pertaining to music." Furthermore, he added, "no matter how well [the organist] played, or how well the Choir sang, when the first of May came around [the traditional date on which contracts were signed], there would be something wrong somewhere." Bristow's activity as a church organist and choir director—like his employment as a teacher or work as a theater musician—was quite unexceptional for a nineteenth-century musician. Playing the organ at services was probably the easiest part of the job; as Bristow observed, "There is not much to say about the career of any organist, simply as an organist. The subject is threadbare." But there were plenty of other responsibilities for a music director: to recruit potential choir members; audition and hire professional singers for a quartet; nurture and mold ensembles and navigate the inevitable personnel issues; choose repertoire, purchase scores, and teach the compositions; conduct performances; maintain the organ and the music library; and satisfy the minister, the congregation, and the unpredictable music committee. But such positions provided a regular (albeit usually small) salary, exposure to the general public, and valuable experience as a conductor and composer of sacred music. And Bristow must have found such work gratifying, for he held positions as a church music director for almost his entire career. In addition, he wrote sacred music—lessons, sentences, anthems, services, hymns, organ compositions, and larger choral works—during much of that time.[1]

Music for established congregations had grown in importance in America during the first several decades of the nineteenth century, as the New England singing-school movement of the late eighteenth and early nineteenth centuries was beginning to be supplanted (especially in urban areas) by the sacred music reforms of Lowell Mason (1792–1872), Thomas Hastings (1784–1872), William Bradbury (1816–1868), and others. This reform movement started to transform what was performed and heard in churches, as well as the styles of sacred music that American composers wrote. But during Bristow's formative years in the 1830s and 1840s, the choral music heard on special occasions, especially Christmas and Easter, was still dominated by hymns and four-part, mainly homophonic, and hymn-like pieces, and only occasionally included anthems, motets, or set pieces from Europe.

By the middle of the century, in fact, a divide opened among American churches in terms of their incorporation of music into regular services. Many urban congregations (especially those of wealthier churches) enthusiastically expanded the role of music during the mid-century and later. They built larger and more spacious churches with interiors that functioned as excellent performance spaces, acquired grander and more sophisticated organs, assembled and supported choirs made up of parishioners, and increasingly hired resident vocal quartets.[2] Other congregations, however, moved in this direction more deliberately and cautiously. As Lee Orr points out, the American branch of the Episcopal Church "remained steadfastly low church" during the mid-century period, partly as a reaction against the "Papist" influences introduced by an influx of Irish-Catholic immigrants.[3] As a result, during the 1850s and 1860s, very little of the liturgy in Episcopal or Protestant Episcopal churches (the venues for most of Bristow's activities) included music, except on special feast days. We also know very little about the everyday music that Americans heard on regular Sundays, since most choral music scholars have focused instead on the music that accompanied special events. It is likely, however, that short pieces—hymns and chants (the type that Bristow harmonized and put together into collections) and possibly some organ preludes or interludes—were the musical selections that most congregants heard every Sunday in New York churches during this period.

One 1906 publication about music used at Trinity (Episcopal) Church in Manhattan during the second half of the nineteenth century provides valuable insight into the increasing use of music at mid-century and later by such congregations.[4] Arthur Messiter, the author of the study, explains that the practice of reciting the Nicene Creed was adopted by the Trinity congregation in May 1861; at Christmas services later that year a carol was sung both before the service and after the sermon. In 1864 the Trinity Psalter was introduced, and in December of that year the church inaugurated a chancel organ to accompany a choir. More frequent incorporation of sung psalms started in August 1866, and processional hymns were introduced on All Saints Day that same year. In 1867 the church fathers instituted a daily choral service, two years later the collection *Hymns Ancient and Modern* (published by Novello in 1861) was introduced to the congregation, and by 1870 the parish adopted a new Trinity Parish Psalter of single chants.[5] November 1873 saw the inauguration of an annual service at which the combined choirs of the Parish sang; on the 4th of July 1876 there was a performance of a Te Deum accompanied by an orchestra, and by 1879 the choir started to sing a Magnificat on the first Sunday of each month. Throughout the rest of the century, there was similar gradual addition of more music in terms of quantity, complexity, and size of performing forces, until by the 1890s the British Oxford movement (which encouraged, as John Ogasapian and Lee Orr write, "more refined choral singing, larger organs, more dignified hymns, and professionally trained directors and organists") was in full swing in the United States.[6] Music gradually became a much more regular component of weekly Sunday services.

## Bristow's Church Jobs

This increased interest by American congregations in musical performance generated practical jobs for many working musicians and created a market for their compositions. Bristow is an excellent example, and his career as a church musician is illustrative. Although most sources report his employment as an organist or choir director (or both) at St. George's (Episcopal) Chapel, Holy Trinity Church (Harlem), First Collegiate Reformed Church (Harlem), and the Church of the Divine Paternity, more recent scholarship suggests that his activities in this realm were even more extensive than this list suggests. (See table 2.)[7] During the early part of his career (late 1840s through the 1850s), in fact, he had already enjoyed engagements at three different churches. The earliest was St. John's Chapel (a part of Trinity Parish), located on Varick Street. Bristow claims to have been organist at a church where the assistant minister became a bishop, and the Rev. Jonathan Mayhew Wainwright (1792–1854)—who was assistant minister of St. John's Chapel—left that position in 1852 to become bishop of the Dioceses of the Episcopal Church.[8] Bristow left St. John's shortly after Wainwright departed, for that year

**TABLE 2.** *Bristow's Church Positions*

| Church | Denomination | Location | Dates |
|---|---|---|---|
| St. John's Chapel (Trinity Parish) | Episcopal | Varick Street, facing St. John's Park | 1846(?)–1852 |
| St. Mark's Church-in-the-Bowery (?) | Episcopal | East 10th and Stuyvesant Square | 1852–1854 |
| St. George's | Episcopal | East 16th and Stuyvesant Square | 1854–1860 |
| St. John's Chapel | Episcopal | Varick Street, facing St. John's Park | 1861–1864 |
| *hiatus* | | | 1865–1866 |
| Church of the Covenant | Presbyterian | Park Ave. and 35th St. | 1866–1869? |
| Zion Protestant Episcopal Church | Protestant Episcopal | Madison Ave. and 38th St. | 1869–1871 |
| Holy Trinity Church | Episcopal | 5th Ave./125th Street | 1871–1873 |
| Zion Protestant Episcopal Church | Protestant Episcopal | Madison Ave. and 38th St. | 1874(?)–1878 |
| St. Mary's Church | Episcopal | Alexander Ave./141st Street | 1878–1879 |
| Holy Trinity Church | Episcopal | 5th Ave./125th Street | 1881–? |
| First Collegiate Reformed Church | Dutch Reformed | 191 East 121th St. Harlem | 1885–1889 |
| Church of the Divine Paternity | Universalist | 5th Avenue/45th Street | 1889–1891 |
| 23rd St. Baptist Church | Baptist | 23rd St. and Lexington | 1892–1893 |

Note: Citations for these positions are in the text.

he is identified as the organist of St. Mark's (possibly St. Mark's Church-in-the-Bowery).[9] In 1854 Bristow took up a similar position at St. George's Church on East Sixteenth Street at Stuyvesant Square, where the Rev. Dr. Stephen Tyng, a popular and renowned preacher in the evangelical wing of the Episcopal Church, was minister from 1845 to 1878. Bristow not only played the organ but also conducted both congregational singing and a professional quartet; he remained with the church until spring 1860.[10]

By February 1861 Bristow, described as "formerly of St. George's," apparently returned to St. John's Chapel. His merits as organist for this congregation were described as "well known"; moreover, the church "choir"—a quartet that included his future wife, Louise Holder—executed their music with "much beauty and grace." An article in *Dwight's Journal* identified him as organist there in 1864 and further reported his intention to introduce a boys choir.[11] In March 1865, however, the composer purchased a rather puzzling classified advertisement in the *Daily Herald* that read: "A First-Class Choir, with Organist, Desire to negotiate with some church for an appointment from the 1st of May; appropriation required $2,500. Inquire of Geo. F. Bristow, 147 10th Street."[12] This unusual notice indicates that the forty-year-old musician had a group of singers with whom he was working closely—probably a small choir—and that he was in search of a position for all of them. The salary requested suggests a choir, since at St. George's Church Bristow and a professional quartet had been paid $1,600 (Bristow and the soprano, $500 each; the other singers $200 each).[13]

Fortuitously, an experience that Bristow describes in his "Life of a Musician" explains this advertisement. The incident "happened in a certain church of which he was organist." The years 1864–1865 were a transitional period at St. John's, for there was a ministerial change, which resulted in the rector's daughter being put in charge of the church's music department. This young woman preferred "more operatic" music for the services and decided to hire a professional "quartette choir" to replace the newly established choir of men and boys that Bristow had been training. As a result, she "summarily dismissed all of [the musicians] but the organist," who did not "appreciate . . . her condescension," so he "dismissed himself." Bristow noted that after resigning from the church, he "rested a while from playing and devoted himself to composing," which suggests that the attempt to find a position for both an organist and an established choir was unsuccessful. It does reveal, however, that Bristow was an enterprising music businessman.[14]

By 1866 Bristow was once again employed, this time at the Church of the Covenant, a Presbyterian congregation at Park Avenue and Thirty-fifth Street.[15] The denomination of this church, however, is somewhat outside Bristow's norm, for his usual employment suggests a preference for either Episcopal or Protestant Episcopal congregations (his funeral, for example, was held at the Episcopal Church of the Holy Faith and the church service music he wrote is likewise appropriate for that denomination). How, or if, the music he chose for the Presbyterian congregation differed from what he normally programmed for Episcopal services is unknown. It is interesting, however, that although Bristow clearly preferred working for Episcopal congregations, the beneficiaries of many of the vocal and instrumental charity concerts that he either organized or participated in (throughout the 1860s and later) represented a wide variety of Christian denominations, including Episcopal, Methodist Episcopal, Protestant Episcopal, Baptist, and Roman Catholic churches.[16]

Evidence about Bristow's church jobs from the 1870s is somewhat murky: newspaper reports suggest that he served as organist and conductor at the Zion Protestant Episcopal Church at Madison Avenue and Thirty-eighth Street between 1869 and 1871 and between 1874 (?) and 1878, which indicates a tenure of some eight years. But he is also identified (1871–1873) as the organist at Holy Trinity Church in Harlem.[17] Perhaps he held simultaneous posts in several churches or returned to Zion after two years elsewhere. The general picture, however, is of an energetic individual who sometimes held positions for lengthy periods and at other times had to scramble for jobs. Bristow was organist from 1878 to 1879 at St. Mary's Episcopal Church in Mott Haven (about twenty blocks south of his home in Morrisania, then in Westchester County), and during the 1880s worked at two different churches in Harlem: Holy Trinity Church (again) at 125th Street (starting in 1881; terminal date unknown) and at the First Collegiate Reformed Church (191 East 121st Street) from around 1885 to 1889. His penultimate known paid position was with the Universalist Church of the Divine Paternity (1889–1891), a wealthy Manhattan congregation under the leadership of the Rev. Charles Henry Eaton (1852–1902), a noted lecturer and advocate for liberal thought and social progress.[18] Brian Bailey reports that no orders of service survive from Bristow's two years at the Universalist church, so there is no further information on the nature of music performed during regular (non-holiday) services for that congregation. (See below for Christmas and Easter services in 1890.) His final known position was at the Twenty-third Street Baptist Church (Twenty-third and Lexington), the first Baptist congregation he served. How long he remained there is unknown. According to George Henry Curtis, however, Bristow continued to serve during the 1890s as "an organist and conductor of a church choir," but no additional conclusive information has come to light.[19]

Tracking down Bristow's professional activities as an organist or choirmaster is needle-in-a-haystack work. Church archives, when they exist, tend to be limited to records of baptisms, marriages, and deaths; vestry minutes; sometimes names of congregants; and activities of ministers, deacons, or other officials—not the identities of employees. Furthermore, only rarely is the matter-of-fact occurrence of music in regular church services reported in print, which makes the music of religious services a perfect example of an almost invisible but important element of professional music making in the American soundscape prior to the advent of recorded sound.

## Music for Holy Days and Regular Services

In contrast to the lack of information about music performed for regular Sunday services, journalists frequently reported on the religious services for major Christian holy days (Christmas and Easter), and sometimes included names of musicians, comments about the caliber of performances or performers, and lists of compositions. Such accounts confirm the fact that Bristow regularly played works for organ (voluntaries, processionals, and recessionals) during such services. His responsibilities included rehearsing with and directing church choirs that increasingly, in the 1860s and into the 1870s, consisted of a quartet of professional musicians, a practice that became commonplace in affluent churches during the second half of the century. Occasionally, such reports mention a choir of some dozen or more singers, primarily parishioners. Bristow, for example, conducted a choir of eleven, including his ten-year-old daughter, Estelle, at Christmas in 1878, and an ensemble of seventeen, including his wife, Louise, and nineteen-year-old stepdaughter, Nina, for an Easter service in 1877.[20] Many churches continued to have such congregational choirs; one reporter noted in 1872, for example, that the "choir" (a quartet) under Bristow's direction "will be assisted by a large number of ladies and gentlemen of the congregation" in order "to give the proper effect to the sublime music selected for these services."[21] On rare occasions Bristow enlisted members of some of the large social choirs that he conducted. For example, in 1869 "a large chorus from the New York and Morrisania Harmonic and Mendelssohn Union Societies" performed in the Christmas service at Zion Church.[22]

If the handful of extant comments about Bristow is typical, he was highly regarded as both an organist and a choirmaster. An article about Easter services at St. George's Church in 1860 noted that "the music at this church, under the direction of Mr. George F. Bristow, is of the finest in the city"; a year later Bristow's "merits" were described as "so well known [that] we will not speak of them in detail on the present occassion [*sic*]."[23] In 1871 the assessment of Bristow by the *Herald*'s critic Myron Cooney (1841–1898) was similarly positive in an account of the Easter celebration at Holy Trinity Church in Harlem. "The services were of the usual order," he noted, but "one of the best features was the music. The organ, under the clever touch of Professor George F. Bristow, gave forth its sweetest strains in the worship of God, and the choir [actually a quartet] is of a high order." Six years later, Cooney described Bristow, then organist of Zion Church, as "the representative composer and virtuoso of America [who] has given to the church many grand works which have attained a world wide reputation."[24] In the early 1890s—by which time Bristow had been playing in church services for over forty years—the *Herald* ran a feature about the most important organs in New York. In a discussion of the instrument at the Church of the Divine Paternity, the reporter noted that "the music is a great feature of the service," and that "Mr. Bristow's manipulation of an organ that some younger artists . . . claim has outlived its usefulness, is a performance worth listening to."[25]

Reports about music performed for Christmas or Easter suggest that Bristow typically programmed works by both European and American composers. The former, unsurprisingly, included Handel (especially selections from the *Messiah*), Haydn (*The Creation*), and Mendelssohn. The Americans included Dudley Buck (1839–1909), one of the most successful and popular composers of sacred music in nineteenth-century America, as well as forgotten individuals such as James Remington Fairlamb (1838–1908), organist and prolific composer of both secular and sacred works; Samuel P. Warren (1841–1915) a Canadian-born organist and composer active in New York; and Robert Mosenthal (1834–1896), a German-born violinist, organist, conductor, and composer of anthems, part-songs, and sacred and secular songs.[26] Bristow also regularly programmed his own compositions. The type of music he chose for Easter is suggested by the works he conducted in 1872 at Holy Trinity Church in Harlem. In addition to various hymns and psalms, the selections included "The Trumpet Shall Sound" (for trumpet solo) and the soprano aria "I Know That My Redeemer Liveth" (both from the *Messiah*); "The Heavens Are Telling" (chorus from *The Creation*); Buck's anthem *Christ Our Passover*; a Te Deum and Jubilate by Fairlamb; Gloria by Mosenthal; and two works by himself: an organ voluntary from his first oratorio, *Praise to God* (1868) (as a processional) and "Gloria tibi," perhaps one of his many sentences.[27] His choice of works by these local musicians is further evidence of his continued support for American composers.

By the early 1890s, however, Bristow's choices were more heavily Eurocentric, a reflection both of changed American tastes but also of presumably greater resources, for at the time he was working for the wealthy Church of the Divine Paternity. The 1890 Easter service for that congregation, for example, included an organ processional from the overture to *Les Huguenots* (Giacomo Meyerbeer); "Oh! Thou, Whose Pow'r Tremendous" (for solo, chorus, and harp), an adaptation of the prayer "*Dal tuo stellate soglio*" from Rossini's *Moses in Egypt* (*Mosè in Egitto*); "The Trumpet Shall Sound"; and, as recessional, a selection from Weber's *Euryanthe* (possibly the version transcribed for organ by Samuel Warren in 1885).[28] The only other works by Americans were all by Bristow: a Te Deum in E-flat major, from his *Morning Service*, op. 19; Gloria Patri (probably the final chorus from his first oratorio), and his arrangement for quartet of "I Lay My Sins on Jesus," a song attributed to Adrian Van Vliet that Bristow later transcribed (1893). The Christmas service that same year was even more heavily dominated by European compositions, for it featured works by Gounod, Mendelssohn, and the British composer John Farmer (1836–1901). The sole American work was Bristow's 1887 Christmas anthem, *Light Flashing into the Darkness*, op. 73.[29]

## Bristow's Compositions for Church Services

The works described above are only a sample of the many sacred compositions that Bristow wrote; his first such work was Sentence No. 2, op. 15, from 1852; the final one was probably his Easter anthem *Except the Lord Build the House*, op. 79, presumably from 1894. He wrote a wide variety of pieces for performance in church services, including compositions for full choir and soloists (odes, anthems, and his two oratorios, all accompanied either by organ or full orchestra), works for organ and SATB (choir or soloists), hymns and chants, and organ pieces intended for church use, including interludes from his early years at St. John's, published in *Melodia Sacra* (1852), *Six Pieces for the Organ*, op. 45 (1883), and *Six Easy Voluntaries for the Cabinet Organ*, op. 72 (1887).

The vast majority of his religious pieces, however, are for voice, and many are purely utilitarian. For example, like many organists of the time, Bristow compiled collections of music for congregational or choir singing. In the early 1850s, he was asked to harmonize new selections that were added to *Music of the Church: A Collection of Psalm, Hymn, and Chant Tunes Adapted to the Worship of the Protestant Episcopal Church in the United States*, a revision of a compilation by the Rev. Jonathan Wainwright and originally published in 1828. Apparently after Wainwright was made bishop, he turned to Bristow and asked (or hired) him to harmonize the new tunes. Three other sets of utilitarian sacred music are similar: all are SATB arrangements of tunes, some a cappella and others with organ accompaniment. The undated *St. John's Collection* (no opus number), is a compilation of hymns (choir and organ) that he presumably used while organist at that church early in his career (or in the 1860s). The other two sets are collections of harmonized hymns and chants, both compiled in 1867 while he was working at the Church of the Covenant. One is titled *Hymns and Chants*, op. 44, and consists of fourteen hymns and twelve chants, all arranged for SATB; the second, larger, but untitled compilation [*Hymns and Chants*] includes slightly over one hundred short chants and hymns (mostly the former), also harmonized. Only some of the tunes have titles, composers, and texts; neither set was published. All of the collections, however, are copied in clean and beautiful calligraphy. Bristow also wrote a handful of his own hymns, as well as several sacred songs for SATB and piano (such as "There Is Joy Today," "O Bells of Easter Morning," and "Holy Night"); most of the latter appeared in the 1880s in the New York monthly *Tonic Sol-fa Advocate*. He also composed several short works for organ and SATB (for either choir or quartet) for use in the Episcopal service, including *Four Offertories*, op. 48 (1870) and three sentences (short Episcopal calls-to-prayer), opp. 15 (1850), 23 (1853), and 40 (1866; revised 1891).

Bristow wrote a number of medium-size multimovement sacred pieces, including four *Morning Services*: op. 19 in E-flat major (Te Deum, Jubilate, and Kyrie Eleison, 1855), op. 51 in B-flat major (Te Deum and Benedictus, 1873), op. 54 in C major (Te Deum and Jubilate, 1878), and op. 58 in F major (*Easy Morning Service*, 1881) as well as two *Evening Services*, op. 36 in D major (Bonum est and Benedic Anima mea, 1865) and op. 56 in G major (Cantate Domino and Deus misereator, 1885). Movements from several of the services (especially the Benedictus and various Te Deums) show up fairly regularly either in sacred concerts or in church services during the 1870s, 1880s, and early 1890s, both at churches where Bristow was organist and elsewhere.[30] The *Morning Service in E-flat*, op. 19, is a good example of this category of sacred music. In three movements, this work was first performed on May 15, 1857; the Te Deum was dedicated to the Rev. Stephen Tyng, rector of St. George's Church while Bristow worked there.[31] The composer must have thought highly of this composition, however, for he published the first movement almost thirty years later (1888) and was still using it in the 1890s (for example, on Easter Sunday in 1890 at the Church of the Divine Paternity). It is written in four-part harmony with organ accompaniment (*con pedale*), with vocal parts in English (despite the Latin movement titles) that would have been reasonable for the church choirs he conducted. The harmonic structure is fairly conservative, with short sections in the dominant (B-flat), subdominant (A-flat), relative minor (C minor) and both its parallel major (C) and minor subdominant (F minor). Textually, the work is sectional, with straightforward, fairly homorhythmic, chorale-style writing alternating with the occasional contrapuntal entrance. There are also two solo sections (one each for bass and soprano) and a triumphant finale of a more complex contrapuntal texture that must have been inspiring to congregants and a thrill for the choir to perform. The work fits well with Delmer Rogers's assessment of Bristow's Episcopalian service compositions, the ranges and tessitura of which fit easily the vocal abilities of the average church choir members with whom he worked.[32]

Bristow's four anthems were also performed fairly frequently. They include *Christ Our Passover*, op. 39 (1866) and *Once More We Greet with Gladsome Hearts*, op. 77 (1893) (both for Easter); *Light Flashing into the Darkness*, op. 73 (1887) (for Christmas); and *Except the Lord Build the House*, op. 79 (1894). Rogers suggests that Bristow's anthems followed the pattern of English works of that style—that is, recitative and aria sections that alternate with choral segments. But while both the Christmas anthem and *Christ Our Passover* are sectional, neither features recitative. *Light Flashing into the Darkness*, for example, is in four sections, marked *Allegro ma non troppo presto* (D minor); *Andante* (D major); *Allegro* (G minor), and *Grandioso* (D major). The *Andante* section features a soprano solo and the *Allegro* is marked "quartette," but the majority of the work (including the *Allegro*) is scored for soprano/tenor duet, with the occasional addition of the altos and basses. There are fermata rests at the end of each section, but the work is apparently intended to be performed without pauses. The work is a setting of a text by the Rev. Joachim Elmendorf, pastor of the First Collegiate Reformed Church, which is where Bristow was working when he wrote it; the piece is dedicated to the Right Rev. Henry C. Potter (1834–1908), who was then bishop of the Episcopal Diocese of New York.[33]

Bristow's most important sacred choral works are his two oratorios, *Gloria Patri* (*Praise to God*), op. 31 (1860), and *Daniel*, op. 42 (1866), as well as the *Mass in C Major*, op. 57 (1885). All three are clearly sacred, but all should be considered concert works rather than compositions intended for performance in religious services, although individual movements from each—like separate movements of the anthems—were performed in church services during Bristow's lifetime. These works are discussed in chapters 4 and 6.

# 4 | The 1860s

## *Personal and National Agony and Triumph*

**THE 1850S CLOSED ON A TRIUMPHANT** public note for George Bristow, but his personal life was more complicated. As Victor Yellin describes in his account of the composer's divorce, Bristow and his wife, Harriet, had separated ← sometime during the 1850s because of her numerous infidelities, which continued even after he had pleaded with her "to abandon her intimacy with other men." According to court documents, she found this "impossible to do," so he consented to her request for a physical separation. He supported her financially for a while but later testified that he found her choices to be "utterly abandoned and wicked" and ended even this connection. Bristow's attorney argued in 1863 that this was justified because she could support herself as a musician and enjoyed "an ample income independent of her allowance" from her estranged husband.[1]

The public image of a successful and happy professional musician during the mid to late 1850s, then, was only part of Bristow's reality during this period. The situation must have been both humiliating in the close-knit musical world of New York and morally distressing, for Bristow makes abundantly clear in his "Life of a Musician" that he considered music and religious faith to be inextricably linked. "Some have said 'music is the hand-maid of religion,'" he wrote. "No greater truth was ever uttered." This statement, when combined with his regular employment as a church organist and the copious amounts of sacred music he wrote, suggests a deep faith and attachment to organized religion that would have made his wife's behavior intolerable.[2]

The divorce was not completed until 1863. Why Bristow waited so long to sever legal connections with his wife is puzzling, although perhaps he was sufficiently distracted by his numerous professional activities during the period that he put it out of his mind. It is also possible that he was reluctant to embark on divorce proceedings, which would inevitably lead to a public trial, with its taint of dishonor and notoriety. That situation, however, changed in the early 1860s, when he met Louise N. Holder (1836–1922), a young woman who would eventually become the love of his life. Holder, née Westervelt, was a soprano and a member of the quartet and choir at St. John's Chapel when Bristow was rehired by the congregation in 1861 as organist and choir director. The composer had probably already met Holder, for (as described in chapter 3) she had sung at his March 1859 Testimonial Concert. Furthermore, he was surely acquainted with the family of her husband, Charles A. S. Holder (ca. 1834–1858), whose father, Charles J. Holder, was a manufacturer and merchant of prizewinning pianos and whose firm was located at 118 Spring Street, only four blocks from the Bristow, Morse & Co. piano and melodeon wareroom at 423 Broadway. (See Interlude D.) It is highly likely that the piano manufacturers and merchants active in New York during this period were at least acquainted with one another.[3]

In September 1858, however, the younger Charles had died of yellow fever while visiting relatives in Galveston, Texas, so when Bristow and Louise were thrown into close contact with each other at St. John's Chapel, she was a young widow with a two-year-old daughter, Nina Louise (b. ca. 1857), who lived in Brooklyn with her parents and siblings.[4] Apparently Bristow was smitten. A surviving short note that fellow choir member James W. Good wrote to her, "Bright & Early," on February 11, 1861 (the day after her twenty-fifth birthday), hints at both the budding relationship and the camaraderie within the ensemble. He reminded her that St. John's Chapel would be holding services on the morning of Ash Wednesday (two days hence) and continued, in a playful tone, "Will the fair one with the Golden Locks attend? Our worthy organist thinks it best to do so, in which we all acquiesce. Knowing that you are with us in the *Spirit*, we trust you may also be in *body* on that sacred day." He signed the note, "In tremendous haste. Yours as ever. I mean of course devotedly, as your fellow says, J. W. Good.[5] Apparently Good and Bristow worked closely together, for Good, who was active in other church choirs, had performed the composer's double quartet "I Will Arise" (from his *Sentence* in E-flat major, op. 23) at a benefit concert in 1853.[6]

Another extant letter, dated August 1862 and written by Bristow to Louise (who evidently at the time was in the country recovering from an undisclosed ailment), is also revealing. Addressed to "Darling Kitten," the missive is replete with references to "sweet darling," "sweet one," and "sweet love"; it also includes instructions to "kiss Nina for me a great many times." In a tone of casual familiarity that one might expect from a man writing to his fiancée, the letter also reveals that the composer was then living with the Westervelt family in Brooklyn. The casual teasing banter in the letter clearly suggests an understanding between Louise and George; other references indicate that her parents and siblings enjoyed his company and had essentially accepted him into the family fold.[7]

The divorce was finalized on October 19, 1863. Harriet was prohibited from marrying again during Bristow's lifetime, but the composer had the right to remarry "as though the said defendant Harriet N. Bristow was actually dead."[8] A final extant letter is from several months later, when Bristow reminded Louise that he had been "so overjoyed" at this decision that he had immediately hastened to her home to give her the good news. This happy ending to his miserable first marriage should have set the stage for the wedding that both he and Louise apparently wanted. But as Yellin relates, the months immediately following the divorce were somewhat rocky for the couple. In this same letter, written in January 1864, Bristow mentions that some of his acquaintances were trying (for some unknown reason) "to prejudice me against you." To make matters worse, other unnamed individuals were spreading malicious rumors about *him* to *her*, including the erroneous information that he was not permitted to marry for two years. To this he responded vehemently, writing, "Whoever told you that, told you a barefaced lie. I am free as air, to do what I please, marry when I please." This impassioned letter was in response to one that Louise apparently had written to him; it clearly suggests Bristow's fear that he was on the verge of losing her. He reminded her of the "happy, most happy hours we have spent together, when there seemed but one thought, one heart, one being," and assured her of his commitment and devotion. He ended the letter with an unambiguous statement of his true feelings: "Louise, I love you."[9] Both letters provide insight into Bristow's humanity, personality, and character.

→ George Bristow and Louise Holder were married on September 1, 1864, presumably at the home of her parents in Brooklyn.[10] In the January letter, Bristow had expressed his intention to purchase a new house for his bride during the summer of 1864; presumably after the September wedding, the couple moved from Brooklyn to Morrisania in Westchester County. Because of its station on

**FIGURE 2.** Engraving of the village of Morrisania in 1861. The numbers indicate the homes of prominent residents. According to Elizabeth Green Fuller, *Index of Personal Names in J. Thomas Scharf's History of Westchester County* (Valhalla, NY: Westchester County Historical Society, 1988), the Bristows lived at the southeast corner of Forest and George Streets. A map of Morrisania in *Henry's Directory of Morrisania and Vicinity* (1853–1854) indicates that their home was catty-corner from the estate of R. H. Elton, indicated by the number 22 in the engraving. (The two sources are in the collection of the New York Historical Society; the illustration is used courtesy of the Westchester County Historical Society.)

the New York and Harlem Railroad, it had grown into a busy village by 1860, although it was still close to the country. (Fig. 2 shows Morrisania in 1861.)[11] Whether or not George adopted his stepdaughter, Nina, is unknown, although census records indicate that she took the name Bristow; he and Louise had one additional daughter, Estelle Viola (1868–1946).[12]

## Performance Activity

Bristow's work as a performer continued apace as the 1850s segued into the 1860s, even as the country fell apart. As a violinist, he performed regularly with the

Philharmonic Society orchestra, which increased the number of its subscription concerts from four to five in its 1858–1859 season, and again in 1868–1869 from five to six—which it maintained for the rest of the century; the ensemble also performed three public rehearsals per concert during Bristow's tenure.[13] He was a member of the first violin section of the orchestra and throughout the decade was consistently ranked just below the concertmaster, Joseph Noll. During this period he also served on the orchestra's board of directors (1857–1858 and 1858–1859 seasons), as vice president (1865–1866), and as president (December 1866–April 1867). According to William Thoms, Bristow resigned from the latter post prematurely to show his "utter disapproval" of the Philharmonic's treatment of an American pianist, John Nelson Pattison (1845–1905), whose scheduled appearance with the orchestra was preempted by the British pianist Sebastian Bach Mills (1838–1898); this is another example of Bristow's consistent support for American musicians.[14] He also continued to perform with the orchestra of the Philharmonic Society of Brooklyn (he had joined when it was formed in 1857); this ensemble relied heavily on instrumentalists from the Philharmonic Society across the river. (It also borrowed the ensemble's conductor, Eisfeld.) From its start, the Brooklyn orchestra presented four concerts per season as well as twelve public rehearsals.[15]

Bristow continued to perform publicly as a church organist (see Interlude B) and as a pianist. The latter role was mostly as an accompanist for concerts given by visiting or local singers, such as a benefit concert in January 1868 at Ittner's Hall in Tremont (Westchester County, fairly close to Morrisania), during which amateur singers performed to the accompaniment of George Bristow, "who presided at the piano in his usual efficient manner." Occasionally, however, Bristow participated in other types of events farther away from home, such as a church social in July 1861, billed as a "Grand Social Reunion of all Denominations" and held at Snug Harbor on Staten Island.[16] The pattern established in the late 1850s, however—performance activity dominated by conducting—continued in the subsequent decade. Such appearances included numerous regularly scheduled and special concerts with either the New York Harmonic Society (until 1863) or the Mendelssohn Union (1867–1871), which are discussed below. In addition to these regular choral performances, he also continued to conduct a wide variety of benefit concerts, church-related socials, amusements, celebrations, and other special events.

During the first half of the decade, much of the activity in this realm was related to numerous nationalistic or patriotic concerts intended to raise funds for the war effort. One particularly grand event that Bristow organized was a special concert given by the Philharmonic Society orchestra at the Academy of Music

on May 25, 1861, "in aid of the Volunteer Fund." The "committee of arrangements," headed by Major General John A. Dix (secretary of the treasury, governor
of New York, and major general in the Union army), included ministers, military
leaders, and a large number of prominent gentlemen from the city as well as
many important New York musicians. The Harmonic Society provided the chorus,
the orchestra was from the Philharmonic Society, and Bristow conducted both.
The lengthy potpourri-type program (twenty-two numbers) included two of his
works: the "Vivandière Song" and the chorus "God of Battles," both from *Rip Van
Winkle*. Interspersed among the selections by Handel, Vincenzo Bellini, Saverio
Mercadante, and others were a large number of patriotic and "war-like" pieces,
including "Columbia, Gem of the Ocean"; Jerome Hopkins's "Union Hymn"; a
patriotic song titled "To Arms! To Arms!" by William F. Otten; "My Country 'Tis
of Thee"; and "The Union, Right or Wrong," attributed to Wallace. The concert
ended with all four verses of "The Star-Spangled Banner," sung by four of the
female stars and the audience. Advertisements promised that the flags of Forts
Sumter and Moultrie would be on display. According to William Fry, the concert
attracted "a very full and select audience" and was "altogether a complete success."[17]

There were many other war-related concerts and benefits. Bristow, for
example, performed as a pianist in a concert that benefited the McClellan Rifles,
arranged a performance of his "Grand Te Deum" (see below) to celebrate military victories by the Union army, and participated in a Wounded Soldiers Benefit
and concerts in aid of sick wives and children of "deceased and absent soldiers."[18]
He also participated in numerous events that raised money for the US Sanitary
Commission, an important private relief agency created by federal legislation in
1861 to provide support for sick and wounded soldiers.[19] In June 1864 Bristow
organized a benefit performance with personal resonance: a "Grand Concert for
the Benefit of the Widow of Lieut. Frank Boudinot," a soldier who had been one
of the members of the Pyne and Harrison Opera Company, with whom Bristow
had worked during the summer of 1855. That Boudinot and Bristow were more
than nominal acquaintances is suggested by the existence of several inscribed
cabinet photos of the singer in the family materials that are now in the Bristow
Collection at the New York Public Library.[20]

Bristow's efforts in this realm were unflagging throughout the war. He also
wrote two overtly patriotic compositions during the period. *Keep Step with the
Music of Union* (SATB and orchestra; also a song with piano accompaniment published in 1861) is a setting of a poem by the American poet and attorney William
Ross Wallace (1819–1881), one of his several "fervently patriotic songs" from
the early 1860s that became widely popular. Bristow's version is an illustration

both of the rash of songs that were produced and disseminated during the Civil War and of the composer's nationalistic musical inclinations during that period. Lawrence explains that the song was "the mandatory patriotic offering" at the Harmonic Society's annual rendering of the *Messiah* at Christmas 1861, but it was undoubtedly also performed at other patriotic concerts.[21] Bristow's efforts in this realm were probably an honest expression of his own sense of patriotism but could also be interpreted as a means to assuage his own conscience for not volunteering himself for military service—although he was thirty-five years old in 1861, which would have been considered elderly for military activity at the time (the average age of Union soldiers during the war was twenty-six). In fact, not only was age on his side but so was his profession, for teachers were exempt from the draft.[22]

The second overtly nationalistic piece from this period is the *Columbus Overture*, op. 32, written in January 1861, hence predating the beginning of Civil War hostilities. Originally intended as the overture to an opera that Bristow never completed, the work is programmatic and Americanist. The Philharmonic Society first performed it (under Eisfeld) in an "extra" concert on April 2, 1864, as part of a Metropolitan Fair held to raise funds for the US Sanitary Commission. It was the only "American" composition on a program that one might have expected to be patriotic in orientation. The orchestra played the overture an unprecedented second time on November 17, 1866 (under Bergmann)—the sixth time that the orchestra had performed a Bristow composition (and the fourth in a subscription concert). Both performances were described on their respective programs as premieres; the program for the second concert, however, included a detailed note about the piece.[23]

The composition, according to this program, presented "in dramatic form, a series of tone pictures, illustrating some of the incidents connected with the discovery of this continent by Columbus, without . . . pretending to follow all the events, or to introduce them in strict order." As such, it is another example of a nationalistic overture. In D major, the composition is sectional, although from the piano arrangement it is not clear if the sections constitute actual movements or if the overture was intended to be played without stop.[24] Henry Watson congratulated Bristow for his "brilliant success," noting that the overture "is clear and definite in design, pure and artistic in form," with "well chosen" subjects and a "marked character." The "brilliant freedom" and "power of contrast and . . . delicate coloring," Watson continued, "stamps Mr. Bristow with eminence as a composer," an assessment that was ratified by the "highly critical Philharmonic audience," which rewarded him with extended applause at the end of the performance. Several years later (1870), William Cadwallader Hudson (1843–1915) chastised Bristow for using timpani for "ordnance duty" but otherwise praised the composition as a "fluent, and melodious work, in which a succession of good themes are well worked up."[25] If frequency of performance is a guide, this overture was one of Bristow's most successful pieces: some of the many repeat performances were by the Philharmonic Society of Brooklyn (1870), at the Music Teachers National Association conference in New York (1885), and as part of a concert at Brighton Beach (1889) organized by Anton Seidl (1850–1898).[26]

The number of benefit concerts, special events, concert series, and the like that occurred in New York during the second half of the decade increased significantly after the end of the Civil War as the country itself experienced an extraordinary time of economic prosperity. Reconstruction of the destroyed infrastructure of the South, expansion of the railroads, and an unparalleled wave of immigrants from both Europe and Asia (coupled with significant internal migration) led to unrestrained growth in the entire national economy and an unprecedented period of economic expansion in most of the country. This created an insatiable demand for amusement and entertainment of all types, in New York and elsewhere.[27] It is interesting, however, that during this period Bristow's activity in the realm of extra concerts and entertainments decreased markedly. Perhaps his regular jobs as a teacher, conductor, and church organist meant he no longer needed to rely on such activities for income. He may also have wanted to concentrate on solidifying his new family, which included his stepdaughter, Nina, and, after 1868, his new daughter, Estelle. The family's relocation to Morrisania also meant that Bristow had to take into consideration the time and expense required of travel into and out of the city for performances or rehearsals.[28] By mid-decade, in fact, Bristow had begun to reorient some of these activities northward by participating, for example, in performances by the (unknown) Union Harmonic Society of Morrisania, in concerts at National Hall in Harlem, and at such events as the benefit concert at Ittner's Hall in Tremont mentioned above.[29] Whatever the reason, the level of Bristow's activities in what we would today call the "gig" economy diminished significantly during a period when such activities overall had become more commonplace. He took advantage of this freed-up time, however, to focus more exclusively on composition.

## Sacred and Secular Choral Compositions

George Bristow continued to conduct large massed choirs during a majority of the 1860s, either as director of one of the major New York choral societies or at the helm of ad hoc ensembles assembled for short-term engagements, special celebratory concerts, or benefit performances. His experience as a choral conductor undoubtedly whetted his appetite for writing for such ensembles. By directing rehearsals and conducting hundreds of concerts, he became thoroughly acquainted with many of the standard European works for large choral forces. This type of work also gave him extensive firsthand familiarity with the abilities and limitations of amateur choristers and a ready vehicle for the rehearsal and performance of his own choral compositions. In fact, both of his two oratorios—among his most important sacred choral works—date from the 1860s and were premiered by standing choral societies of which Bristow was director.

## PRAISE TO GOD, OP. 31

One of Bristow's most gratifying conducting experiences with the Harmonic Society must have been the premiere of his *Praise to God*, op. 31, on February 19, 1861.[30] The work, which he called an oratorio, is scored for full orchestra (pairs of winds, pairs of horns and trombones, tuba, timpani, strings, and piano or organ), SATB soloists, and choir; it was written for the Harmonic Society and was dedicated to its president, E. M. Carrington. Although divided into different sections, it has neither a libretto nor a dramatic narrative. Rather, it is a setting of the texts to the Te Deum and Benedictus of the Episcopal morning service; these words, in fact, appear on the first page of the manuscript's full score but are crossed out. Bristow was soundly criticized for his nomenclature in contemporary reviews. As Jerome Hopkins (writing as Timothy Trill) observed, since there is "no variety in the dramatis personae, nor is there any plot," it is more technically a cantata.[31] Other critics agreed, pointing out that the Te Deum is singularly nondramatic, which made its use as the text for a vocal composition all the more challenging.

Several critics also commented on Bristow's reliance on old-fashioned models for this work. "Every page" of the oratorio, the *Albion* critic noted, "reveals the devotion of a classicist who has studied thoroughly the school in which he belongs and believes implicitly in its tenets"; that school, he continued, is the "Handelian standard." Theodore Hagen, writing in the *Review and World*, likewise complained that the oratorio was backward-looking. Bristow's "motives," he wrote, "his modulations, his whole treatment indicate this." Choral director Brandon Moss, in fact, suggests that because of striking similarities in the text setting, Bristow may have been influenced by the *Dettingen Te Deum*, which was performed at the Crystal Palace in London during 1859 (the centenary of Handel's death) and was the topic of some journalistic attention in the United States during that period. On the other hand, William Fry disagreed completely with his contemporaries, writing bluntly that "the style of the music is modern. The accompaniments are elaborate, and partake largely of the spirit of Spohr and Mendelssohn, without being copies of any school." Bristow, he continued, "is perfect master of the *entrain* of dreamy harmony of the present epoch. . . . The whole work," he concluded, "will compare favorably with the classics, besides being free from old-fashioned crudities."[32]

The oratorio opens with an expansive instrumental introduction, followed by vocal movements that include nine choruses; solos for bass (2), tenor, alto, and soprano; a trio; two duets; and two quartets. Several critics decisively praised the orchestral writing; one wrote of "excellent instrumentation throughout," and Watson described the composition in general as "a masterly work . . . marked by bold and brilliant treatment, chorally and instrumentally."[33] Critics also praised the performance, which was under Bristow's direction. As Fry pointed out, the "execution of the choruses was entrusted to fresh, youthful voices and . . . the soloists all performed their most interesting parts well"; several of the movements elicited "hearty encores." Jerome Hopkins was positively effusive, calling the performance "the best I ever listened to from the time-honored honest old 'Harmonic'"; he concluded that it "did great credit to all concerned."[34]

In general, despite the harping about an inappropriate text and overreliance on older forms, the assessment was positive. The *Albion* critic concluded that the work was "the best of [its] kind that we have heard or seen, after the great masters" and that as a composition it "deserves to rank as a great production." Hopkins agreed, suggesting that *Praise to God* "should . . . be hailed with acclamation by all the choral societies in the country as a new, fresh, and easily comprehended work; at all events it certainly deserves to be." Moss points out that this premiere may have been the first performance of an American grand concert work based on a liturgical text.[35]

The Harmonic Society repeated the oratorio on February 28 and March 14, and Bristow pulled it out for a fourth performance a year later on April 21, 1862, when it was billed as "A Grand Te Deum" in celebration of "Recent Victories of the National Army" (presumably Grant's successes in Tennessee). Vera Lawrence suggests that this 1862 concert was the composer's "swan song" as conductor of the Harmonic Society, and in fact the following September the society announced Bristow's resignation, which was sudden and without explanation.[36] It occurred in the midst of rumors in the press that the older organization was on the verge of merging with the Mendelssohn Union, a younger and smaller choral society in Manhattan.[37] In fact, George Washbourne Morgan (1822–1892), founder of the younger society, was immediately named new director of the Harmonic Society, and Bristow, after a run of almost twelve years, was no longer connected with an organization that he had helped to mold. Hopkins, writing in the weekly *New York Dispatch*, recognized this and praised the steadfast composer and conductor for his efforts on behalf of the older organization; as he put it, the Harmonic Society "has existed so long" because of Bristow's "ability and perseverance."[38]

After leaving the Harmonic Society, Bristow took a five-year hiatus from directing a large choral society. As he remembered, "After I left the Harmonic Society . . . I devoted my time to work which was, if not more congenial, at least more profitable, that is, playing and teaching."[39] He also could have included composing, for newly freed from his responsibilities at the Harmonic Society, he completed not only his oratorio *Daniel* but also several other large compositions, including one of his *Evening Services*, op. 36 (1865), his Easter anthem *Christ Our Passover*, op. 39 (1866), and, with Francis Nash, the first iteration of their text *Cantara, or Teacher of Singing* (1866).

As he later remembered, however, in 1866 "that *ignus fatuus* 'glory' tempted me again to exchange personal profit for the applause of the public," for the Mendelssohn Union came knocking on his door, offering him the position of conductor.[40] That organization, which had been founded in 1854 by Morgan and Henry C. Timm, was smaller than the Harmonic Society (at its inception the singers numbered eighty-five) and duplicated some of the older organization's repertoire (e.g., *The Creation*, the *Messiah*). But the younger ensemble had quickly made a mark in the New York choral community, and presented serious competition to the Harmonic Society by featuring newer and more interesting works, including oratorios by Michael Costa (*Eli*, 1855) and Mendelssohn (*St. Paul*, 1836); incidental music by Mendelssohn (*Athalie*, 1845) and Beethoven (*Ruins of Athens*, 1811); Rossini's *Moses in Egypt* (*Mosè in Egitto*) (1818) (performed as an oratorio); and the "romantic symphony/cantata" *Hiawatha* (1859) by Robert Stoepel (1821–1887).[41] Bristow, however, turned them down. "I declined," he explained, "on the ground that I could not afford to give up the time necessary for such an exacting position." But they countered with an offer that he could not refuse: the premiere performance of his new oratorio. "That settle[d] it," he remembered. "I could not resist the temptation of having my work presented to the public judgment." He took over the position and during his first season at the helm continued the organization's trend of presenting new choral works: he chose for the union's four regular concerts that year—including the premiere performance of *Daniel*—Mendelssohn's *Psalm 42*, op. 42 ("As the Hart Pants") (1837–1838), Beethoven's oratorio *Christ on the Mount of Olives* (1803), and the cantata *St. Cecilia's Day* by Johannes van Bree (ca. 1850).[42]

In fact, in the autumn of 1867, Bristow was clearly on a creative roll. In addition to his new compositions and directorship of the Mendelssohn Union, he had also been honored (in late June) with another testimonial—a ceremony in the Steinway rooms, where he was presented with a "superb oil painting of himself, painted by Mr. B. [perhaps Benoni] Irwin." (See fig. 3.)[43] This was evidently

**FIGURE 3.** Portrait painted by B. [Benoni?] Irwin (1840–1896) and presented to Bristow at a testimonial in June 1867. (Oil on canvas. National Portrait Gallery, Smithsonian Institution; gift of Mrs. Louis T. Edwards.)

a Masonic event, for the master of ceremonies was Robert D. Holmes, Grand Master of the Free and Accepted Masons, who gave an eloquent speech that summarized Bristow's career. Many musicians were present to wish him well and celebrate his successes. Henry Watson noted that "no testimonial of admiration and esteem was ever more cordially tendered, or more entirely deserved. Americans," he continued, "should be proud of their one representative man in music."[44]

One unhappy personal experience in the midst of these positive developments in 1867 was the death (from chronic rheumatism) of Bristow's father, William, at his home in Brooklyn on August 18, 1867. The obituary noted that one of William Bristow's survivors was "his eldest son," who was described as "one of the best composers this country has yet produced."[45]

### THE ORATORIO OF DANIEL

The Mendelssohn Union's performance of Bristow's second oratorio opened its 1867–1868 season. Bristow's composition created an undeniable buzz among New York music lovers as soon as it was put into rehearsal. Watson, for example, kept his readers informed about its progress during the fall, reporting on a "splendid rehearsal" of the work on December 5 and predicting two weeks later that the oratorio would "add great brilliance to the high reputation which Mr. Bristow has already acquired by his works."[46]

Unlike Bristow's first attempt in the genre, *Daniel* is a true oratorio. The libretto was written by his friend, business partner, and attorney William A. Hardenbrook, who inscribed his title page "This libretto for the Oratorio of *Daniel* completed and presented to his friend *George F. Bristow* by Wm. Hardenbrook, New York, January 10, 1862." An inscription on the final page of the holograph ("Finished, September 1866") suggests a lengthy gestation period.[47] But Bristow probably did not commence work on the music immediately, as he was already busy with other compositional commitments during this four-year period, which was (as we have seen) an emotionally turbulent time for him. David Griggs-Janower suggests that he turned his full attention to this piece only in 1865 and completed his setting of the first part in 1866.[48] A notice in the *American Art Journal* in July 1867 observed that Bristow was "enjoying the vacation at his house in Morrisania, and is putting the finishing touches to his new and fine oratorio of 'Daniel.'" This timeline dovetails closely with Henry Watson's statement some five months later that Bristow had devoted "nearly two years to its completion."[49]

The libretto is from the Book of Daniel (from the Bible), with biblical and nonbiblical interpolations; the focus is the Babylonian captivity of the Jews. Bristow used only a portion of Hardenbrook's three-act libretto, focusing on part 1

("Nebuchadnezzar") and dividing it into two sections comprised of eighteen and ten discrete movements, respectively.[50] There are roles for eight soloists: soprano and mezzo (the two angels), high tenor (Azariah), tenor (Meshach), baritone (Daniel), and three basses (Nebuchadnezzar, Arioch, and Abednego). There are six arias in the oratorio, most of which incorporate elaborate melismas; this, as Howard Smither points out, differs from the usual practice of Handel, Mendelssohn, or most English oratorio composers.[51] The most obvious example of vocal display is number 7 ("He that dwelleth in the secret place," for Angel I) sung by the Scottish soprano Euphrosyne Parepa-Rosa (1836–1874), the featured star at the premiere performance. In ternary form, it commences (after a short recitative) with a stately and solid *Allegro spiritoso*, the melody of which is repeated. After a forthright and emphatic orchestral interlude, the soprano reenters, this time more urgently (*Andante grazioso*) before returning to the A strain. There are many coloratura passages throughout the aria, with long-held notes on $G^2$ and A-flat$^2$ as well as a thrilling climb to $B^2$ in the soprano's final, dramatic, phrase. There are also several ensembles: for a male quartet comprised of Daniel and the three young men Azariah, Meshach, and Abednego (baritone, high tenor, tenor, and bass, numbers 6 and 10); another quartet for Angel I (soprano) and the three men in the fiery furnace (16); and a trio of these three after they have been released from the fire (17). Griggs-Janower suggests that Bristow's close-harmony writing for male ensemble was probably influenced by Schubert, Schumann, and Mendelssohn, although only one of the works that he cites as a possible model (Schubert's *Nachthelle*, D. 892) is known to have been performed in New York before 1867, and that composition is for tenor soloist, male chorus, and piano.[52]

Almost a third of the individual numbers are for SATB chorus: six in the first half and three in the second. Bristow's choral movements are demanding, musically satisfying, and stylistically reminiscent of both Handel and Mendelssohn (or perhaps Handel via Mendelssohn). The chorus also functions in a dramatically effective manner: sometimes as the Israelites and other times personating the Babylonian people; its main function is to reinforce the moral of the story.[53] The finale to act 1 (18) is a good example. The movement starts with a segue from the triumphant male trio, the members of which have just been rescued from the fiery furnace; it is an expression of joyous happiness and relief that the God of the Israelites has demonstrated his superiority over the god of the Babylonians. The work starts (*Allegro con spirito*) with an expression of triumph ("How excellent, how excellent") mostly in four-part harmony with the orchestra providing appropriate accompaniment. At measure 44, however, a powerful fugue commences, with the vocal parts doubled, and emphasized, by the orchestra. The movement eventually builds to a climax with continued reiterated statements of the text—"Oh! Lord, is in the heavens and thy faithfulness reacheth unto the clouds"—until the ensemble achieves the final statement of the text and sings it emphatically, powerfully, and with long-held notes. After that *fortissimo* climax, the orchestra concludes the movement with a joyous coda.

Bristow's vivid and skillful orchestral writing is particularly strong in *Daniel*. The ensemble is comprised of pairs of winds, four horns, three trombones, timpani, organ, and strings. (One movement also calls for triangle and a pair of cymbals.) This orchestra lacks only the trumpets and tuba of Mendelssohn's ensemble for *Elijah*, which Bristow had conducted with the Harmonic Society numerous times (especially in the late 1850s) and that clearly was his model. He used his orchestra skillfully to help convey the emotion inherent in the text. As Howard Smither observes, early in act 1 (in number 5) he uses a key change, an expansive melody, and powerful orchestral accompaniment to portray the heroic nature of Daniel's character. His orchestral writing also demonstrates a mastery of mid-century harmonic language. Although key relationships are fairly standard (mostly third-related), he frequently uses nonharmonic chords for modulating and exploits fully diminished seventh chords and the flat supertonic for dramatic effect. As Griggs-Janower points out, Bristow's harmonic vocabulary was expansive and exploited "the full palette of tonal and harmonic relations" typical of the mid-century European harmonic language.[54]

The premiere performance of *Daniel* was on December 28, 1867, with the composer conducting. He later remembered enjoying "the satisfaction of standing before my fellow citizens in Steinway Hall at the first production of 'Daniel' with a magnificent chorus . . . an orchestra of fifty good musicians and the glorious Parepa in the principal soprano role." The chorus numbered one hundred, and the orchestra was comprised of sixty (not fifty) instrumentalists, including organist John P. Morgan. The most famous soloist was Parepa-Rosa, who was in the midst of her second American tour and enjoying phenomenal success in concert and oratorio performances.[55] The audience was reportedly "large and discriminating," and critical reception in the press ranged from congratulatory to wildly enthusiastic, the latter frequently tinged with American pride. The correspondent to *Dwight's Journal*, although unhappy about several of the performers, called the work "most carefully written and scored" and noted that "many of the numbers are melodious and pleasing." The critic for the *New York Evening Mail*, on the other hand, was much more enthusiastic, describing the oratorio as "at once the most ambitious and the most successful composition yet produced in America." Watson (who in the early 1870s would contribute the libretto to Bristow's secular cantata *The Pioneer*) agreed with the *Mail*, writing that the premiere performance of "an original grand Oratorio by a native composer" was "one of the most important events in the musical history of America." The composer, he continued, "had produced a great and lasting work" and "an unquestionable success, receiving a public endorsement more prompt and decided than has been accorded to a work of its class since the production of Mendelsohn's *Elijah*."[56] After the second performance, on January 30, 1868 (with a smaller audience, because of inadequate advertising and the illness of audience-magnet Parepa-Rosa), Charles Seymour noted that the "favorable impression" created by the first performance "was more than confirmed on this occasion." He pointed out that Bristow's "melodies are delicious; his concerted pieces are ingenious but clear, and his recitatives are powerful dramatic statements." The composer's orchestral writing, he continued, was "more free and operatic than in any other oratorio with which we are acquainted," and the choruses "are striking from their harmonic treatment." *Daniel*, he concluded, was the work "of a master whose judgement is calm, his invention fresh, and his knowledge perfect."[57]

Happily, the critical commentary about *Daniel* was completely devoid of the type of complaints concerning similarities to European works that had marred the reception of Bristow's earlier instrumental compositions, despite the marked similarities to Mendelssohn's *Elijah*. Both the correspondent to *Dwight's* and Henry Watson noted the resemblance to Mendelssohn's style, but their observations were couched in positive terms. The former commented that "the orchestral accompaniment to the chorus in A minor (No. 13) is excellent, somewhat Mendelssohnian in character; indeed there are strong suggestions to that master throughout the entire oratorio"; Watson observed that the opening chorus in unison recitative "will inevitably recall the opening of 'Elijah'" but "only as to form . . . for subject and treatment are entirely Mr. Bristow's own." He also asserted that "the work bears the mark of strong individuality."[58] Perhaps the difference was in genre; the positive reception for *Praise to God*, another vocal work, had also been devoid of the sniping comments about European derivation. It is also possible that American critics no longer felt the need to demonstrate their own cosmopolitanism and familiarity with European composers and compositions. Furthermore, critics were increasingly observing growth in Bristow's musical voice; Watson, for example, wrote that *Daniel*—in comparison with his earlier works—exhibited "a greater maturity of thought and style, greater freedom in handling his material, [and] a broader manner and a more impassioned expression."[59] It is also feasible that this perception of the composer's musical voice allowed critics finally to recognize that his style, in fact, was a dialect within the broader Western European musical language. Or maybe the change reflected a combination of all of these elements.

Bristow was surely gratified at the reception to this major composition. Unfortunately, however, despite critics' confidence that *Daniel* would "find its way to the great cities of the country" (Seymour) and that the new oratorio "will live with the few other great choral works which the world endorses" (Watson), Bristow's oratorio did not enter the repertoires of American choral societies, probably because he was unable to secure its publication.[60] Today, however, *The Oratorio of Daniel* is considered not just one of the composer's major accomplishments but an important composition that deserves a place in the repertoires of modern choral ensembles. According to Howard Smither, *Daniel* "is musically significant in the European sense" and "worthy of performance today." And conductor and choral music scholar David DeVenney agrees, writing that the music of Bristow's oratorio "is of high quality and originality" and that *Daniel*, as a work, "marks a high point in the history of American choral music."[61] Perhaps its day will eventually come.

## Secular Choral Music

The language that Bristow's contemporaries used to discuss *Daniel* is a clear reflection of the esteem in which oratorios were held in America during the second half of the nineteenth century. A much more popular genre, however, was the cantata (and its closely related form, the ode). Americans—both audiences and performers—actually preferred cantatas, as shorter, less operatic, and less formal works than oratorios. During the 1860s, '70s, and '80s, they also tended to be secular (sacred cantatas would become popular during the 1890s). An ever increasing demand for cantatas was fueled by what Lee Orr calls the "astonishing growth of community choral groups" that sprouted up, mushroom-like, all over the United States starting around 1860. The choral music craze was also fueled by the already noted availability, and affordability, of scores for cantatas and oratorios by European composers (which was aided by growth in printing technology and distribution networks) and by a widespread celebration of American triumphalism in all of its forms. The latter led to a demand for choral works that were nationalistic and laudatory, and American composers readily complied. Thurston Dox, for example, identifies more than two hundred nineteenth-century American cantatas written during the second half of the century—a repertoire that Orr describes as "democratic music," for although these works could be mastered by amateur choristers, they also conveyed a sense of musical sophistication that was gratifying to both singers and listeners and that fostered appreciation of America as a noble and heroic nation. One of the most important early composers of secular cantatas was George Frederick Root (1820–1895), who helped to establish the genre in America. Root wrote sixteen such works, including *The Flower Queen* (1852, for children; see Interlude C), *The Haymakers* (1857), and several overtly nationalistic cantatas such as *The Pilgrim Fathers* (1854) and *Our Flag with Stars and Stripes* (1896).[62] Dudley Buck, another of Bristow's contemporaries, also wrote several cantatas, but most other American works in this genre date from the 1880s and later.

Bristow frequently conducted performances of cantatas by both the Harmonic Society and the Mendelssohn Union. Examples include the American premiere of the new cantata *The May Queen* (op. 39, 1858?) by Sterndale Bennett (1816–1875), put on by the Harmonic Society in 1860, and an already noted performance by the Mendelssohn Union of Johannes van Bree's *St. Cecilia's Day* (ca. 1850) in 1868. Such compositions also show up occasionally in special individual concerts in which Bristow participated; a good example is a Grand Musical Festival at the Brooklyn Academy of Music in early 1870 during which "various choral societies" (including the Mendelssohn Union) performed Mendelssohn's cantata *Athalie*.[63] Bristow's own output of secular choral music during the 1860s was light, but his conducting activities apparently whetted his appetite for writing secular choral works, for he would produce two major compositions in this style during the 1870s: *The Pioneer: A Grand Cantata*, op. 49, and *The Great Republic: Ode to the American Union*, op. 47. Both are discussed in chapter 5.

| Interlude C | **Pedagogy II** |
|---|---|

## *Teaching in Schools*

IN 1854 BRISTOW STARTED A LIFELONG CAREER as a teacher in the New York Public Schools.[1] His first position was as a teacher of music at the Female Normal Institute, a training school for teachers. This appointment was apparently temporary, however, for after a year Bristow's friend George Henry Curtis returned to New York after a brief reassignment and resumed that position, and Bristow turned his attention to the education of young children (rather than teachers). He started in 1855 at Grammar School No. 44 on North Moore Street in the city's Fifth Ward, not far from where he was living at 429 Broome Street, near Broadway.[2] Like all music teachers in the public schools, he taught simultaneously in numerous different schools, located in the Fifth, Tenth, and Fifteenth wards, all within easy walking distance of his residence.[3]

### Music in the New York Public Schools

Bristow's career as a public school teacher started around the same time that public educators in New York began to take music more seriously as an academic subject. Before 1854 there were neither teachers nor a curriculum for music in the schools; music itself, although occasionally proposed as a subject matter to the board of education, was generally dismissed as mere recreation. This situation began to change only in the mid-1850s, inspired in part by a growing national interest in music education, as indicated by the activities of Lowell Mason in the Boston schools and efforts by Mason, George Frederick Root, William Bradbury, and others to publish articles and organize singing conventions and teaching institutes, primarily in the Northeast.[4]

The entire New York City public school system underwent a significant restructuring in the mid-1850s, and the first president of the newly reorganized board of education recommended that music be incorporated more thoroughly into the curriculum because such instruction helped to instill "taste and discipline" in students; moreover, learning "carefully chosen songs" contributed to students' quality of life.[5] A substantial later report confirms this change, for it notes that by 1855 pianos had been introduced into some of the boys primary schools, "having heretofore been provided in part only for the female departments." This change "greatly influenced the discipline of the schools, and rendered them pleasant, cheerful, and attractive, besides introducing a beneficial vocal training."[6] But acceptance of music as a part of the curriculum was a slow process. After another school board reorganization, in 1855, the newly appointed temporary chairman denounced "ornamental education" (such as music, drawing, and languages) as unnecessary indulgences that were "simply robbing the taxpayers" and insisted that teachers should focus exclusively on reading, writing, and basic arithmetic. In fact, Bristow later claimed in a report to the Music Teachers National Association (MTNA) that even as late as 1885 many principals and teachers in the school system exhibited "indifference to the teaching of music"—but mostly (in his opinion) because they lacked knowledge about music pedagogy.[7] Clearly, New York's music teachers faced an uphill battle during the second half of the century.

Music pedagogy in the public schools was by all reports a difficult job, with or without administrative support. Bristow pointed out that many of the schools in which he taught did not have pianos, which meant that a teacher "had to take his violin, if he could play on it, and *fiddle do, re, mi*, for the musical benefit of the rising generation." If the teacher could not play a portable instrument, he had to use his voice or "any and every device to interest and improve the pupils." Nor was there adequate time devoted to music instruction. The maximum amount allotted to musical pedagogy per week was eighty minutes in the primary schools and one hundred minutes in the grammar schools (Bristow taught in the latter), plus ten minutes of music instruction per day by the regular classroom teacher (except on the day of the music teacher's visit). This meant that students in primary schools had two and a half hours of music pedagogy per week; students in the more demanding grammar schools had three hours.[8] In addition, when the music teacher visited, he or she typically taught the students from all classes of a particular grade level, crowded into a large room. Bristow reported that in one school he had taught anywhere from 128 to 181 students in a large room that measured 17 feet by 17 feet, which meant that students were "packed like herrings in a box." On the other hand, however, as education historian Diane Ravitch reports, during the late 1860s the New York schools in general were "desperately overcrowded," so this characteristic was not limited to music instruction. According to the *Evening Post*, in the 1860s many public school classrooms (designed to accommodate between fifty and seventy students) had between 100 and 150 students, all under the supervision of a single teacher.[9]

Bristow taught both boys and girls. The grammar schools were mostly gender-specific, although some were mixed. In 1869, for example, New York had forty grammar schools for boys, forty-two for girls, and nine that accommodated both genders.[10] Bristow taught in two girls grammar schools: No. 7 (on Chrystie Street) and No. 47 (at 36 East Twelfth Street). He also taught at four schools that served both males and females: No. 10 (on Wooster Street near Bleeker), No. 20 (160 Chrystie Street), No. 42 (Allen Street near Hester), and No. 44 (North Moore and Varick Streets). The school system was also segregated by race, and African American pupils were significantly underserved: in 1869 there were only four "colored" grammar schools (two each for boys and girls), as well as three "colored" primary schools.[11] Bristow did not teach any of these students.

The overwhelming majority of his pupils were foreign-born. In 1885 Bristow described New York as "perhaps the most cosmopolitan city on the globe, containing Germans, Irish, French, Italians, Poles, a few English, . . . and here and there an American." In most of the neighborhoods where he taught, "we scarcely hear a word of English spoken in the streets," and his pupils heard no English "from the time [they] leave school until they return to it again."[12] New York children attended neighborhood schools, and the population of Manhattan during the second half of the century was heavily immigrant. One demographic study of a specific New York neighborhood (the Seventeenth Ward) is quite revealing. This ward was part of a large segment of the East Side known as "Little Germany" or *Kleindeutschland* (which included wards Ten, Eleven, Thirteen, and Seventeen), and a large number of residents were German-speakers. There had been such an influx of German immigrants into this area in the 1840s and early 1850s, in fact, that by mid-decade "Little Germany" was the third-largest urban enclave of German speakers in the world, surpassed only by Vienna and Berlin. But there were also many Irish, as well as natives of thirty-seven other countries in the British Isles, Europe, South America, Asia, and the Caribbean. Over 60 percent of Seventeenth Ward residents were foreign-born, and the percentage of immigrants who were of prime child-bearing age (between twenty and thirty-four years old) was even higher, at 83 percent. Most children in the ward were born in the United States and spoke English, but as Bristow pointed out, it was "reasonable to infer how bewildering" it was for both pupils and teachers to deal with a multiplicity of languages and cultures within the classroom.[13]

## George Bristow's Leadership in the Public Schools

Three of Bristow's schools (Nos. 7, 20, and 42) were located in the Tenth Ward, that part of *Kleindeutschland* populated primarily by Prussians, which suggests that approximately half of Bristow's elementary-age pupils—with whom he worked closely for decades—were first-generation German immigrants. This, of course, is further evidence that Bristow was not virulently anti-German, since such a bias would have made his workaday existence quite unpleasant. His other three schools were located in the Fifth and Fifteenth wards, which were also overwhelmingly populated by immigrants. Nearly 24 percent of the populations of both of these wards, for example, were native Irish.[14]

Under these circumstances, most music education in the elementary grades consisted of teaching songs by rote, a style of education that Bristow called "the prevailing epidemic at this time." The goal, he wrote, was to prepare students to perform at receptions where they recited memorized texts and sang songs for the "delectation of parents, school boards, principals, and teachers in general." An example of one such public demonstration occurred in 1867, for a delegation from the Baltimore schools. The pupils, according to Ravitch, "displayed their prowess in calisthenics, reading, singing, and simultaneous recitation, regulated by the music of a piano" and very much impressed the visitors. The demonstration created the impression of well-disciplined and accomplished students who performed their tasks with a "precision . . . that was remarkable." Bristow dismissed this approach as not true music pedagogy but noted that rote singing was not "altogether useless," for although teachers were "not allowed to instruct the pupils" in real music, they nevertheless "in many cases taught them classical music, especially in the 5th, 10th, 13th, 15th, 18th, and 20th wards." Bristow's schools were located in three of these wards.[15]

As examples, he noted that students in the Tenth Ward schools learned such pieces as the Credo from Haydn's Third Mass, Schubert's "The Wanderer," the celebrated "Singing Lesson" by Valentino Fioravanti (1764–1837), and "many other operatic choruses and selections." The "greatest achievement" of this nature, he noted, was a concert by students from the Girls' Grammar School No. 47, which included the Gloria from Mozart's Second Mass and the act 1 finale from *Lucrezia Borgia* and a chorus from *The Martyrs*, both by Donizetti; the female chorus from the *Paradise and the Peri* (*Das Paradies und die Peri*) by Schumann; the opening chorus from Flotow's *Martha*; "and other pieces of like character." It was, he reported, "our pleasure to listen to."[16] Bristow was the music teacher at these schools.

The composer used these two concerts as examples of the type of repertoire that he taught to grammar school children during his tenure, and it is clear that these were not isolated samples. Students performed regularly at receptions, spring commencements, and benefit concerts. The commencement and promotion exercises were elaborate affairs in which all the students participated; they were also described in detail in newspapers. Fifth Ward School No. 44, for example, held "one of the most imposing and well-arranged displays connected with [the] public schools" in early July 1855: the ceremony included promotion exercises for all of the ward's primary and grammar school students. School officials, including representatives from the superintendent's office, were present, and the ceremony included short speeches, recitations by some of the children, instrumental performances, solo and ensemble singing, and choral performances, including a hearty rendition of Henry Russell's "A Life on the Ocean Wave" by the whole school, including "many of the fair visitors."[17] Accounts of commencement ceremonies at Bristow's other grammar schools during the 1860s confirm the general musical content of such events and suggest that sometimes selections were much more demanding than Russell's strophic song. The commencement exercise for Ward School No. 42 (July 1865), for example, included the anthem "Come Let Us Sing Unto the Lord," adapted to the "celebrated and difficult Cannon [*sic*] from Haydn's Imperial Mass" (*Mass*, H. XII, 11, in D minor), which was performed "with precision, promptitude and spirit, and reflected great praise upon the pupils and their teacher, Mr. George F. Bristow."[18]

Students also regularly performed in public concerts, including benefits. Bristow reported that his pupils gave concerts to raise money "to purchase first-class pianos," a strategy that evidently was successful, even at twenty-five cents per ticket. In both 1855 and 1856 students at one of his schools held benefit concerts to purchase pianos; the latter concert, in May 1856 and at the Broadway Tabernacle, featured sixteen hundred children.[19] Almost a decade later, during the Civil War, pupils of Bristow's three Tenth Ward schools performed several times (in April 1864) at the Metropolitan Fair for the benefit of the US Sanitary Commission. The children sang unidentified "musical selections" for a crowded and appreciative audience and performed every afternoon for the duration of the fair. The performances attracted many children as audience members, both with the singing and with "a mammoth magic lantern" that was exhibited in the darkened room.[20]

The Tenth Ward school board also granted Bristow permission to have children from his schools "assist" him in a "Grand Juvenile Beethoven Festival" in June 1870, as part of the centennial celebration of that composer's birth. Since the Tenth Ward was heavily German-speaking, this celebration of German culture must have been an easy sell to the local school board, although Bristow assured parents that preparation for the festival would not interfere with "the studies of the pupils."[21] The event was held at Steinway Hall on June 16, 20, and 22, and featured—in addition to the children—several eminent vocal and instrumental soloists. The first concert included four hundred girls and two hundred boys from Grammar School No. 42 (students from the other two schools were featured on the other evenings); they sang seventeen pieces, including several solos and two choral selections each by the boys and the girls. Apparently only the adult soloists performed works by Beethoven. But the event must have been a tour de force for Bristow: all of the children were reportedly seven years of age or younger; the girls were dressed in white and had flowers in their hair; the boys, dressed in dark clothing, sat "with great decorum in the back seats" on the stage. The program was "finely performed throughout," in front of a hall that was "densely crowded." After it was over there was a "a great rush for the stage," where the well-behaved children "sat quietly waiting to be claimed by their parents."[22] Bristow's ability to train such a large number of very young pupils from three different schools for impressive performances in three separate concerts over this short period of time is remarkable.

The Juvenile Festival took place in conjunction with "The Great Beethoven Centennial Music Jubilee," held at the American Institute Coliseum (cap. 22,000) for six nights (June 13–18). These performances were mounted by a choir of 3,000, an orchestra that numbered between 350 and 550 instrumentalists, four brass bands, and the personnel of six opera companies (including such vocal celebrities as Clara Louise Kellogg [1842–1916], Euphrosyne Parepa-Rosa, Caroline Richings [1827–1882], William Castle [1836–1909], and others). The event had all the trappings of an extravaganza orchestrated by Patrick Gilmore (who was the organizer), and reviews and advertisements regularly refer to his "Great Peace Jubilee" held in Boston the previous June. In late May, Jubilee advertisements had named Bristow as "choral maestro and conductor," but his name disappeared from the ads in early June; apparently he was replaced by James Pech and his

Society of Choirs. It is entirely plausible that Bristow decided that participation in both events was too much, especially as the first juvenile concert conflicted with one of the Jubilee performances. His choice—to work with children instead of the luminaries engaged for the Jubilee—seems completely true to his unassuming character and reflects both his passion for teaching children and devotion to music. As noted in one of the first announcements for the Juvenile Festival, "Mr. Bristow, feeling that the present year should not be allowed to pass without some respect being shown to the memory of so great a man, has taken this step to show that even children desire to commemorate that event."[23]

Bristow's remarkable success in creating support for music education in New York was not accomplished in a vacuum, for he worked in solidarity with many of the other music teachers. His close friend George Henry Curtis, for example, was also a longtime public school educator, as were George Petit, George Rexford, and his singing-textbook collaborator, Francis Nash (who was both a fellow-teacher and a neighbor, since he also lived in Morrisania).[24] By 1860, in fact, Bristow, Curtis, Nash, and Petit were in charge of music pedagogy in twenty-two different schools. The teachers helped each other out, especially in the implementation of concerts and other public performances. One excellent example is a performance in December 1856 of George Frederick Root's new cantata, *The Flower Queen*. The event, at the Academy of Music, featured the boys of Grammar School No. 11, under the direction of Mr. J. C. Woodson, the school's music teacher. Both William Mason and Bristow lent their support.[25]

By the late 1850s Bristow had earned a solid reputation in New York as a positive force for music education in the city's public schools. The frequency and success of his students' concerts contributed to this reputation and kept his name in front of the public. As a critic wrote in a review of one such concert held in 1865, "Mr. Bristow has added much to his reputation as a teacher by this pleasant exhibition."[26] The increasing visibility of schoolchildren performing music also helped to propel changes in the place of music in the curriculum. In 1865, in fact, the board of education adopted a new bylaw that required music teachers in the primary and grammar schools to provide not only "exercises in vocal music" but also instruction of students in the highest grades in the "science" of music—that is, musical notation.[27] In response to this, Bristow and Nash created *Cantara, or Teacher of Singing* (New York: A. S. Barnes and Co., 1866), a "Complete Musical Textbook for Schools of Every Grade." The book is divided into two sections: part 1 is a tutorial on the rudiments of musical notation, with forty graded exercises; part 2 consists of fifty sight-reading exercises of increasing difficulty.[28] Whether or not many schools adopted the Bristow/Nash text is unknown, but the fact that a second, expanded edition (*Cantara No. 2*) was released within two years and that both volumes were reprinted (in 1870 and 1873), suggests that there was a market for such texts—which was clearly the New York schools, for the preface to the first version explicitly states that the book had been compiled "with special reference to the new By-law of the Board of Education of the City of New York." Furthermore, both editors were identified on the title page as "Teachers of Music in the Public Schools of New York." Certainly Nash and Bristow must have used the texts in their own classrooms.

The movement toward overhaul of the school's music curriculum gained momentum in 1873 when the school board decided to undertake structural changes, including a graded and unified curriculum for all of the city's schools, specific evaluation techniques of students' progress, and the creation of a new position: the assistant superintendent of music. In December the board appointed a subcommittee of Bristow, Nash, and one additional individual to travel to Boston and observe the pros and cons of that city's efforts.[29] Their report (March 1874) points out both positive and negative aspects of Boston's approach to music pedagogy. In response, the board created several new positions: a director of music and eight assistants. Bristow was nominated as music director (at the rank of assistant superintendent); others were tapped to be assistant directors. The board, however, failed to ratify any of the nominations.[30]

This inaction opened the door for complaints and petitions, which poured in from teachers, principals, and others who objected to the overall proposal. But Henry Watson, in an unsigned editorial in his *Journal*, pointed out the root problem: "Practical men look upon the study of music as an idle, nay, an almost worthless accomplishment."[31] In February 1876 the board repealed the substantive proposal, which meant that music education in the schools was back to where it had been in 1865. In May, Bristow requested a leave of absence. How long this lasted is unknown, although he participated in the commencement exercises of Grammar School No. 42 in May 1877, which suggests that he probably resumed teaching by spring of the 1876–1877 academic year.[32] The school system finally adopted a graded music curriculum in 1879, about which Bristow wrote at some length in his 1885 address to the MTNA. He praised the goals but, based on the amount of time allotted to music education per day, deemed them "absurd" and completely unfeasible.[33]

The school system did not create the office of supervisor of music until 1897, one year before Bristow's death. Frank Damrosch (1859–1937) was appointed to the position, and although several authors of Bristow's obituaries seemed certain that he had been at least an assistant supervisor under Damrosch, Thurston Dox was unable to find any mention of such a position. As Dox points out, "Perhaps those authors [wanted] to offer some fitting and historically reasonable expression of respect for this stalwart American musician."[34] Bristow, however, spent the rest of his career as a classroom teacher, eventually serving in the public schools for forty-three years. His tenacity is not altogether surprising, because the New York schools did not offer their teachers any kind of retirement until the 1890s, so many of them—like Bristow—continued to work until they were physically unable to do so.[35]

## Private Institutes and Conservatories

In addition to teaching schoolchildren and private students, Bristow was regularly associated with many of the private music schools and academies that emerged in New York during the middle- and late-century period. This was a fecund period for private music academies in the city; newspapers are full of advertisements for such establishments, some of them studios set up by individual teachers, others fully incorporated academic institutions recognized by the State of New York. The history of these academies, conservatories, or schools—and their impact on musical life in the city—has been almost completely ignored by music historians, but a brief overview of Bristow's activities in this realm provides a glimpse into this aspect of musical life in New York.

Many of the conservatories that emerged during the mid-century period disappeared almost as quickly as they were established, but others were more permanent. An important early example of the latter is the Cooper Union for the Advancement of Science and Art, a college established in 1859 as a free school for working-class students that is still going strong in modern New York. Founded by the industrialist, inventor, and philanthropist Peter Cooper (1791–1883), the school reflected his belief that education was "the key not only to personal prosperity but to civic virtue and harmony"; it was supported by rent revenue from stores and offices located elsewhere in the Cooper Union building. The Union also boasted of a large hall that could seat nine hundred and that presumably also generated income.[36]

Several reports of student concerts held in 1862 confirm that Bristow was at least briefly associated with the Cooper Union. The first was a complimentary concert, held in April 1862 by "pupils of the Cooper-Union Music Class" and dedicated "to their teacher, George F. Bristow." It included performances by five singers, a flutist, clarinetist, and the "full chorus of 250 of the Cooper-Union Music Class." A month later Bristow assisted at commencement exercises for the institute, and graduates included over 100 students from his class. Also in May 1862 Bristow organized a vocal concert that featured several well-known local singers and a chorus of 250 of his music students; the event raised funds for the many sick, wounded, and needy soldiers who were being transported from Southern battlefields to New York City on hospital ships. A similar "Wounded Soldiers' Benefit" was held in December 1862 and again included significant participation by his music class. It is not clear whether the Cooper Union music class was a chorus or a singing class, nor do we know if Bristow taught at the Union before or after 1862. These bits of ephemeral information, however, reveal another of the myriad musical activities that were a normal part of the New York cultural scene at mid-century and that were part of Bristow's busy life.[37] His participation in this organization is not surprising, however, for Peter Cooper's attitude about the value of education dovetailed closely with the composer's.

In September 1866 Henry Watson, editor of his eponymous *Art Journal*, wrote a laudatory article about what he called the city's newest musical educational organization, the National Conservatory of Music, and observed that in 1866 the city had three such institutions—the Cooper Union and the National and New York Conservatories.[38] In 1866 the National Conservatory was thriving, with some fifteen hundred pupils and twelve well-known music faculty members, including Bristow, who was professor of theory and composition and the newly named musical director of the conservatory. Watson, a staunch supporter of the composer, described Bristow as "one of our most eminent musicians, and one who has had a vast experience in the education of the young." He continued, "A more experienced man could not have been chosen. He is every where popular, and, as an American Musician he has won the highest respect, not only in his own country, where he takes the lead, but in Europe, where his name is well known." Watson also noted that Bristow had recruited "some of the first and best teachers in the country" and moreover expressed confidence in the "continued and permanent success of the National Conservatory."[39] Advertisements and notices of concerts, soirées, and the appointment of faculty members suggest that the National Conservatory had a strong presence in the city, although it may have suffered some setbacks, since it changed location frequently. Bristow was connected with the school until 1871. Whether or not he was consistently on the faculty during that four-year period is unknown, as is the length of his tenure as music director of the organization. In September 1873 the National was incorporated into the New York Conservatory.[40]

Bristow apparently took a hiatus from teaching in private institutions during 1871–1875, but in the latter year he accepted a position at the Grand Conservatory, which had been established in spring 1874. Described in a notice as "the Great American Composer," Bristow joined this faculty in January 1875, teaching "the rudiments of Music and the art of singing at Sight."[41] Later that same year the conservatory announced the formation of a "Grand Choral Society" to perform with the Philharmonic Society. Whether or not anything came of this plan is unknown, but Bristow, described in glowing terms as "perhaps the most able leader of a chorus to-day in America," was announced as the conductor of that ensemble.[42] By 1880 the school offered classes in "all branches of Vocal and Instrumental Music: Piano, Organ, Harp, Violin, Flute and all other string and wind instruments; Harmony and Composition &c., Elocution and Oratory," and three years later could boast of forty-five professors. The Grand Conservatory was still going strong at the end of the century, although Bristow had long since ceased working for the institution.[43]

By 1878 Bristow, whose choral conducting had tapered off, ramped up his private pedagogical activities, primarily with a new organization, the New York College of Music, which that year had been granted authority from the State of New York to give diplomas and confer degrees. Over the years, Bristow had worked for various private schools, which was perhaps the reason he felt compelled in December 1878 to take out a personal ad (under the heading "New-York College of Music") and declare, "As my name has appeared with various musical conservatories, I now beg to state that the above college is the only one where I teach and has the authority to use my name."[44] In October he was teacher of organ, sight-singing, and choral singing (with a focus on "oratorios, cantatas, masses, and other vocal compositions"); in 1879 he added classes in theory, harmony, and organ to his schedule.[45] By 1880 the college had established a Chorus School, under the supervision of Theodore Thomas, who was on the board of directors; Bristow was named as his assistant but by 1882 was identified as the chorus master (he also taught piano, vocal sight reading, and organ). The Chorus School, according to an 1880 announcement, was "organized by the College for the purpose of giving everybody, no matter how small their means, an opportunity of having their voice cultivated and to learn to read at sight, the terms being $5 [roughly $130 in 2019 currency] a quarter."[46] Bristow was a prominent member of the faculty for six years, during which time the institution regularly added to its faculty renowned performers such as the pianist Rafael Joseffy, violinist Edward Mollenhauer, and others from the Philharmonic Society orchestra. He apparently retired from the college after the 1883–1884 academic year.

The justification given by the New York College of Music for the establishment of its Chorus School fit well with Bristow's generous attitude about music education; it also echoed the goals of two other educational organizations for which he had worked—Henry Meiggs's American Musical Institute and the Cooper Union school. As already mentioned, he had written in the 1860s that that his goal in life was to do "all that I can for art" and that he was interested in helping "ordinary human beings" to learn about music. He accomplished this goal admirably as a public school teacher; as William James Henderson (1835–1937) wrote in Bristow's obituary, "Most of the public school boys of the last thirty or thirty-five years know something of his work" because of his pedagogical efforts. But the fact that over the course of his career he taught not only in the public schools but also in three different private institutions that echoed his belief in the power of music and that made it possible for those of limited economic means to participate in musical endeavors suggests that he was deeply interested in reaching out to adults as well as children, including perhaps the parents of his pupils, most of whom came from working-class families. His unstinting pedagogical efforts— coupled with his decades-long work as a church organist, director of amateur church choirs, and attempts to make it possible for lower-income individuals to purchase pianos (see Interlude D)—suggest a generous nature and a deep belief in the power of music. Henderson succinctly summarized his character: "He was a most earnest man, filled with a real love for his art and self-sacrificing in his labor for its benefit."[47]

# The 1870s

## A "Manly and Patriotic" Composer of "Native Independence and Originality"

**THE 1870S MARKED THE MIDPOINT** of Bristow's career. As a mature and established composer (he was fifty years old at mid-decade), his stature in the New York music world was both secure and widely acknowledged. His freelance or short-term engagement activities, which had diminished significantly in the mid-1860s, no longer made up an important part of his professional life. But his profile as a highly recognized performer nevertheless remained constant throughout the decade, as measured both by appearances in regular concerts (as an orchestral violinist, a church organist, and a choral conductor), and in occasional special events (as an organist, a conductor of performances that featured his students [see Interlude C], and in intermittent special performances, musical congresses, and benefit concerts). As a composer, the sheer number of new compositions declined during the decade, but his public reputation nevertheless grew as the result of three major new works: a cantata, an ode, and his fourth symphony. The number of concerts that featured his works, both new and old, remained steady throughout the decade.

## Bristow as Performer

Regular responsibilities with two orchestras required a significant commitment of Bristow's time. As already mentioned, during the 1870s the Philharmonic Society of New York gave six concerts per season as well as three public rehearsals per subscription concert. The schedule for the Brooklyn orchestra was similar: five concerts per year (a sixth was added in 1879–1880) and three public rehearsals for each subscription performance. For most of the decade, then, the concerts for these two orchestras alone totaled forty-four over the course of a six-month season (November to April), not counting any special events, benefit concerts, or other activities in which both ensembles sometimes engaged.

Bristow also had regular performance-related responsibilities as the music director of the Mendelssohn Union (a position he relinquished in 1871), the Harlem Mendelssohn Union (1871–1873), and the historically elusive Centennial Choral Union (1875). Although the first of these societies gave few regular concerts during the early 1870s, it nevertheless participated in several high-profile events, which suggests continued activity: three performances of the *Messiah*, two in November 1870 that featured the Swedish soprano Christine Nilsson and American soloists Annie Louise Cary (1841–1921, contralto), George Simpson (dates unknown, tenor), and Myron Whitney (1836–1910, bass), and the third in January 1871 with an all-American cast of soloists (Louise Kellogg, contralto Jenny Kempton [1835–1921], Simpson, and Whitney). There was also a "Grand Concert" in February 1871 with some of the same artists and, a month later, Nilsson's return engagement singing in both the *Messiah* and *The Creation*.[1] The union's activities diminished during 1871–1872, although the organization did give another performance of the *Messiah* in October 1871, featuring Parepa-Rosa, Zelda Seguin (1848–1914), George Simpson, and Aynsley Cook (1831 [or 1836]–1894), after which, according to Henry Krehbiel, it fell apart.[2] Bristow almost immediately took over directorship of the Harlem Mendelssohn Union (1871–1873), a choral society that was located much closer to his home but about which almost nothing is known. And in 1875 he became conductor of the Centennial Choral Union, a society organized by the entrepreneur/manager Lafayette F. Harrison that performed with the German soprano Thérèse Titiens (1831–1877) in the *Messiah*, *Elijah*, and a concert of miscellaneous works in October and November 1875, as well as a testimonial concert for Bristow in December. (See below.) The organization subsequently disappeared.[3]

Critics continued to comment positively about Bristow's conducting abilities. In his review of the *Messiah* performance (with Nilsson) in 1870, for example,

Myron Cooney described the assisting ensembles as "a finely-trained and evenly-balanced chorus" and "a capital orchestra," under the direction of "one of the best conductors in America, George Bristow." He went on to say that the performance was marked by "the nicest shading of expression from *pianissimo* to *fortissimo*, a thing unheard of before in oratorio choruses here, and the most perfect accord and unanimity through the most intricate passages." John Rose Green Hassard (1836–1888) of the *Tribune* was similarly laudatory of the Nilsson performance the following March; he pointed out that "the Society has improved greatly under Mr. Bristow's management." The unknown critic of the *Times* praised the performance that featured Parepa-Rosa in October 1871, writing that "the choruses were given with unusual precision," the orchestra was "handled with a keen eye to the value of contrasts," and the difficult writing in the oratorio "has never been read with more clearness and finish, though *pianissimo*, on the same platform."[4]

Bristow was occasionally invited to play in an organ concert series at Plymouth Church in Brooklyn that was held throughout the 1870s; the weekly Saturday performances featured well-known organists from New York, Brooklyn, and elsewhere and regularly attracted hundreds of auditors. (The cost of admission was ten or fifteen cents per performance.) The repertoire was also varied. A March 1871 concert that featured "the celebrated composer" George Bristow and several singers, for example, was described as "mainly in the popular school of melody" and appropriate for "the general taste"; it included performances of "The Last Rose of Summer" with variations, Rossini's *Semiramide* overture, a "grand fantasia" on *Lucia di Lammermoor* (all presumably transcribed for organ), and several ballads and a vocal duet.[5] Also in 1871 Bristow organized and performed in a series of "Grand Concerts" at Zion Protestant Episcopal Church in Manhattan, where he was director of music. The first such concert featured selections from Bach, Rossini, Haydn, Beethoven, and Franz von Suppé; performers included Bristow on organ and a quartet of singers.[6] The vast majority of Bristow's performances during the decade, however, were functions of his regular jobs: school activities, orchestral performances, concerts by choral societies, and organ playing in churches.

The handful of concerts and special events in which Bristow participated during the mid-1870s illustrate some of the continued diversity of musical activity in the city as well as his standing in the musical community. His lack of serious engagement with New York social choirs after about 1873 (excepting the short-lived Centennial Choral Union) perhaps illustrates a reorientation of his priorities; he was, in fact, thoroughly occupied with pedagogy, orchestral performances, and composition during this time. But his almost complete lack of special concert activity might also reflect more than his personal disengagement with such endeavors, for during the mid-1870s New York (and the rest of the country) was in the throes of the worst economic crisis that the nation had ever faced. The Panic of 1873, which occurred in late September, burst the bubble of economic prosperity that the country had enjoyed since the end of the Civil War. This period of prosperity, and a related explosion in entertainment activity, had relied on a dangerous level of speculation: American bankers, and the government, had borrowed heavily from European lenders for both the Civil War and the postwar economic expansion. In response to unsettled economic conditions abroad, European banks began to call in these loans in the early 1870s, and American financial institutions could not pay their debts, which precipitated the Panic and a subsequent Long Depression. Banks and trust companies failed, businesses went bankrupt, and tens of thousands of American workers were laid off. In some parts of the country the effects of the financial downturn lasted well into the 1880s; in New York the worst effects were felt in the middle years of the decade.[7]

## Performances of Bristow's Compositions

Despite the repercussions of the Panic, Bristow's identity as an accomplished composer of all types of works grew during the 1870s, an assertion that is confirmed by journalistic comments. In the first year of the decade, for example, William Hudson of the *Brooklyn Daily Eagle* wrote a positive review of a *Columbus Overture* performance by the Philharmonic Society of Brooklyn on February 26, 1870. After praising the work as "deserving attention for its intrinsic merit," he described it as "the production of an accomplished American musician, in a department of effort in which America is as yet singularly impoverished. Mr. Bristow," he continued, "derives solitary eminence from the fact that he is the only American composer who has written an overture worthy of a place in a Philharmonic programme."[8] In fact, as noted in chapter 4, this was the third time this particular overture had been played by a Philharmonic Society—twice by the New York orchestra and once by the Brooklyn ensemble. Furthermore, the first composition by Bristow to enjoy a public performance—twenty-three years earlier, in 1847—had been his first overture, played by the New York orchestra. Nineteenth-century New York critics had remarkably short memories, especially about the accomplishments of American composers and the development of American musical culture.

In reality, a growing number of Bristow's compositions were performed during the decade. There were older pieces (sacred compositions, overtures, and his opera) as well as some new works. The sacred pieces were showing up more regularly in church services throughout the city, which reflected his growing body of such works and his increased identity as a solid composer. The *Columbus Overture* was also heard several times in the 1870s in addition to the performance just described. And *Rip Van Winkle* was revived by the company of Caroline Richings, an American soprano who played an important role in the remarkable renaissance of vernacular-language opera in the United States after the Civil War.[9]

Critics praised Richings's decision to produce an American opera, although the company's experiment was not successful. The troupe resurrected the work after its slumber of fifteen years and mounted it in early November 1870 as part of its season at Niblo's Theatre. Henri Drayton (baritone, 1822–1872) sang the title role, Susanna Drayton (mezzo, ca. 1822–after 1872) was Dame Van Winkle, and tenor William Castle and soprano Richings performed the love interest characters of act 2.[10] Several lengthy reviews essentially replicated the critical observations of 1855, calling the melodies of the opera genial and clever and the choruses sprightly, and pointing out (as before) the overall lack of drama in the music. Hassard of the *Tribune*, however, noted the major impediment that doomed the revival: in the intervening years since Wainwright had written his cobbled-together libretto, the Irish playwright and actor Dion Boucicault (1820–1890) had created his own adaptation of Irving's story, which the extraordinarily popular actor Joseph Jefferson (1829–1905) had made into his signature role. "No other Rip van Winkle," Hassard wrote, "is likely to be tolerated in New-York while Jefferson lives or is remembered." (In fact, Jefferson was at that moment appearing in the play at Booth's Theatre.)[11]

Several critics, however, used this performance of an old Bristow work to highlight both the progress he had made since writing the opera and the damage that resulted from Americans' well-documented disregard for their own composers. Seymour, for example, noted that the old work gave "little proof" of Bristow's current "creative powers" and complained about the lack of "encouragement . . . afforded to native composers," pointing out that although Bristow's style had matured in the intervening years, he had not been encouraged to write another opera. The critic for *Leslie's* agreed, commenting that "it is a matter of regret that [Bristow] has [had] no opportunity for a further development of his unquestionable talent" and noting that "we should like to hear an opera of Bristow's now, when his style is matured." He expressed hope that "this good melodist and excellent master of instrumentation" might try his hand at another opera.[12] About eight months later, *Leslie's* reported that the opera was being translated into Italian and that Christine Nilsson was interested in singing the role of Alice. Although this seems rather improbable (Nilsson performed the standard continental repertoire written or translated into Italian, not English comic opera), Bristow later told Travis Quigg that Max Strakosch (1835–1892)—manager of the Italian opera company that included Nilsson—had arranged for a translation of the opera but had never performed it.[13] Although there are scattered materials in the New York Public Library collection that indicate the composer's continued interest in the genre, Bristow never completed another opera.

## Compositions of the 1870s

As suggested, in terms of numbers of pieces completed, the decade of the 1870s was the least productive period of Bristow's entire career, even including the 1890s. He wrote only a handful of shorter works, such as sacred choral compositions (see Interlude B) and several songs. There were no works for either piano or organ. But he was hardly idle as a composer, for during the decade he produced two of his most significant secular choral compositions: *The Great Republic: Ode to the American Union*, op. 47 (1870–1876), and *The Pioneer: A Grand Cantata*, op. 49 (1872), as well as his fourth symphony, the *Arcadian*, op. 50 (1872) and an orchestral transcription, *Fantasie Cromatica con Fuga*, op. 53 (1879). The latter was his final work performed (in April 1880) by the Philharmonic Society of New York.

### THE GREAT REPUBLIC: ODE TO THE AMERICAN UNION

*The Great Republic*, op. 47, was published in piano/vocal format in 1880, and as a result Rogers assigned that date as its compositional year. But as Brian Bailey discovered, the work's overture was performed in 1873 (see below) and the ode's opus number, which is lower than that of two compositions known to have been completed by 1872 (*The Pioneer* and the *Arcadian Symphony*), suggests that Bristow had at least started work on the ode in 1870 or 1871.[14]

Another paean to the United States, it is a setting of "The Great Republic Is No More" (1861), by the poet, editor, abolitionist, and clergyman William Oland Bourne (1819–1901). Although mostly forgotten today, Bourne was well known at mid-century for his patriotic verses; "The Great Republic" was published in 1864 in his collection of nationalistic poems titled *Poems of the Republic*.[15] Bourne apparently wrote the poem after reading a pronouncement in the London *Times* (following the secession of South Carolina) that "the Union is dead. The Great Republic is no more." His verses refute what the poet called a "premature utterance."[16]

The first half of the eight-page poem is a lament that elucidates the world's disappointment that the "glorious land," "Freedom's vision," and the "Great Republic" are "no more." At midpoint in the poem, however, the "freemen" take up the cry "to arms, to arms," to which millions respond. In the last three pages Bourne changes to a more forceful and emphatic meter and eventually employs an almost call-and-response format, with the narrator exhorting his comrades to action and the chorus responding, "Arm, brothers, arm! / For the strife be ye ready! / with an eye ever steady! / Arm, brothers, arm!" The poem ends with three linked quatrains that proclaim "the glorious dawn" and a "rapturous birth of Freedom out of woe," culminating in a triumphant proclamation: "The clouds may gather, and the storm be long / And lightnings leap across the darkened sky, / But Freedom lives to triumph over wrong / It still will live, for Truth can never die!"

Bristow's setting commences with a quasi-programmatic overture, followed by fourteen vocal numbers with parts for reader, vocal quartet, SATB chorus, and orchestra. The composer wrote the ode for possible performance as part of the 1876 Centennial Exhibition, as indicated by a letter he wrote in August 1875 to the Philadelphia music publishers Lee and Walker inquiring about the identity of the director of music for the upcoming event. He explained that he had "just completed a composition" for orchestra, solos, choruses, and quartets, "written to a poem by Wm Oland Bourne" that would be "very suitable . . . for such an occasion." The publishers forwarded the letter to Simon Gratz (1840–1925), a prominent Philadelphia attorney who was involved in planning the exhibition and who clearly answered Bristow, for the composer responded to him on August 18, assuring Gratz that "there is a total absence of the spread Eagle business about it, in fact it is a *very sensible work*." An overture, he continued, "preceeds [*sic*] this poem, which is of a purely national character and then is followed by Choruses, Solos &c, portraying the sentiment embodied in the words, thereby forming a rather interesting story, and fully in keeping with so great an event as the coming one."[17]

Bristow's ode, however, was not chosen for performance. Theodore Thomas, director of the music committee, arranged for modest commissions awarded to only two American composers: John Knowles Paine (1839–1906), who wrote a hymn, and Dudley Buck, who composed a cantata. The major commission for the event—for five thousand dollars (approx. $123,000 in 2019 currency)—went to his idol Richard Wagner, who dashed off a completely forgettable "Centennial March" that the conductor nevertheless programmed almost twenty times during the year.[18] Bristow subsequently withdrew his piece, perhaps in reaction to this overt snub of American composers; as the *Brooklyn Union* reported in April 1876, the composer had written a "large work . . . expressly for the Centennial," but "having . . . become so disgusted with the management . . . declines allowing it to be performed."[19]

Bourne's poem is not particularly dramatic, and Bristow's setting, according to David DeVenney, consists of mostly homophonic writing for the singers, some "rather cumbersome" recitative, and occasional brief interruptions by the orchestra.[20] The first known performance was on May 6, 1890, in a concert by the Euterpe Choral Society (in Association Hall at Twenty-third Street and Fourth Avenue); it was repeated on February 23, 1891 (at Lenox Lyceum on Madison Avenue), and again on May 6, 1892 (at an otherwise unidentified "Music Hall"). Two of the concerts were benefits for the annuity fund of the Teachers' Mutual Benefit Association. The single extant review deemed the composition itself "monotonous," although the critic praised one of the solo quartets and called the finale—a setting of the poem's final triumphant quatrains that relies in part on the tune of "The Star-Spangled Banner"—"delightfully refreshing." Although the 1860s sentiments expressed in the poem (and the ode) were rather dated by 1890, the audience at this benefit performance nevertheless "applauded with vigorous patriotism."[21]

The *Great Republic Overture*, in contrast, became one of Bristow's most popular compositions. Patrick Gilmore featured it in his Fourth of July concert in 1876 at Philadelphia's Independence Hall, perhaps as a deliberate snub of Thomas's choices; a critic for the *Music Trade Review* later remembered that the work "created a furore." A critic reporting from Philadelphia (possibly Myron Cooney) called the overture "a work in which Americans may well take pride" and described Bristow as a musician "who incontestably occupies the first place among American composers." The premiere performance, however, had occurred several years earlier, at a New York concert on March 1, 1873, by that city's Musical Fund Society, which was, according to Cooney, "a benevolent organization, principally composed of members of the Philharmonic Society."[22]

An expansive one-movement composition in E-flat major, the *Great Republic Overture* is scored for pairs of winds (plus piccolo), brass (four horns, two trumpets, three trombones, tuba), percussion (timpani, cymbals, tambour, triangle), and strings (including contrabass). Cooney wrote that the opening's "grand and massive" phrases are repeated throughout the movement but with "lovely little interludes for the reeds and strings sandwiched between them." The patriotic mien is most overtly stated toward the end, he continued, with the introduction of the first bars of "Hail Columbia" in the basses "as a foundation to various subjects and rich harmonies"; he found this use of the popular tune, however, somewhat jarring. Otherwise, he noted, there was much to praise. He described Bristow's approach as having "more of a descriptive, or Berlioz, element . . . than may be found in the other works of this eminent American composer" but then added that "it never degenerates to the mere programme . . . standard," for Bristow never loses sight of "the true aim of a musical work, continuity of thought and unity of idea." George Curtis, writing much later, called the overture "beyond question one of the most effective of Bristow's orchestral works" and described how the themes in the overture "musically cover in quick succession the desolation, and the subsequent rejoicing after the final victory at Appomattox." He disagreed with Cooney, however, by praising the "brilliant contrapuntal treatment in the base [sic] of our most dignified national air."[23]

In addition to the performances mentioned above, the overture was also heard in a concert celebration of Washington's Birthday (February 1876) and in an 1879 performance by the Philharmonic Society of Brooklyn (its symphonic premiere).[24] In a review of the latter, the critic for the *Music Trade Review* dismissed the overture as "entirely out of place in a Symphony Concert," although he admitted that it was "a work that will excite the American masses." He also conceded that he had it found it "expressive" when performed at Gilmore's Garden (on the site of the future Madison Square Garden). In fact, Gilmore programmed it frequently during the 1880s and 1890s, on national holidays like the Fourth of July and on riverboats. The New York Manuscript Society mounted a reprise of the orchestral version in 1895.[25]

## PIONEER/ARCADIAN SYMPHONY

Bristow completed his other large secular work, *The Pioneer*, op. 49, "A Grand Cantata for Solos, Chorus, and Orchestra, preceeded [sic] by a Symphonie, for Orchestra Alone," in 1871 or 1872, so he clearly was working simultaneously on both this and the *Great Republic Ode*.[26] During its gestation period, he split *The Pioneer* into two individual works: the cantata (with the original name) and a symphony (op. 50), with a new name, *Arcadian*. The manuscript full score of the symphony has *The Pioneer: Symphonie for Grand Orchestra*, with "Pioneer" crossed out and "Arcadian" written in with pencil.[27]

The cantata is a setting of the poem "The Pioneer, or, Westward Ho," by critic Henry Watson. When Bristow actually started to work on his cantata is unknown, but it may have been as early as the late 1860s, for Watson had originally offered his poem to William Vincent Wallace as the subject of a cantata; he gave it to Bristow sometime after Wallace's death in 1865.[28] Another example of musical nationalism, *The Pioneer* is a celebration of the heroism of American pioneers and their triumph over various adversities (the monotony of traveling across the plains, the wilds of nature, a prairie fire). The cantata calls for a vocal quartet, SATB chorus, and orchestra; it includes recitatives, arias, duets, and choral numbers. The vocal parts suggest that Bristow strategically utilized the orchestra throughout; the instrumental score, however, does not survive. Evidently *The Pioneer* was never performed, and since only a portion of the holograph survives, a reconstruction is not possible.

Delmer Rogers dismisses the work as "a tedious composition with little dramatic, musical, or textural worth," but it is not clear on what musical evidence he based this assessment.[29] The prose is stilted in a manner typical of mid-century vocal works, but the surviving materials nevertheless reveal the rather insular world inhabited by both Watson and Bristow, and perhaps by many other Americans of the period. A distaste for the natural world and an attitude that it must be conquered, for example, is enlightening to the twenty-first-century reader and is revealed in the opening recitative for bass soloist: "day follows day and still before us lies / a boundless, dread monotony of plain / dread to the heart and sickening to the sight / the painful labor of this trackless way." At one point a child sings, "Father, father, all is so strange / rivers so mighty and mountains so high / Ever and ever the dark forests range / ever and ever the dark forests range." Later in the cantata a "monarch oak" is suitably felled by "the leveling axe in the hand of the bold Pioneers." Such sentiments clearly embody the somewhat old-fashioned concept of Manifest Destiny: the obligation of Americans to expand westward and conquer both nature and the land's current inhabitants. An attack by Native Americans that is successfully repulsed is not part of the cantata (it is heard as the third movement of the symphony), but the pioneers' ultimate success is clearly portrayed as the will of God. The most obvious crisis they face is a wildfire ("from the forked flame every living thing madly flies / already comes its hot and searching breath / and on its blast rides the destroyer, death"), which is snuffed out by "torrents of rain [that] pour from the pall-like heav'n . . . by mighty winds the hurrying clouds are riv'n / and back upon itself the raging flame is driv'n." God has spoken and His people are grateful: "The danger past, let us with one accord and humble hearts give thanks to God on high." The entire cantata, in fact, is imbued with Christian religiosity.

## THE *ARCADIAN*

The impetus for carving a stand-alone symphony out of this larger hybrid work was a one-hundred-dollar commission (about $2,150 in 2019 purchasing power) that the Philharmonic Society of Brooklyn offered to Bristow in October 1872 for a new symphony. The composer, as a practical musician, may already have been wondering about the performance viability of his hefty composition.[30] The fact that there were only four months between the commission and the symphony's premiere performance (February 1873) likewise supports the suggestion that he dismembered the almost completed hybrid work to fulfill the commission. Several critics censured the orchestra for the modesty of its honorarium; Hudson, for example, pointed out that "Miss Kellogg and Phillipps" (soprano Louise Kellogg and contralto Adelaide Phillipps [1833–1882]) "get three or four hundred dollars for singing two or three songs for our popular concerts" and suggested that one hundred dollars for a full symphony was pretty meager. On the other hand, he noted, this was "probably the first instance in the history of the art in this country in which any similar society have [sic] ever offered a dollar to a composer for an original composition," which was probably true.[31]

The symphony's new name was likely in honor of the Arcadian Club, a new social organization for artists, actors, writers, musicians, and critics that had been founded earlier in the year; Bristow was a member of the club's council.[32] The E-minor work is scored for flutes, clarinets, oboes, bassoons, and piccolo; four horns, two trumpets, three trombones, and tuba; timpani, cymbals, triangle; and strings. Bristow used the triangle and cymbals only in the third movement, which also features his first solo orchestral writing for the trumpet. The tuba mostly doubles the third trombone, but there is true chorale-like writing for brass choir (three trombones and tuba) in the second movement. The four movements, marked Allegro appassionato, Adagio, Scherzo: "Indian War Dance," and Allegro con spirito, portray the story of the cantata but in an impressionistic manner. The work's premiere, by the Philharmonic Society of Brooklyn (February 8, 1873), was under Carl Bergmann, although it had already been heard in several public rehearsals.[33]

The *Arcadian* is more overtly programmatic than is Symphony No. 3; Bristow, in fact, provided a synopsis of each movement that suggests how the work's formal structure conveys the narrative. Shadle posits that a programmatic symphony by Joachim Raff—*Im Walde*, first played by the New York orchestra in January 1872—was Bristow's inspiration; he also provides a persuasive table that compares the two works.[34] He does not consider, however, the symphony's original intended function as the prelude for a grand narrative cantata, which certainly played a role in its programmatic character. It is possible that Raff's programmatic symphonies, which Bristow knew well, encouraged him in the ultimate decision to extricate the "grand symphonie" from the cantata. But its pictorial nature was probably a fait accompli by the time the Philharmonic Society orchestra played *Im Walde*.

The first movement of the *Arcadian*, in sonata form, predictably commences with a melancholy viola solo, perhaps illustrative of the desolate plains. The orchestra takes up one of the theme's inherent gestures, develops it briefly, then launches into a *furioso* transition before introducing a second theme that is contrasting and lyrical. An expanded development follows, which several critics grumbled was too long. But Bristow's goal was to convey the journey of immigrants through "the unbroken waste, with its weariness and monotony," and evidently he succeeded. There is a full orchestral recapitulation before the viola returns with its subdued melody to finish the movement, a technique that Bristow had also used before. The second movement, Adagio. "Motive Tallis' Evening Hymn," quotes a tune by the sixteenth-century English composer Thomas Tallis (ca. 1505–1585) that could still be found in the *Protestant Episcopal Hymnal* at mid-century. In B minor, the movement opens with a restrained theme played by the horns, bassoons, and clarinets, with subdued accompaniment by the strings; the full orchestra repeats this theme before the Tallis hymn emerges in four-part harmony, played by the brass choir. Shadle suggests Schumann's *Rhenish Symphony* as inspiration. Another plausible source is the tradition of trombone choirs used in sacred services by Moravian congregations in Pennsylvania, which Bristow might have known.[35] This movement was intended to convey a weariness at the end of the day as the travelers join in a communal hymn before sleeping. Bristow's skillful orchestration in this lovely movement highlights both wind and brass instruments that play not only four-part harmony but also lyrical countermelodies to the strings.

The third movement "Indian War Dance" is a scherzo with trio, in A minor (with modal inflections), and ostensibly suggests an Indian encampment, where (according to the program) "the savages are engaged in a war dance, preliminary to an attack." The work starts with disjunct melodic fragments—a 3–2–1 gesture followed by an upward leap and a trill by the clarinet that is punctuated by a crash of the cymbal. The movement proper starts at measure thirteen with a pulsating rhythm in the strings (and cymbal) to accompany an almost playful dance-like tune in the winds, followed by whirling in the strings. As Michael Pisani points out, this descending melodic gesture is similar to what Robert Stoepel used in his *Hiawatha*.[36] The clarinet trill is perhaps meant to represent a shriek, the whirling strings a circular dance, and the B theme—played by low strings and answered by syncopated and *sforzando* crashes by the rest of the orchestra—a fight. The trio, in contrast, has a resolute melody in the brass, played against a rising ostinato in the low strings, perhaps suggesting the emigrants' rebuff of the attack. The result is a movement that is deliberately pictorial (unlike the rest of the symphony) but in which Bristow relied on some tried-and-true musical signifiers of "exoticism": the modal melody, clarinet (reed instrument), and cymbals of Turkish Janissary bands. The character of this movement, in fact, suggests a composer who had never heard a Native American tune and had almost no idea what one might sound like. The final movement, also in sonata-allegro form, is in the parallel major key of E and is unabashedly heroic, joyous, and spirited (even raucous), suggesting not only the emigrants' survival of the attack but also a triumphant celebration at the end of their journey.[37]

George Bristow was at the top of his game in early 1873, when he was completing this symphony and preparing for its premiere. In late 1872 Cooney had written a congratulatory essay about the progress of instrumental music in the United States in which he commended the Brooklyn orchestra for "bringing out a true American Symphony, the work of the first of American composers, George Bristow." He pointed out that "instrumental music in New York will compare favorably with any other city in the world" and forecast that "the tidal wave of progress in this direction may lead to results which . . . may not now [in the present season] be entertained even for the most sanguine."[38] News of the commission and impending premiere performance of this new work, in fact, created a buzz, and critics—especially in Brooklyn—expressed excitement and support for the composer. William Hudson wrote proudly that Bristow "is almost the only American who has made his way into the German orchestral stronghold, but he has not surrendered himself, as a composer, to German subjects. On the contrary, he has maintained native independence and originality which prove at once his manliness and his patriotism." Another critic commented that the symphony "is eminently American" and that the composer treated the topic "ably and truthfully."[39]

But these same critics had a change of heart once they heard the work in rehearsal. Hudson, in particular, resurrected old and drearily familiar complaints in two lengthy essays. In the first he directly contradicted the sentiments he had expressed earlier by denouncing programmatic and nationalist music, arguing, "Art is cosmopolitan [and] it ought to make no difference in our acceptance of a good thing whether it is the work of an American or a Hindoo" (or, he might have added, a German). Furthermore, he continued, "it is simply impossible for [Bristow] or anybody to describe a journey across the plains or anywhere else." This dismissal was echoed by the critic for *Dwight's*, who wrote that "any composer . . . who writes 'programme music,' either does not rightly comprehend his art, or is setting a trap to catch the applause of unreasoning and unmusical people." Both journalists overlooked the fact that Bristow's symphony (with the exception of the third movement) was intended to be impressionistic rather than a blow-by-blow account of specific events. In his second essay, Hudson resurrected the trope that all American music is derivative, calling the symphony "frequently reminiscent." He granted that Bristow was not exactly "a conscious plagiarist" but noted, "Here there is a faint flavor of Wagner, there a suggestion of Schumann, and once a hint of Liszt." Then, in a breathtakingly patronizing statement, he described the veteran and accomplished musician as "a student" and that "the fruits of his studies appear in his writing."[40]

After figuratively marking their territory, however, both critics—in a remarkable showing of two-handedness—took it all back. Hudson predicted that "the 'Arcadian' will be pronounced a fluent and finished work," the effort of "an accomplished musician, well educated in orchestral effects," and a skilled orchestrator. And the critic for *Dwight's* conceded that aside from the "very objectionable feature" of programmatic writing, he "could speak of the Arcadian Symphony in terms of almost unqualified praise," for most of its themes were "fresh and original," interest throughout was "well sustained," and "the instrumentation . . . masterly." This whiplash style of critique should have been absolutely infuriating. But perhaps Bristow, who was described frequently as unassuming and patient, dismissed such inchoate critiques as not worthy of his attention and instead took pleasure from the praise, both written and from audiences; the auditors at one of the rehearsals enthusiastically called out the composer (who was playing violin in the orchestra) at the end of the first, third, and fourth movements.[41]

Bergmann was sufficiently impressed, in fact, that he scheduled another performance a year later (February 14, 1874), this time by the Philharmonic Society of New York; it elicited much less carping and more genuine praise, as well as so much applause that "'George' was fairly intoxicated with happiness and accepted the congratulations of his friends." The *Times* critic called the symphony "a tone-picture of decided merit"; Cooney wrote that it was "a genuine American work"; and a critic in *Appleton's Journal* noted that in addition to its "intrinsic excellence, the work is of double value, as it is by an American musician on an American theme."[42] Some defended the "programmatic" approach as an attempt by Bristow to combine elements of classicism (musical form) with the narrative approach of the more progressive styles. As John Hassard put it, the *Arcadian* was "something very different from [program music]—conceived in a higher spirit, and executed with a true musician's appreciation of the beautiful and poetic." Mr. Bristow, he continued, "has not attempted to be picturesque, but has . . . confined his art to its proper functions, and has not tried to do with it what it was not created to accomplish." Shadle suggests that in this manner, Bristow was doing in America what Raff had done in Europe.[43]

The *Arcadian*—or reports about it—spread word of Bristow's compositional prowess to England. After the winter 1874 performance, the British composer and critic William Howard Glover wrote to the *London Musical Standard* from New York and described Bristow (whose Second Symphony had been played for British audiences in 1854 by Jullien) as "one of the few genius American musicians who really deserve the title" and the symphony as "admirably conceived, developed, instrumented, and most effective." Bristow, he concluded, "may well be proud of his work, and his country-men may well point to him as a proof that they possess a man quite able to hold his own against many greatly inferior composers, who, mainly owing to their Teutonic origins, are lauded to the skies—especially in New York."[44]

### THE BACH TRANSCRIPTION

One of Bristow's final compositions of the decade was not actually an original work but rather a transcription for orchestra of Johann Sebastian Bach's *Chromatic Fantasy and Fugue*. It merits inclusion here if for no other reason than it was the final Bristow work that the Philharmonic Society performed. It was completed in 1879 and dedicated to Theodore Thomas, who conducted the premiere performance on April 24, 1880. It was not well received. Although several critics praised Bristow's work on the composition, most contended that an orchestral adaptation of an organ composition was a travesty and took both Thomas and the orchestra severely to task for performing it. Frederick Schwab (1844–1927) of the *Times* recommended that if the Philharmonic Society "wishes to do honor to Mr. Bristow, let them play one of his numerous original works."[45]

## More Evidence of Esteem

Two notable events that occurred in 1875 bookended the middle year of the decade. In March the *Arcadian Symphony* was performed as part of an "American night" concert at the Conservatory of Music in Baltimore (today's Peabody Conservatory), along with works by three other composers active in New York— Alfred Pease (1833–1882), Otis Bardwell Boise (1844–1912), and William Bassford (1839–1902).[46] According to the *Baltimore Sun*, the auditorium was well filled with an enthusiastic audience. The critic's muted enthusiasm for the repertoire reflected his sense that there was not yet "any distinctive character in our home music," but he did concede that the concert "was a great success, and gives hope that the day is but far distant when we may boast of a national school of composers." He deemed the first movement of the *Arcadian* "the most artistic part of the work," called the second movement "the most attractive," and described the "Indian War Dance" as both "barbaric enough" and "professedly savage." The concert in general "showed evidence of native genius"; Bristow, he concluded, "may be considered . . . established as an American composer of the highest merit."[47]

**FIGURE 4.** Etching of a portrait painted by George Rockwood (1832–1911), a prolific New York photographer who introduced the *carte-de-visite* to the United States. The etching was made in 1879 by Henry B. Hall (1808–1885), a well-known New York engraver who lived on the same street in Morrisania as Bristow (Scharf, *History of Westchester County, I: 836*). There is a damaged copy in the Bristow Collection.

On the far end of the year was another Grand Testimonial Concert (Bristow's third), given at Steinway Hall on December 15, 1875. (See fig. 4 for an 1870s portrait of Bristow.) None of the advertisements for the concert identifies the organizers of the event, but a large number of "distinguished artists" (singers, pianists, an organist, a violinist) joined forces with the Centennial Choral Union and a grand orchestra, which resulted in a concert by more than four hundred performers, with Bristow conducting. The featured works included selections from the *Messiah*, Rossini's *Stabat Mater*, Alfred Pease's two-piano arrangement of selections from *Faust*, organist George Morgan's arrangement of "America," vocal selections from Mercadante's *Il Bravo*, the Bach *Chaconne* for violin, and overtures from *Oberon* and *William Tell*. Strangely, although there was a large crowd, which "gave every indication of satisfaction," there were no works by the guest of honor.[48] The two events attest to the continued esteem in which Bristow was held by his contemporaries, both in and outside of New York.

# Bristow as Businessman and Musical Authority

**OVER THE COURSE OF HIS CAREER,** George Bristow engaged in a wide variety of music-related activities in order to support himself and his family. Many of those engagements—performing, teaching, and composing—have already been described. But there were a number of other business-like activities that he undertook at different times in his life that are worth examining briefly for what they reveal about the varied types of money-generating endeavors that were available to nineteenth-century New York musicians like Bristow. Most of his activities in this realm involved the piano.

## Pianos and Melodeons

During the mid-1850s, Bristow partnered with a "Mr. Morse" and George Hood to establish a retail business at 423 Broadway that sold pianos and melodeons. This endeavor was launched in April 1854 with an announcement that the partners "have leased and refitted the well-known ware-rooms heretofore occupied by E. G. Bradbury, and will keep constantly on hand a large and splendid assortment of the very best Pianos to be found in the market." Secondhand pianos were also for sale. The firm of Geo. F. Bristow, Morse & Co. continued to advertise their stock for the rest of 1854. Advertisements disappeared after the end of the year, but the company, now located several doors away at 419 Broadway, was still listed in the *New York City Directory* for 1855–1856. During this time Bristow was living on Broome Street, about three blocks away from his wareroom.[1] He later confessed to Travis Quigg, however, that Morse and Hood had supplied the "expertise and business savvy" and that he had put up the capital: savings of five thousand dollars ($157,000 in 2019 currency) to underwrite the business. Unfortunately, it was unsuccessful, and it took the composer some time to dig himself out of debt. Later, when asked if he wanted to accept some pianos on consignment, he responded that he "would hereafter stick to fiddling, as that was the only music business he understood."[2]

By 1863, however, Bristow was back in business, now in partnership with his friend William A. Hardenbrook, the librettist for *The Oratorio of Daniel* and a businessman and attorney. The firm of Bristow and Hardenbrook began advertising in January 1863. First located at 765 Broadway (later at 147 East Tenth St.), the firm sold "the new style of Parlor Grand Pianos, unique in design, unrivaled for beauty, and superior to all others." They also offered "a fine assortment of square pianos," secondhand pianos, and melodeons and harmoniums, and rented studio space on the side.[3] Bristow apparently maintained this partnership with Hardenbrook even after he moved to Morrisania; the final directory entry for the firm is in 1867–1868.

## Pianos II: Testimonials

Like many other well-known musicians in New York, Bristow lent his name to "testimonials" in support of various instrument manufacturers. Such endorsements surely included an honorarium, probably small, but nevertheless another method that allowed musicians to earn some money from their renown. As early as January 1860, Bristow's name appeared in advertisements for Steinway pianos; other eminent New York musicians also supported this brand, including Carl Bergmann, Henry Timm, William Mason, Sebastian Bach Mills, U. C. Hill, Robert Goldbeck, and George Morgan. This association of respected musicians with a particular brand suggests the emergence of an increasingly effective marketing strategy for selling musical instruments, not unlike the similar use of performers to sell particular sheet music imprints "as sung by" favorite singers. Bristow contributed testimonials to advertisements for Weber, Chickering, and Bradbury pianos; Carhart and Needham parlor organs; and several other musical endeavors.

In 1867 the Weber piano factory boasted that the "two principal Musical Conservatories" in New York—the National Conservatory (Bristow was director) and Edward Mollenhauer's conservatory—had both recently engaged the Weber firm for the exclusive use of its pianos in their studios.[4] Such testimonials by Bristow continued into the 1870s but definitely peaked in the 1860s.

## Pianos III: United States Mutual Pianoforte Association

Another piano-related activity—one that clearly reflects aspects of Bristow's character and his belief in the importance of music—was his service as treasurer of the United States Mutual Pianoforte Association, an otherwise unknown organization, chartered in 1867. Its goal was to make "first-class pianos" more readily available to the general public by selling "high quality pianos" to "subscribers" through monthly installments of "only $10." This amount (roughly $178 in 2019), the notice pointed out, was less than it cost to rent a good instrument. The association held monthly piano "distributions" (and musical soirées) from May to December 1867. The first event took place in May 1867 and included musical entertainment, a speech by the association president, and the distribution itself—which apparently entailed bidding, for the two winners each paid fifty and sixty dollars ($891 and $1,070 in 2019), respectively, and agreed to pay off the balance in monthly installments. Further distributions were held later in 1867, after which all mention of the organization disappears from the historical record. Any extra money that the association earned through subscriptions was plowed back into the organization itself, thereby further reducing the stated price of the pianos.[5]

Bristow's participation in this apparently nonprofit endeavor reflects again his genuine interest in promoting the dissemination of music and musical instruments among New Yorkers, a commitment that he stated clearly in the final paragraph of his autobiographical sketch. "Young men," he wrote, should not "throw away their time and money in frivolous nonsense, such as billiard playing, and the like" but instead should "learn to sing, or play, [for] there would be some use in that, something elevating." In general, he believed strongly that "everybody should learn music either to play upon an instrument, or [to] sing," a conviction that suffused his life and work and explains his lifelong devotion to the art as a creator and performer, merchant of musical instruments, and teacher.[6]

## Pianos IV: The Centennial Exhibition of 1876

As we saw in chapter 5, Bristow was unable to convince the program committee of the 1876 Philadelphia Centennial Exhibition to include performances of his *Great Republic* as part of the celebration. But he participated in the event in another guise: as a judge of pianos. The experience, unfortunately, was not entirely propitious.

The centennial fair was *the* American go-to event of the decade. The first world's fair ever held in America, it was timed to celebrate the country's one-hundredth birthday. Nearly ten million people visited the exhibition over the course of six months (May 10–November 10, 1876), and there were plenty of cultural events, foods, and entertainments to keep everyone amused. In reality, however, the major focus of the exhibition, as for all such international fairs, was business. The official title was the International Exhibition of Arts, Manufacturers, and Products of the Soil and Mine, and it attracted exhibitors from thirty-seven countries. Despite the strong international showing, however, the vast majority of exhibitors were from the United States, perhaps because of the continuing effects of the Long Depression. Nevertheless, thousands of dealers, exhibitors, and manufacturers took advantage of the event to introduce their products to the millions of visitors and to compete (sometimes unfairly) for the thousands of medals.[7]

Many of the items on display supported a growing American leisure culture, and since the cultivation of music was a major aspect of that culture, representatives from the American music industry were out in force. Although exhibitors of musical instruments included manufacturers and merchants of banjos, brass instruments, harps, violins, cellos, basses, organs, and drums, the vast majority on display were pianos (upright, square, and grand)—a clear reflection of that instrument's status as both an indispensable component of a proper middle-class parlor and a symbol of culture and respectability. The fair featured sixty-four piano exhibitors from nine countries; two-thirds of them were American.[8] The group of judges for musical instruments consisted of only four individuals: General H. K. Oliver (1800–1885), an organist, singer, and Massachusetts politician; Julius Schiedmayer (1822–1878), co-owner of a Stuttgart piano factory and a judge at earlier European fairs; F. P. Kupka, an Austrian musical amateur who also had been an earlier judge; and George Bristow. The composer later claimed to be the only musician, but all of them had musical experience.[9]

The Centennial Commission established a judging system for this fair that they hoped would eliminate the charges of favoritism and corruption that had plagued earlier events. There were medals but no distinctions (gold, silver, and bronze), as this was considered arbitrary. As Bristow explained, "We could not compare one maker's piano with that of another in our report"; judges instead were tasked with examining musical instruments and writing recommendations for the Centennial Commission, the members of which would read the reports, compare them, and decide whether or not the instrument deserved a medal.[10] There were several major problems with this system. First was a general perception that some of the judges were either corrupt or predisposed toward particular firms. Schiedmayer, for example, was favorably disposed toward the Steinways, and Bristow, "whether he deserved it or not," was thought to favor the firm of Albert Weber (1829–1879). Second was a great deal of improper fraternizing between makers and judges, clearly intended to influence the reports. The diary of William Steinway (1835–1896), for example, reveals that he or other members of his firm met at some point with all four of the judges.[11] Third were reports of conversations among the judges (some even involving manufacturers) about reports that were supposed to be impartial. Finally, so many medals were awarded that almost all of the exhibitors could claim victory—and they did. As a result, the newspapers were full of ads in September and October that proclaimed "unanimous award of the highest honors" to Steinway, Weber, Knabe, Decker Brothers, and other firms.

But then exposés started to appear, and while some of the four judges had clearly crossed lines, it is possible that Bristow found himself caught up in the fray and was deemed guilty by association. It is impossible to know whether—or to what extent—he may have engaged in activities that were not aboveboard, but he had a strong reputation of integrity; he also had defenders. Myron Cooney, for example, expressed support for the composer. "We are loathe to believe," he wrote, "that Mr. George F. Bristow, who is included in the charges against the judges, would do any wrong himself in a matter of this kind or consent to it in others." Bristow, in the crossfire, quickly submitted a letter that was published several days after one of the exposés, in which he "most emphatically" defended himself. "When I accepted the position as judge," he wrote, "I did so with the most earnest intention of doing justice to all, and, being the only musician in the group, did my duty to the best of my ability." He continued: "I went there as an honest man; as such I have returned. I repel the covert charge of having allowed either money or friendship to influence my opinion as infamously and maliciously false, and invite a thorough and most searching investigation of my actions as a judge of the Centennial Commission, group 25."[12] In a companion column in the same issue, Cooney again defended the composer, stating emphatically that "Mr. Bristow's letter was not necessary to make us believe in his integrity."[13] The situation, however, continued to spiral out of control after the conclusion of the exposition, and piano manufacturers filed lawsuits against one another in 1877 and again in 1880. Bristow must have rued the day he ever agreed to serve as a judge for this event.

Most of Bristow's business-related activities were more positive than this stint as a judge. The wide-ranging types of engagements, however, are interesting for what they reveal—again—about the variety, multiplicity, and ubiquity of music in American society during the middle of the nineteenth century.

# 6 | The 1880s and 1890s

## *A Stalwart Educator and Composer*

**DURING HIS LAST TWO DECADES,** George Bristow focused on teaching and composition. At mid-century he had been one of the most influential and active composer/performers in the rather small and insular musical community of New York City, but during the 1880s and 1890s his position changed significantly, primarily because the city itself was transformed into an urban area that was neither small nor insular. By 1880 Manhattan had unequivocally crossed the million-person mark, with a new population total of 1,206,300—a 28 percent increase over its size in 1870 and over 40 percent larger than its nearest American competitor, Philadelphia (847,170). The city experienced a leap of 26 percent a decade later, to a total of slightly over 1.5 million. (The real change would occur in 1900, after the 1898 consolidation of all five boroughs, when the city's population exploded—at least on paper—to 3,437,202).[1]

Musical activity likewise grew dramatically as the city began to take its place as a major cultural center of the Western world. One measure was an increase in the number of venues dedicated to art-music performances. The Academy of Music continued to be an important performance space until the mid-1880s, and Niblo's Theatre was used for concerts into the early 1890s. But the Academy of Music was supplanted in 1883 by the new Metropolitan Opera House, and other concert venues, frequently connected with the showrooms of piano manufacturers, also appeared, including Chickering Hall (Fifth Avenue and Eighteenth Street, 1875), Steinway Hall (Fifth Avenue and Fourteenth Street, 1866), and Carnegie Hall (Seventh Avenue and Fifty-sixth Street, 1891). There were also numerous other venues, such as Lenox Lyceum and Association Hall (as mentioned in chapter 5), that have been mostly forgotten.

The foreign-language opera companies that performed at the Academy and the Metropolitan continued to attract the most important European operatic luminaries active on the continent; the city also hosted countless troupes that performed English-language opera, comic opera, *opéra bouffe*, operetta, and the newer forms of spectacle, extravaganza, and musical comedy, all of which included music. The established orchestras active in the city included the Philharmonic Society; New York Symphony Society (1878–1928); Theodore Thomas's various ensembles (including the Philharmonic, 1878–1891); and orchestras led by Anton Seidl, including the Metropolitan Opera orchestra (1885–1891), the Philharmonic (1891–1898), and the Seidl Orchestra and Seidl Society Orchestra in the 1890s.

Choral societies were increasingly active as well. German-language societies such as the Liederkranz (founded 1847), the Arion Society (1854–1918), and numerous similar organizations proliferated; others included the Mendelssohn Glee Club (1866– ) and the Oratorio Society of New York (est. 1873).[2] Bands and wind symphonies continued to be an important part of the musical culture, and music publishing firms flourished, many of which churned out reams of popular sheet music that was disseminated from Tin Pan Alley. The city was also still a magnet for European performers, who used New York (as they had done throughout the century) as a base for their American concert tours.

A published summary of the 1889–1890 New York musical season provides a compelling glimpse into the increasingly rich and sophisticated state of classical music performance (George Bristow's world) in New York City during the 1880s and 1890s. The summary, titled "Live Musical Topics," was written at the midpoint of that twenty-year period (April 1890), probably by *Times* critic William James Henderson. He reported that the three dominant orchestras active in the New York area during the just completed season (the Philharmonic Society, the Symphony Society, and the Philharmonic Society of Brooklyn) had each given six concerts and six public rehearsals.[3] In addition, the Boston Symphony had mounted four concerts, the Harlem Philharmonic Society three concerts and three rehearsals, and an orchestra under Frank van der Stucken (1858–1929) three performances. There had also been testimonial or benefit events involving orchestras, a series of concerts by the Thomas Orchestra, and "a dozen orchestral concerts in which pianists were the chief figures," resulting in some seventy-five orchestral concerts between early October 1889 and late April 1890. Moreover, there were eight important choral concerts by the Oratorio Society, as well as additional performances by the Arion Society, Palestrina Choir, Mendelssohn Society, Metropolitan Musical Society, Rubinstein Club, and several other choral organizations, totaling around thirty major choral performances. There were fewer chamber ensemble concerts but "almost innumerable" piano performances by such visiting stars as Eugen d'Albert, Hans von Bülow, Otto Hegner, Vladimir de Pachmann, and Adele aus der Ohe. Opera lovers in the city could also choose from fifty performances of opera in German and twenty-one in Italian. (As was typical of critics during the time, however, Henderson ignored performances of operettas, *opéras bouffes*, and continental operas translated into English.) The visiting continental operatic luminaries included sopranos Adelia Patti, Emma Albani, Lilli Lehmann, and Inez Fabbri; tenors Francesco Tamagno and Luigi Ravelli; bass Emil Fischer; and baritone Theodor Reichmann. Henderson pointed out that this total enumeration of concerts omitted "all the song recitals, benefit concerts, and other scattered entertainments of miscellaneous nature" that also had been heard. Furthermore, he added, the season had not been "uncommonly rich" but rather a "fair-average New York season"—one that nevertheless represented a remarkable wealth of musical activity.[4]

In general, American musical culture—at least classical or art music—was now thoroughly a part of the Western European cultural scene. Since the 1870s, young American performers and composers had regularly traveled to Europe for training, which provided them with a patina of respectability that was almost indispensable in this increasingly Eurocentric music world. By the 1880s, then, the performers and composers who dominated New York's music scene were either transplants, visitors from Europe, or Americans who had gone abroad for their education. George Bristow, a homegrown musician who had carved out his entire career in New York, had never considered European "credibility" to be important. Now, however, it made a difference in terms of visibility in his hometown. New York in the 1880s was also gradually becoming a cultural outpost of Bayreuth: important critics were Wagnerians; the opera company at the Metropolitan in 1884–1885 performed its first German season; Theodore Thomas was determined to teach American concertgoers to love Wagner's music whether they wanted to or not; and Anton Seidl—a true Wagner acolyte—arrived in 1885 and helped to create a Wagner mania in the city in the 1890s.[5] This latter development, however, left Bristow behind, for he was not a Wagnerian, and his views about music and musical style—which in this context were undoubtedly old-fashioned—set him apart from mainstream musical trends in New York, especially in the late 1880s and into the 1890s.

An excellent example of Bristow's disconnect is an 1885 incident when he was asked to respond (via written comments) to a debate on the merits of Wagner's music between the Rev. Hugh Reginald Haweis (visiting from Britain) and the Italian opera impresario James Mapleson. The Nineteenth-Century Club, the event's venue, was "packed to suffocation by well-dressed ladies and gentlemen who crowded into every corner, pushed in front of each other, trod on each other's toes, and in a general way manifested a burning desire to be in the vanguard of intellectual progress." Haweis spoke on "Wagner and His School" and Mapleson—whose Italian opera company at the Academy of Music was facing serious opposition from Anton Seidl's German troupe—spoke in defense of Italian-language opera. The impresario was convinced that Wagner's music dramas were no match for the Italian school and that the current interest was a fad that would quickly fade. Bristow, who limited his comments to instrumental music, insisted on the superiority of the older school of German composition, noting that Beethoven had produced "sublime musical effects with simple materials," which, in Bristow's opinion, was clearly the mark of a superior composer.[6] But although Americans (and New Yorkers) of the mid-1880s were divided on Wagner's merits (many critics were adherents; many audience members disliked his music dramas), Wagnerism was the coming wave, and Bristow was not a part of it.[7]

Nevertheless, George Bristow continued to maintain his presence as a respected, admired, and venerable figure. One journalist described him in 1888 as "the doyen of New York musicians" and "the most distinguished of American composers"; critic William Thoms agreed, writing ten years later that Bristow was "one of the most renowned of American composers." Bristow also enjoyed yet another "Grand Testimonial Concert," at Steinway Hall on February 22, 1887, which included a chorus of three hundred "juvenile voices." Frederick Schwab of the *Times* described the honoree of this event as "one of the most prominent of resident musicians."[8] Such accolades suggest that Bristow continued to flourish. But he did so on his own terms, by pursuing a pattern that he had followed for most of his life: as a patient, unassuming, and generous individual who remained steadfast in his work as an educator, performer, and composer. As his friend the composer and educator George Curtis wrote in 1893, even after "half a century of constant professional labor," Bristow still "walks his daily round of duty in the New York schools, attends to his weekly rehearsal as organist and conductor of a church choir, is ready at reasonable notice to organize musical entertainments for benevolent objects [and] to act as organist, violinist, pianist, accompanist, leader of an orchestra, or lecturer upon any department of music from ballad singing to the highest forms of opera and oratorio."[9]

## The Gradual Eclipse of a Performance Career

Bristow still continued to appear in occasional benefit concerts but to a lessening extent. Sometimes he played keyboard, such as an organ recital that preceded a lecture by the Rev. Henry Ward Beecher at Steinway Hall (1880), or a patriotic "Grand Promenade Concert in Commemoration of the Departure of the Seventh Regiment for Washington in 1861" (1890).[10] He also appeared as a conductor— sometimes (as noted in Interval C) in events that involved students, sometimes at benefits or concerts associated with his church jobs. One such high-profile event occurred in 1890 when he organized (and conducted) sixty selected singers and an orchestra of twenty-five in a performance of the *Messiah* at the Church of the Divine Paternity.[11]

He also continued to work occasionally with large choral ensembles, although his days as the music director of choral societies were over, especially since choral conducting in New York was now dominated by mostly European-trained conductors. Nevertheless, he kept his hand in by collaborating with several of these higher-profile conductors. As already described, during fall 1880 he began to work as Theodore Thomas's assistant in the latter's newly formed Chorus School at the New York College of Music, where he also served as the chorus master for four years. And in 1890 he collaborated with Anton Seidl to recruit, audition, and rehearse some 150 vocalists who made up the "Philharmonic Society Singers" in preparation for a series of three grand concerts that marked the semi-centennial of the orchestra's founding. The final concert of that event, held on April 23, 1892, was described as "one of the most daring and successful concerts ever undertaken in New-York" and included a performance of Beethoven's Ninth Symphony, the chorus for which had been "organized and trained by Mr. George F. Bristow."[12] The composer's most significant conducting tasks during this period, however, were the premiere performances of his *Jibbenainosay Overture* in 1889 and his final symphony, *Niagara*, in 1898.

The most important shift in Bristow's performance activities during this period was his resignation from the Philharmonic Society orchestra in spring 1882, after almost forty years in the first violin section of the most important orchestra in New York.[13] He resigned for financial reasons, which he explained in a letter dated February 4, 1882, and addressed to the secretary of the Philharmonic

Society. He wrote that it was "with regret that I cannot attend to the rehearsals required by the Philharmonic, as it would be a serious loss to me in the omission of lessons. I am very sorry," he continued, "but I cannot help it." His "salary" as a member of the quasi-cooperative orchestra was clearly not sufficient to cover the amount of time for both performances and rehearsals. Since his main source of income was from teaching, the choice was evidently clear. His final concert was on March 11, 1882.[14] Whether or not he continued to perform for the Philharmonic Society of Brooklyn is unknown.[15] But his resignation from an orchestra that had been such an important part of his life marked the end of an era, for both Bristow and, arguably, for the Philharmonic Society. Apparently, however, he left the orchestra without any public acknowledgment of his long years of service.

### THE MANUSCRIPT SOCIETY

Although the number of his performances declined dramatically after the early 1880s, Bristow continued to participate in music-related organizations that supported the work of American composers. The Manuscript Society was the final such organization with which he was associated. Organized in 1889 "to advance the interests of American Musical Composition, and to promote social intercourse and friendly feeling among its members," the society grew quickly and eventually included "most of the leading composers of New York," such as Edgar Stillman Kelley (1857–1944), George Chadwick (1854–1931), Arthur Foote (1853–1937), and Horatio Parker (1863–1919), many of whom were significantly younger than Bristow.[16] Perhaps this explains why Bristow was not a charter member of this organization; his name does not appear on the membership roster, in fact, until the fourth season (1893–1894). The following year he became a member of the board of directors (1894–1896) and of the music committee (1894–1897).[17] The society, in return, supported Bristow by performing at least five of his compositions over four years: the *Jibbenainosay* (called a tone poem) (December 12, 1894), Benedictus from the *Mass in C Major* (January 8, 1895), the *Great Republic Overture* and *Seventh Regiment March* (August 27, 1895), and the *Niagara Symphony* (April 11, 1898).

## Composing in the 1880s and 1890s

During the final two decades of the century, Bristow was extraordinarily productive as a composer. As already suggested, he continued to write sacred and pedagogical pieces; he also returned—after a long hiatus—to several genres of smaller works (songs and piano pieces). Moreover, he extensively revised *Rip Van*

*Winkle*, wrote a final stand-alone overture, *Jibbenainosay* (1889), and produced two significant large-scale compositions: the *Mass in C Major* (1885) and his fifth symphony, *Niagara* (1893).

Bristow had started his compositional career by writing songs and piano works, to which he returned during his final decades. Over the course of his career, he wrote more than forty songs (not counting selections from *Rip Van Winkle*); some were sacred, others were secular.[18] Some fifteen of these works are from the 1840s and 1850s, five were written during the 1860s and 1870s, and another fifteen were never published and have no dates. So his reengagement in the final two decades—when he wrote nine songs, all of them published—is worth noting. Almost half are hymns; the rest are "sentimental" in nature (for example, "My Mother's Old Portrait," "Only a Little Shoe," and "Woman's Love") and perhaps were written mainly to keep his hand in that branch of the business; the production of sheet music, after all, was a major revenue stream for many composers of popular songs.

Bristow also wrote a fair number of late piano compositions (mostly character pieces). Over half of his estimated forty-five known works for piano date from before 1858; most were written in the 1840s. During the 1860s and 1870s he almost completely ignored the most popular instrument of the century, but eventually he returned to the fold, writing twelve piano compositions between 1883 and 1895. They were primarily character pieces, such as *La Vivandiere* (1884); *Dream land*, op. 59 (1885); *Impromptu*, op. 76, (1894); three morceau characteristics titled "Plantation Pleasures," op. 82, and "Plantation Memories" Nos. 2 (op. 83) and 3 (op. 84?); and an incomplete piece titled "A Walk Around for the Piano."

*Dream land*, a very appealing and satisfying character piece, is Bristow's best-known piano work, for there is a modern recording.[19] In G-flat major, the work is appropriately fantasia-like, opening with a delicate wash-of-sound arpeggiated filigree in the upper reaches of the piano that is blurred with the pedal. This continues as accompaniment to a middle-register legato melody (in clear-cut antecedent/consequent phrases), somewhat reminiscent of the styles of Sigismund Thalberg or Louis Gottschalk. The piece eventually transitions to a contrasting middle section, ostensibly in D major but harmonically adventurous and with several delightfully unexpected twists. This middle section features a singing melody introduced in the pianist's right hand that eventually transitions to the left. After the return of the opening theme and dreamy arpeggiation, the piece somewhat surprisingly ends with a coda of forthright marcato block chords, reminiscent of Robert Schumann's pianistic style.

The "Plantation Memories" are longer and more virtuosic than *Dream land*, and their genesis is worth some speculation. It is quite possible that these pieces, like his late songs, simply represent a return to earlier styles. As described in chapter 1, several of Bristow's first piano works from the 1840s were inspired by blackface minstrelsy—variation sets based on tunes that were popular and well known at the time. Bristow's decision to return to this general theme almost fifty years later with his "Plantation Memories," however, was plausibly prompted by different circumstances: the vigorous discussion in the American musical community about using American folk music (including "negro" tunes) as the basis for an American musical voice. As several scholars have suggested, this conversation predated the heated response to Antonín Dvořák's controversial admonition to American composers, in May 1893, that "the future music of this country must be founded on what are called the negro melodies, [which] must be the real foundation of any serious and original school of composition in the United States."[20] A week after the *Herald* published Dvořák's statement, an unknown New Yorker (identified as "A. Thompson") wrote a response, protesting that while "this idea may be original with Mr. Dvorak," in reality "George F. Bristow advanced that theory ten years ago and was laughed at for it. Bristow's idea," he continued,

> was that the American school of music would partake more of the character of negro melody in the South than the so-called negro melodies sung at minstrel shows. . . . To prove Bristow's claim [as] the first to put forth this idea, about five years ago he wrote a piano piece called a "Walk Around" (a decidedly original composition). Also in a new symphony Bristow has put a "breakdown." So you see it is only just that . . . Bristow, an American and one of our best musicians, should be recognized as the first to put forth this idea.[21]

Bristow, of course, was hardly the first American composer to use "negro" melodies in his compositions. Anthony Heinrich's 1820 "Barbeque Divertimento" (especially Part 2: "The Banjo") and Louis Moreau Gottschalk's 1850s compositions come immediately to mind as early examples; Elsworth Phelps's acclaimed (but now forgotten) *Emancipation Symphony* (1880) likewise relied heavily on such tunes.[22] But there seems to be some merit to the claim that Bristow likewise was exploring this idea in the 1880s. I have located no evidence of either his "advancement" of the concept or the scorn that it reportedly elicited, but the holographs of the "Plantation" pieces provide intriguing evidence. Apparently the earliest of the set was originally called "An Ethiopienne: A Walk Around Piece for Piano." Most of this is crossed out on the holograph and replaced with "Plantation Pleasures, a morceau characteristique for the Piano." Also almost thoroughly obliterated on the manuscript is the original opus number, 74. In Delmer Rogers's composition list, opus 73 is assigned to the *Christmas Anthem* (1887) and opus 75 to one of his pedagogical publications (1890), so the original opus 74 "Walk Around" probably dates from sometime between 1887 and 1890, which fits Thompson's "about five years ago" approximation.[23] Bristow eventually renumbered this piece as opus 82, which suggests perhaps that he pulled it out and resumed working on it in the early 1890s, for the second piece in the set, "Plantation Memories No. 2" (originally also titled "Plantation Pleasures"), was given the opus number 83 and is stamped with a copyright date of 1894.[24] "Plantation Memories No. 3" has no opus number (perhaps it should be opus 84?); the opus 82 "Plantation Pleasures" might be considered No. 1 of the three-piece "Plantation" set. There is also an incomplete composition titled "A Walk Around for the Piano" with no opus number; perhaps, as another "walk around," this also dates from the late 1880s.

Evidently Thompson and Bristow were friends, or at least close acquaintances, since the former was aware (in June 1893) of the third-movement "Break Down" in the composer's *Niagara Symphony*, which was not completed until September of that year. It is plausible, then, that in 1893 Bristow, like many others, was irritated both by a European visitor's "ideas" and by the many critics who celebrated Dvořák's "introduction" to American composers of the concept that nationalistic music should be based on folk (especially "negro") melodies—something that many of them had been grappling with for decades. (As we have seen, however, throughout the nineteenth century music critics in the United States had both short memories in relation to American musical culture and a disconcerting tendency to lecture American composers about their craft.)[25] Bristow probably realized that there was little chance that his *Niagara Symphony* (and its "Break Down") would be performed anytime in the near future. So perhaps, as response to Dvořák's "ideas," he decided to pull out his unpublished "Walk Around," retitle it "Plantation Pleasures," write several other "Plantation" pieces, and use them as evidence that Dvořák's suggestions were not particularly new. (None of these pieces, however, was ever published).

"Plantation Memories No. 2," the work that Oliver Ditson copyrighted, is sectional and in D minor. But there is nothing in the piece to mark it as a "walk around" (that portion of a minstrel show during which all the performers prance around the stage), although its tongue-in-cheek quirkiness might represent the comic element of the stage strutting that some minstrel performers undoubtedly engaged in during this portion of the show. "Plantation Memories No. 3," however, does feature some syncopated passages and is essentially a set of variations built on the first strain of "My Old Kentucky Home" by Stephen Foster, a composer whose name appeared frequently in commentary about American folk songs and "negro melodies." Bristow uses the entire keyboard for this bravura work, with octave scalar passages in both hands, difficult sections of chromatic 6/4 chords that descend rapidly in triplets, and segments of alternate-hand rapid-fire arpeggiation. The composition, somewhat strangely for a New York composer, ends with a full quotation of "Dixie"—undoubtedly used to represent the South. In general, however, it is more a virtuosic morceau than either a compositional reinterpretation of spirituals or slave melodies or an evocation of American folk idioms. The two earlier pieces, in contrast, are less virtuosic, rhythmically more complex, and arguably more evocative of syncopated African American music. "Plantation Pleasures" (the former "Ethiopienne") is in E-flat major and commences with a catchy alternating two-against-three rhythmic riff marked *fantastico*. The other (incomplete) "Walk Around" has a cheeky right-hand melody punctuated by staccato notes and comprised of exuberant triplets and embellished dotted rhythmic patterns that become syncopated when paired with the marcato stride-base left hand. All four of these works would benefit from closer examination and performances, especially within the proper historical context.

## Large Compositions

Bristow never seriously attempted another opera, although (as mentioned earlier) there are sketches that suggest a continued interest in doing so. He did, however, undertake a significant revision of *Rip Van Winkle*, completing in 1882 a process that he had started four years earlier. For the revision he worked with the playwright and actor J. W. Shannon. (John Howard Wainwright had died in 1871.)[26] According to Steven Ledbetter, the librettist completely rewrote the spoken dialogue (which Hudson of the *Brooklyn Daily Eagle* described as "stilted and heroic"). Although Shannon retained most of the opera's lyrics, the *Musical Herald* reported that he had "elaborately and largely reconstructed" the libretto.[27] His revisions were mostly to act 2, where he modified the secondary plotline and changed some of the characters. Bristow reworked the score and wrote music for the new second-act lyrics. He also replaced the original overture (frequently played as a stand-alone composition) with an introduction that segues directly into the opening scene. Oscar Hammerstein's English Opera Company listed the opera as an intended offering for 1890–1891, but there is no evidence that it was performed. The New York Banks Glee Club, however, performed selections from the revision in concert at Carnegie Hall, with Bristow presiding at the organ, on December 9, 1898—only four days before the composer's sudden death.[28]

Bristow completed his fourth (and final) freestanding overture, *Jibbenainosay*, op. 64, on May 29, 1886. It is based on *Nick of the Woods; or, The Jibbenainosay: A Tale of Kentucky* (1837), one of the most popular works by the American writer Robert Montgomery Bird (1806–1854). The novel valorizes frontiersmen in the wilds of eighteenth-century Kentucky and portrays their Shawnee adversaries as one-dimensional savages who are viewed with contempt and fear by the backwoodsmen. It is not clear why Bristow chose this topic, although its dramatization had made it an extraordinarily popular melodrama of the time, so the story—like *Rip Van Winkle*—was both well known and a tale of early Americana. The overture was premiered by the Harlem Philharmonic Society Orchestra on March 7, 1889 (with the composer conducting), and enjoyed at least two other performances: July 24, 1893, at the Chicago World's Fair (under Thomas) and, as already noted, in December 1894 under the aegis of the Manuscript Society. The program from the latter concert includes a synopsis (written by George Curtis) that summarizes the main events of the novel. The full score, however, is apparently not extant, so a reconstruction, and any clear idea of how the overture worked musically, is not possible.[29]

### THE *MASS IN C MAJOR*

For more than fifteen years after the successful launch of *The Oratorio of Daniel* in 1867, George Bristow turned away from large sacred choral compositions, so the appearance in 1885 of a final significant work in this realm—his *Mass in C Major*—is somewhat surprising in hindsight.[30] The impetus for this work is unknown, since most of Bristow's other sacred choral pieces were intended either for Episcopal churches or for secular concert performances. In the latter realm his most important effort was *Daniel*, which, although ostensibly a religious piece, was intended for the concert hall and was an example of a genre that some critics in 1868 described as "one of the highest branches of the musical art, equal in importance with the Opera and the Symphony." In fact, Henry Watson had hailed Bristow's success with *Daniel* as the last component of a compositional triple crown: he had "completed the circle of the great styles," Watson wrote, "the oratorio, the opera and the Symphony, proving in all his mastery of the schools."[31] It is entirely possible, in fact, that the self-effacing and unassuming composer was also simultaneously ambitious and had decided to try his hand at a mass precisely because it was one of the two remaining grandiose styles he had not yet attempted. (The other, of course, was a choral symphony.) It is also possible that he had been considering creation of such a work for some time, for in 1874 the *Herald* had published an announcement that "a new Mass by George

Frederick Bristow, will be shortly produced at one of the leading churches in the metropolis," and ten years later a different periodical observed that Bristow had started to write such a work.[32] Whether these references were to earlier, abortive attempts at mass composition or the beginning stages of what would materialize as the *Mass in C Major* is unknown.

There was certainly precedent for such a work in the United States. Several American composers wrote masses for chorus and orchestra during the nineteenth century, including Bristow's father, William, who, according to his obituary, "composed a large number of masses and other sacred compositions." (None are known to be extant.)[33] Today the best-known such nineteenth-century works are the *Mass in D* (1865–1866) by John Knowles Paine and the *Grand Mass in E-flat* (1890) by Amy Cheney Beach (1867–1944). The former, although published in New York in 1866, was never performed in the United States during Paine's lifetime, so Bristow probably did not know it; the latter obviously postdated Bristow's work. There were also five masses (1869, 1874, others unknown) by the Boston composer George Whiting (1840–1923), none of them published, and two later examples (1889 and 1892?) by Frank Dossert (1861–1924).[34] In addition, William Henry Fry wrote a Kyrie Eleison and had started to work on a complete *Mass in E-flat* in the summer of 1864 but never finished the latter work. (He completed its Kyrie and most of the Gloria prior to leaving in November for the West Indies, where he died shortly thereafter.) Bristow might have met Whiting, for that Boston composer studied organ in the early 1860s with George Morgan in New York; it is also possible that he knew of Fry's activities in this realm.[35] It is more plausible, however, that he learned about masses (and many of the standard conventions of mass writing) from the many European masses he had heard or conducted, for a surprising number of such works were performed (in part or in entirety) by New York ensembles during the 1860s, '70s, and '80s. Bristow knew, for example, the famous *Twelfth Mass* by Wenzel Müller (1767–1835), a work that was regularly attributed to Mozart during the period, for he had conducted it as part of Fry's 1853 lecture series. Bristow also conducted masses (or parts of them) at various times at his own instigation. Commencement exercises of Ward School 42 in July 1865, for example, included performance of a text adapted to the canon in Haydn's *Imperial Mass*, and reportedly the Union Harmonic Society sang the entire mass at a concert (which Bristow conducted) in May 1866 at Morrisania Hall. In addition, as choral scholar Brian Bailey has noted, masses by Rossini, Schubert, Weber, and Haydn were heard in the 1860 and 1870s, and the New York premieres of Beethoven's *Mass in C* and *Missa Solemnis* took place in 1870 and 1872. Bailey also points out that during the 1880s, New York church choirs frequently performed individual movements from masses by Haydn, Charles Gounod, Ambroise Thomas, and Francesco Fanciulli, either for special religious holiday services or in concert settings.[36]

Bristow's *Mass in C Major* is a setting of the traditional liturgical texts of the Roman Catholic Ordinary of the Mass (Kyrie, Gloria, Credo, Sanctus/Benedictus and Agnus Dei). His Kyrie follows the repetition in the text and musically is in ternary form. Each of the two longest movements (Gloria and Credo) is divided into sections, as is conventional with mass settings. To distinguish different parts of movements, Bristow made numerous and frequent changes, altering the performing forces, the texture, tempo, meter, and key in different segments. It is clear that he relied on various standard conventions used by eighteenth- and nineteenth-century mass composers (such as those identified above).[37] A number of more or less obvious areas of influence in his work can also be attributed to specific composers. For example, Bailey points to similarities between Bristow's Gloria and the same movement in Müller's *Twelfth Mass*. There are also places in Bristow's work that show the subtle influence of Beethoven's *Mass in C*, as well as several more overt correlations with the *Missa Solemnis*. The latter include Bristow's division of the lengthy Gloria text in precisely the same manner as Beethoven, and similar settings of various passages in both Credos. Furthermore, there are correspondences between the two composers' approaches to their Sanctus and Benedictus movements. In this context, Bailey convincingly challenges Rogers's assertion that Bristow's work was heavily influenced by the religious music of Anton Bruckner.[38]

Although modern scholars can also identify influences in the *Mass in C Major* from other composers, the musical language is Bristow's own. Over the course of some forty years of honing his craft, he had adopted and perfected his own version of the dominant Austro-Hungarian musical vocabulary of the early Romantic period. The tonal language was essentially what he had used in his "Jullien" Symphony in 1853, although now expanded harmonically with the use of more chromaticism and dissonance, as well as modulations via diminished seventh chords, frequently to distant keys. As Bailey points out, Bristow's Mass, "despite its various influences . . . is the work of a mature, confident composer who had found his unique voice."[39] Nevertheless, this musical voice—combined with Bristow's preferred forms (symphonies, oratorios, opera, a mass)—was still essentially conservative within the musical world of the mid-1880s. This orientation is illustrated by the composer's choice of repertoire for his choral ensembles, by his veneration of Beethoven, and by his overt dismissal of the "music of the future" by such composers as Liszt and Wagner. The term "stalwart composer"—

which, as we have seen, has been used by others—thus seems quite appropriate in reference to Bristow.

There is no evidence that the *Mass in C Major* has ever been performed in its entirety, either during Bristow's life or since. By the mid-1880s the composer no longer had access to an ensemble that was sufficiently large to tackle performance of such a composition, and his church choirs probably would have been able to handle only the shorter movements. According to Bailey, in fact, the choir of the First Collegiate Reformed Church in Harlem (at 191 East 121st Street), where Bristow worked from around 1885 to 1889, performed the Kyrie (almost certainly with organ accompaniment) at least three times: on Easter Sundays in 1886 and 1888 and on Christmas Day 1887.[40] The Benedictus movement was also performed in 1895, as mentioned earlier, by the Manuscript Society. The accompaniment was probably for piano or organ, but also with "cello obligato" (a cellist is identified in the program), which was undoubtedly the cello solo from the orchestral accompaniment.[41]

Because there were no concert performances of this massive work, there is no record of contemporary reactions to it; in fact, there probably were no contemporary reactions. If music is not performed, it fades away, which is essentially what happened to Bristow's last major effort in the realm of sacred music. His final major sacred work, then, is another undeservedly forgotten composition, this one by a mature American composer with a well-honed individual voice that had its origins in the musical language of early and mid-nineteenth-century Europe.

### NIAGARA SYMPHONY

Bristow's final orchestral work, his choral symphony, *Niagara*, op. 62, is dated September 1, 1893, although the opus number suggests a genesis in the mid-1880s. In four movements, the work is organized overall into two sections. Part 1 consists of three instrumental movements (Allegro, Adagio, and "A Break Down"); it functions as an instrumental prelude to Part 2: a grandiose finale for soloists and chorus in six sections, the setting of a poem about the mighty cataract.[42] The structural similarity to Beethoven's Ninth Symphony is obvious; in fact, according to critic William Thoms, although Bristow originally considered using the poem as a basis for a programmatic instrumental work, he eventually decided instead to "follow Beethoven and Mendelssohn in their choral symphonies" by writing an instrumental prelude to a final choral movement.[43] Bristow, of course, had already written a similar work: *The Pioneer*, which became his cantata of the same name and the *Arcadian Symphony*. The instrumentation for *Niagara* (pairs of winds plus doubling on piccolo and contrabassoon, four horns, two trumpets, three trombones, tuba, timpani, triangle, organ, and strings), in fact, is almost identical with that for the *Arcadian Symphony*, which adds cymbals and lacks only the contrabassoon and organ.

Modern scholars have suggested numerous probable musical influences. Timothy Cloeter, for example, identifies specific correlations between the *Niagara* and Beethoven's Ninth in his edition of the fourth movement of the symphony; Gregory Fried suggests, in addition, some musical connections with Schumann's Symphony No. 2; and Shadle points out echoes from other contemporary American compositions (by Elsworth Phelps and the German immigrant Louis Maas).[44] All of this, of course, indicates a readily recognizable but conservative musical idiom that was shared by many orchestral composers of the period. The *Niagara* overall is cyclic, but as we have seen, Bristow had also employed cyclic techniques in earlier orchestral works. And although the first movement opens with a theme introduced by solo trumpet (perhaps inspired by Schumann), this partial statement is then completed by somber unison low strings (celli and basses), a gesture that had become something of a signature for Bristow. His three previous symphonies all open with minor-mode unison or solo themes characterized as brooding, ominous, or melancholy and played by low instruments.

According to Thoms, Bristow wrote the symphony to fulfill a promise he had made to an amateur poet, Charles Walker Lord, who was also a public school teacher in Lower Manhattan. Lord approached Bristow sometime in the early 1870s to ask the composer about the appropriateness of a musical setting for a poem he recently had written about Niagara Falls. Bristow read it, was impressed, and eventually decided to use it as the text for a choral symphony.[45] During the late 1860s or early 1870s (when Lord wrote his poem), the appeal of Niagara as a symbol of America was waning. This would have made the poet's tribute somewhat old-fashioned but well in keeping with Bristow's apparently nostalgic orientation during his last decades. The poem is also replete with depictions of natural beauty (including the majesty of the cataracts) and overlaid with a tangible sense of religiosity. By the time Bristow finally wrote the symphony (in the late 1880s or 1890s), however, the country was beginning to emerge as a world power, America was experiencing a newly resurgent sense of nationalism, and Niagara Falls was once again a viable nationalistic symbol. As a result, Bristow's final symphony simultaneously reflects his musical conservatism, deep religious values, and nostalgia—but also a sense of patriotism that was shared by many of his contemporaries.[46] The nationalism is communicated most clearly in the words of the text settings in Part 2, but the very size of the ensemble (the first—and only—performance used over two hundred singers) suggests the magnitude and thunderous sound of Niagara Falls. Moreover, although the instrumental movements are not necessarily programmatic, there are nonetheless definite extramusical suggestions that could be read as depictions of nature, of religion, and of nationalism.

The first movement Allegro, in C minor, is in sonata form. It commences, as mentioned, with a broad and somber theme in the trumpet and low strings. The second theme is appropriately calm and flowing, after which there is a contrapuntal section, perhaps portraying the rapids above the falls. The conclusion of the movement, however, is overtly pictorial. As Thoms described it, "The basses have a running accompaniment, which is taken up at intervals by the other string instruments, until it sounds like the roar of many waters. The harmony is played by the wind instruments, and on the whole produces a grand effect." The second movement—like that of the *Arcadian Symphony*—features a brass-choir-like sound but with two clarinets and two bassoons (instead of the *Arcadian*'s three trombones and tuba) added to the two horns and two trumpets.[47] Thoms likened this to organ music, and certainly the imagery of chorale-like sounds in a large open space reinforces the concept of the spirituality with which the poem is imbued.

The upbeat third movement is the "Break Down" cited by A. Thompson in 1893. Sometimes the movement is labeled a *scherzo*, but Bristow inscribed "A Break Down" on the holograph score, and Thoms stressed unambiguously that the movement was "a Breakdown in character, no matter what it is called, breakdown, scherzo, or anything else."[48] It is something of an anomaly, for it is an exuberant and rowdy dance, and to Thoms it seemed out of place, especially in the context of "the grandeur of the subject." Bristow, however, undoubtedly chose the title deliberately. As a boisterous dance popular in the 1880s and 1890s, a breakdown was associated with African Americans but nevertheless also had roots in such country dances as jigs, hornpipes, and hoedowns. As a result, it is an evocation of the American "folk" (whether African Americans or rural Caucasians of the Southern highlands) and works well as a multilayered musical embodiment of nationalism. The movement has the sectional structure typical of a fiddle tune or a dance. Its introduction is exuberant and syncopated and leads to an opening theme full of scotch snaps, triplets, and leaps. The second motive is contrasting and prominently quotes a popular early nineteenth-century nostalgic song, "Long, Long Ago," by the British composer Thomas Haynes Bayly (1797–1839), which by the 1880s had developed a rather complex racial lineage: it was frequently identified as a slave tune from the antebellum South (it was published in 1839 as "Near the Lake Where Drooped the Willow" with the subtitle "a Southern refrain") but by late in the century had also become a staple in the fiddle-tune repertoire.[49] After this clear-cut quotation, there is another episode that features a calm 6/8 melody played by clarinet that is subsequently treated fugally; a coda based on the opening theme completes the piece. The movement, heard within a major symphony about a natural symbol of the United States, is an excellent example, on several planes, of the various complexities of the American "folk." Since Bristow finished the movement by May 1893, it predated Dvořák's symphony by at least seven months.

The choral fourth movement (Part 2 of the symphony), as Thoms points out, is of an entirely different character, since in this section the topic of the symphony—a depiction of the mighty cataract and extrapolation of nationalistic and metaphysical meaning from that depiction—moves beyond the interpretive imagery of instrumentation and into the more overt depiction of music-with-words. The program distributed at the Manuscript Society performance, in fact, includes Lord's complete poem. (See fig. 5.) Part 2—again, like the fourth movement of Beethoven's Ninth—also functions as a musical culmination of the entire symphony, for Bristow quotes the musical themes of his earlier movements.[50]

The work opens with a majestic and forthright instrumental introduction (marked *Maestoso*) that leads directly to a rendition by chorus (supported by trumpet and trombone) of Nathan Strong's 1799 hymn "Almighty Sovereign of the Skies," an expression of gratitude to God for the beauty of nature; it was sufficiently familiar to the audience that the text was not printed in the program. Bristow set the final strophe of the hymn (which self-referentially exhorts the choir to lift up its collective voice in praise) to the tune of the likewise-familiar hymn "Old Hundredth" (the Doxology). An orchestral interlude leads to No. 2 (marked *Allegro*), where the chorus introduces the subject of veneration: "Niagara! Overwhelm'd with awe and wonder / Thee I behold." A tenor soloist is featured in this segment, and at the end of his first solo statement the chorus returns with another obvious quotation, singing "King of Kings and Lord of Lords" to the melody and accompaniment of Handel's "Hallelujah" chorus. The work continues with a through-composed aria for bass (No. 3, "With reverence I bow," marked *Andante*) that again emphasizes the overall religiosity of the work, with reference to God as the "Great Architect" of "life's cataract." This theme is underscored in the subsequent duet for soprano and alto (No. 4, marked *Allegro*), another through-composed segment. In this complex ode the soprano, then the alto, then both call out four of the five Great Lakes: "Superior, Huron, Michigan, and Erie / With little Clair commingling like Peri." As Denise Von Glahn points out, this comparison of the waters to a sprightly winged spirit from Persian mythology "immediately elevat[ed] the subject from the mundane to the otherworldly."[51] Bristow's picto-

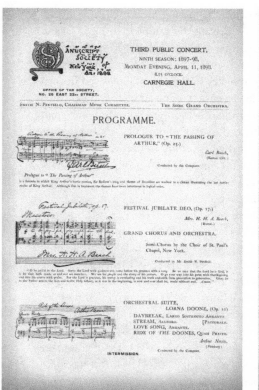

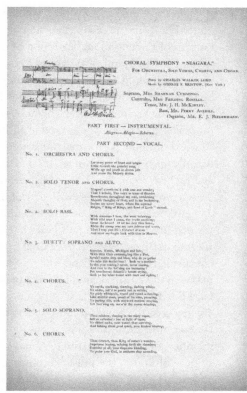

**FIGURE 5.** Pages 1–2 of the Manuscript Society program for the concert on April 11, 1898, that included the premiere performance of Bristow's *Niagara Symphony*. Lord's poem is on the second page. (Manuscript Society of New York. Programs of Public Concerts, 1892–1901. Music Division, Performing Arts Library, New York Public Library, Astor, Lenox, and Tilden Foundations.)

rial use of the orchestra in this section is particularly effective: he employs the instruments throughout to depict the swirling Niagara river, the "waters deep and blue," the fearful leap of the cataract, and the ceaseless roaring of the falls. No. 5 is a complex number that commences with an *Allegro furioso* section for orchestra and chorus to the text of "Ye rapids, sparkling, foaming, dashing wildly"; Thoms describes Bristow's treatment of this section as "the wildest of the wild." After a complex fugato for chorus and orchestra to "Ye giddy whirlpools," the number proceeds to an orchestral interlude followed by a solo for lyrical soprano (marked

*Andante*) accompanied by a brass choir (three trombones and tuba) that uses a quotation from the second movement to illustrate the rainbow and mist at the bottom of the falls. The beginning of the final section (No. 6, "Thou Cataract, Thou King of Nature's Wonders") is again marked *Allegro furioso* and starts *fortissimo* with rapid and brilliant descending scales in the violins, followed in turn by the other strings. The basses of the chorus enter (followed by the full chorus) with a strong statement of the main theme: an exhortation to both the waters and musicians to "to praise your God in anthems thus ascending." The chorus repeats this text but now performed *maestoso*, as at the beginning of the movement, and broadly majestic. The trumpet motive from the opening of the symphony returns, and we hear again the "King of Kings and Lord of Lords" reference from earlier. The symphony concludes with a brief orchestral coda.

Although the composition was finished in September 1893, it was not performed until four and a half years later, in Carnegie Hall, on April 11, 1898. It was the last Bristow work presented by the Manuscript Society and was the final concert in the organization's 1897–1898 season. (See fig. 5.) Bristow's symphony made up the entire second half of a program that also included compositions by Carl Busch (1862–1943), Amy Beach, and Arthur Nevin (1871–1943). The society engaged the Seidl Grand Orchestra, which was to be under the direction of the ensemble's namesake, as well as four soloists, three of whom were performing members of the organization.[52] A massive choir was made up mostly of volunteer singers, although the music committee was authorized in March to hire some additional altos. The vocal ensemble began weekly rehearsals in mid-January, under Bristow's direction.[53] According to both Rogers and Cloeter, this was the largest performance ever given by the Manuscript Society, and the board paid for widespread advertisements and encouraged all members "to show their personal interest in the work" by attending the performance.[54] It was also the organization's first attempt to mount a performance that required a large chorus, and the choice of Bristow's *Niagara Symphony* should probably be interpreted as a mark of esteem for the veteran composer.

Two weeks before the much-anticipated concert, however, Anton Seidl, age forty-seven, suddenly died of gallstone and liver ailments. Plans for the event were thrown into serious disarray. Eventually, the representative composers agreed to conduct their own compositions (except for Amy Beach, whose *Festival Jubilate Deo* was conducted by Smith Penfield), and the performance was held at Carnegie Hall, as originally planned.[55] Neither Rogers, Cloeter, nor Von Glahn located reviews of the concert, but a newspaper notice from April 12, 1898, reports that the concert had taken place as advertised.[56] In addition, Manuscript Society minutes from May 1898 note that "the choral work at the 3rd concert reflected credit on the composer, Mr. Bristow, and on the Society. . . . The honor and standing of the Society has been kept up." There is also information from the treasurer's report to indicate that the society stayed within budget despite significant costs associated with the concert, which suggests the organization sold enough tickets to break even.[57]

The absence of reviews, however, is vexing, especially since this was the composition's single performance. Shadle speculates that the dailies were "swept up by the drumming of impending war with Spain" and hence did not cover it. But an essay on Bristow (possibly by the journal's editor, E. W. Lorenz) in *The Choir Leader* shortly before the composer's death proposes a different explanation. "The 'Niagara,'" he wrote, "was given by the Manuscript Society of New York last spring, and evoked great enthusiasm from all the genuine music lovers present by the wealth of ideas and the wonderful contrapuntal resources it displayed, no less than by its beauty and sublimity." But, he continued, "The purity of form, wealth of melody and classical treatment, did not please the little clique of Wagner-haunted, foreign-bred critics and they did not do it justice in the public press. They are not to be blamed, but rather pitied, that they are unable to recognize good metal unless it has the 'hallmark' of foreign."[58] Although this description fits well Bristow's experience throughout his life (and the experiences, of course, of many other American composers), it does not ring true for William Thoms, who in June 1896 had written an extensive description/analysis of *Niagara* that he called "an impression," for it was based on examination of the score. He reprinted most of this essay on April 2, 1898, just before the premiere, adding as a conclusion, "Bristow's Niagara Symphony is a remarkable work."[59] The language of Thoms's essay seems to indicate a genuine interest in hearing *Niagara*, so it is strange that he did not write a review; perhaps something prevented his attendance. After Bristow's sudden death on December 13, 1898, however, Thoms republished the essay a third time, now retitled "Bristow's Last Work" and commencing with the statement that "this last work from the pen of one of the most renowned of American composers" had been "produced by the Manuscript Society at Carnegie Hall, April 11th, 1898."[60] Clearly, Thoms believed that his earlier analysis of the symphony was adequately detailed and that his preperformance assessment was suitable (even if he had been unable to attend the concert) for a postmortem critique of what turned out to be the composer's farewell performance. We will never know. The concert, in fact, was Bristow's swan song: the final major performance of a fifty-year career as an orchestral and choral conductor and the premiere of his final major composition.

# Conclusion

**GEORGE FREDERICK BRISTOW** had a long and productive life that spanned almost three-quarters of the nineteenth century. He was a successful violinist, pianist, organist, conductor, composer, and educator; he also played a significant role in the development of American musical culture during the nineteenth century. As John Freund (1848–1924) noted in Bristow's obituary, "for over half a century" Bristow was "a prominent figure in the musical life of this country."[1] But Bristow the person has been historically elusive to most scholars. We hear his voice in his music, the autobiographical sketch he wrote in the 1860s, several letters published in newspapers and periodicals, a published address to the Music Teachers National Association, and a handful of interviews, all of them concerned with his professional life. But in this book the only glimpses we have seen of Bristow the man are from the autobiographical sketch he wrote in the 1860s, the series of interviews with Travis Quigg, and the two extant letters he wrote to his future wife, Louise Holder, in the 1860s—both love letters, one happy and playful, the other a cri de coeur written in fear that she had thrown him over.

There are also, however, three additional letters from the composer in the Bristow Collection at the New York Public Library.[2] They have nothing to with his professional activities and normally would not be used in a book of this nature. But the contents of these letters—common, ordinary topics—are valuable precisely because of their mundanity, for they provide a tiny glimpse into George Bristow, the person. All three are from 1898 and are addressed to his daughter Estelle Viola Dearborn, who was thirty years old, married, and with a young son, born in 1897 and named after her father. The three missives reveal aspects of Bristow's personality and character: his desire to help his daughter find a good piano; glee at catching several large fish from the dock in Orient, New York; droll complaints about the weather; affection for his family; and complete and utter fascination with his young namesake. In the first letter, dated February 8, 1898, he tells Estelle that he had found a piano for her (and explains why it was better than another she had considered), after which he launches into a barrage of questions: "How are you? How is the son and heir? How is his pop?" In a postscript he comments that since both daughters are now married, he and his wife are "alone." Then he adds, rather poignantly, "that is just where we started from."

The second and third letters were both written from the Bristows' summer place in Orient, on Long Island, where, as usual, they were spending the summer months. In the first of these, dated July 3, 1898, he gives her the news from Orient. It is, he reports, "Dull. Stupid. Miserable. That expresses it. Heat awful. Mosquitoes, in millions, in fact there is everything here to make you jump into the bay and wet [yourself] all over." He passes on some gossip about neighbors and then asks, "How are you all? The little boy, the Old Man, Swipes, Whiskers . . . and all the other members of the family. . . . It must be very funny to see that Kid splash in the water, he evidently likes it." The elder George was clearly a doting grandfather. The final letter is from August 21, 1898, and Bristow starts by confessing that "when there is nothing to say, it is difficult to say it." He then gloats about catching two three-pound bluefish and instructs her to tell "the Old Man" (her husband, William Dearborn), who will surely be jealous. The topic then turns again to his grandson, George, who was nine months old at the time.[3] "Does he pull whiskers, and noses?" he asks. "Untie neckties as he did mine?" He continues: "He is a fine boy and we all love him. Let him keep on pulling. I can stand it, as long as he can. Kiss him for me,—and when I see him again, I will give him another chance." Bristow then turns somewhat pensive: "How time flies,— only to think, a week from next Thursday will be the 1st of September, the 25th of December will be Christmas Day, the 1st of January will be New-Years, &c, &c"—statements that explain, perhaps, why Estelle preserved these particular letters from her father, for he would not be around for either Christmas or New Year's, or for his seventy-third birthday on December 19, or for any other days.

The heart attack that killed him evidently came without warning.[4] As noted in chapter 6, he had played organ accompaniment for the New York Banks Glee

Club concert at Carnegie Hall on December 9, which included a performance of selections from his revised *Rip Van Winkle*.[5] But he must have fallen ill over the weekend, for when he arrived at Grammar School No. 42 on Tuesday morning, December 13, he told the janitor, "I am chilled to the bone." He went directly into the general assembly room, where he was scheduled to teach, and sat down by the steam radiator. He explained to one of the teachers in the room, "I'm not feeling well. I came here from a sick bed. I've got the grip [the flu]." A few moments later the teacher turned back to Bristow to ask a question, only to discover him sitting with his head inclined on his chest, unconscious. Death evidently ensued "almost immediately."[6]

Most of the obituaries, as is the norm, focused on his professional activities and echo the accolades that have appeared repeatedly throughout this book: Bristow as *the* American composer, a man whose "*Daniel* is, unquestionably, one of the most important compositions in this form yet produced by an American composer"; an "active and influential force in American musical matters"; "one of those who strove to push American music into a place of artistic prominence"; and a teacher whose "whole life [was] devoted to the hardest and most conscientious work in the cause of musical education." As noted in Interlude C, W. J. Henderson of the *Times* emphasized this latter service, pointing out that "most of the public school boys of the last thirty or thirty-five years" were familiar with the composer and his pedagogical activity.[7]

But some also commented on ingrained personality traits, elements that most of the public never saw. One critic called him a "whole-souled, most lovable man"; others described him as "full of a sweet and genial humor that endears him to all who appreciate genuineness" and "a gentleman and a musician."[8] There are repeated references to his steadfast commitment to his art and to the fact that he was "self-sacrificing in his labor for its benefit." William Thoms observed that if American institutions had been "more quick to recognize and foster native talent and genius," the name of George Bristow "would have been a household word throughout the land." But Bristow clearly was not interested in pursuing that type of fame. He was repeatedly described as "modest and unassuming to a fault" and as someone who "despised" the "usual methods of gaining fame and popularity."[9]

The archdeacon of the Episcopal Diocese of New York, who spoke at a memorial service for Bristow, commented on the composer's "genius, his devotion to his art, his unselfish character," and his "touching efforts to inculcate among the young a love of music in all its delightful forms." He continued: "Those who knew him intimately always felt the strongly attractive charm of this composer's personality." Smith Newell Penfield (1837–1920), a composer, organist, and fellow member of the Manuscript Society, wrote to Louise and described Bristow as "one of my warmest and most intimate friends." He summed up his character succinctly: "I have ever regarded him as, more than any other . . . a representative New York composer. Yet he was withal the most modest and retiring of men, far too much for his own interest. He was ever the accomplished musician, the genial gentleman and the quick discoverer of merit in other composers."[10]

But as we have seen, George Frederick Bristow was also a musician whose professional life personifies the development of one type of musical culture in nineteenth-century New York. He was a man who, at one time or another, wore most of the hats of nineteenth-century urban musicians in both America and Western Europe and who was quite skilled at a remarkable number of those varied activities. Furthermore, he was a composer of true ability whose works are, for the most part, undeservedly unknown today. One obituary writer suggested somewhat wistfully that "it may be that, like Schubert, [Bristow's] work will be valued more highly after his death than during his lifetime, and his manuscripts attain the valuation their intrinsic merits deserve."[11] One hundred and twenty years after his death, that still has not occurred. Perhaps someday soon it will.

# NOTES

*About Sources*

Unless otherwise noted, all of the holograph scores cited in this book are in the George F. Bristow Collection (referenced as Bristow Collection), Performing Arts Library, New York Public Library (PAL/NYPL)

BRISTOW COLLECTION, ADDITIONS. This is a file of letters, photographs, and miscellaneous materials from the family that was added to the Bristow Collection. At the time of this publication it is still unprocessed but will be known under this heading after processing.

GOHARI COLLECTION. Genealogical materials and research notes related to William Bristow, George Frederick Bristow, and their ancestors and descendants. Collected by Carol Elaine Gohari, a descendant of William Bristow. Several files of notes and photocopies were given to the author in September 2019 by Jalal Gohari, Carol's widower.

MANUSCRIPT SOCIETY OF NEW YORK COLLECTION. This collection is in the American Music Collection, PAL/NYPL, but segments of it are variously catalogued: some portions under the call number JPF 77, including Minutes (1896–1912) and Clippings (1890–1906) and portions under *MBD (uncat). The Programs of Public Concerts of the Manuscript Society, 1890–1901 are available on microfilm (*ZB561).

All currency conversions are done using the tool at the website of MeasuringWorth.com (https://www.measuringworth.com). At the time of press, the most recent year available for currency calculations was 2019.

*Abbreviations*

ALS            Autograph Letter Signed
PAL/NYPL       Performing Arts Library, New York Public Library for the
               Performing Arts

## BOOKS, ENCYCLOPEDIAS, ARTICLE SETS

| | |
|---|---|
| *AGII* | *New Grove Dictionary of American Music II* |
| *ANB* | *American National Biography* |
| *CHAM* | *Cambridge History of American Music* |

| | |
|---|---|
| *DAB* | *Dictionary of American Biography* |
| *DNB* | *Dictionary of National Biography* |
| *GMO* | *Grove Music Online* (part of *Oxford Music Online*) |
| *MiG* | *Music in Gotham*, https://www.musicingotham.org |
| Lawrence I, II, III | Vera Lawrence: *Strong on Music* |
| *NGDO* | *New Grove Dictionary of Opera* |
| *Odell* | George C. D. Odell, *Annals of the New York Stage* |
| *OfP* | Preston, *Opera for the People* |
| *OoR* | Preston, *Opera on the Road* |
| *ODNB* | *Oxford Dictionary of National Biography* |
| Quigg, *AM* I–VIII | Interviews with Bristow by J. Travis Quigg in *American Musician*: |

AM I, "George F. Bristow," Sept. 15, 1888, 7

AM II, Sept. 22, 1888 (issue not located)

AM III, "Bristow's Reminiscences," Sept. 29, 1888, 7

AM IV, "Bristow's Reminiscences," Oct. 13, 1888, 7–8

AM V, "Bristow's Reminiscences," Oct. 20, 1888, 7

AM VI, "Bristow's Reminiscences," Oct. 27, 1888, 9

AM VII, "Bristow's Reminiscences," Nov. 17, 1888, 5

AM VIII, "Bristow's Reminiscences," Dec. 15, 1888, 5

## PERIODICALS

All periodicals, unless otherwise noted, were published in New York City.

| | |
|---|---|
| *AAJ* | *American Art Journal* |
| *AM* | *American Musician* |
| *Albion* | *The Albion: A Journal of News, Politics, and Literature* |
| *Appleton's* | *Appleton's Journal of Literature, Science, and Art* |
| *DJM* | *Dwight's Journal of Music* (Boston) |
| *JFA* | *Journal of Fine Arts* |
| *Leslie's* | *Frank Leslie's Monthly Magazine* |
| *MA* | *Musical America* |
| *MB* | *Message Bird* |
| *MH* | *Musical Herald* (Boston) |
| *MR&CA* | *Musical Review & Choral Advocate* |
| *MR&G* | *Musical Review & Gazette* |
| *MR&MW* | *Musical Review & Musical World* |
| *MTR* | *Music Trade Review* |
| *MW* | *Musical World* |
| *MW&T* | *Musical World & Times* |
| *NYMW* | *New York Musical World* |
| *SMT* | *Saroni's Musical Times* |
| *WAJ* | *Watson's Art Journal* |
| *WWAJ* | *Watson's Weekly Art Journal* |

## NEWSPAPERS

| | |
|---|---|
| *BDE* | *Brooklyn Daily Eagle* |
| *BDU* | *Brooklyn Daily Union* |
| *BFP* | *Burlington (VT) Free Press* |
| *BU* | *Brooklyn Union* |
| *CIO* | *Chicago Inter-Ocean* |
| *DFP* | *Detroit Free Press* |
| *Mirror* | *New York Evening Mirror / New York Mirror* |
| *NYDisp* | *New York Dispatch* |
| *NYDTrib* | *New York Daily Tribune* |
| *NYEP* | *New York Evening Post* |
| *NYH* | *New York Herald* |
| *NYT* | *New York Times* |
| *NYTrib* | *New York Tribune* |

## Introduction

1. Vera Lawrence, *Strong on Music: The New York Music Scene in the Days of George Templeton Strong*, vol. 1. *Resonances. 1836–1850* (hereafter, Lawrence I). (New York: Oxford University Press, 1988), 424.

2. "With the Amateurs," *BDE*, Sept. 25, 1892; and "Notes of the Week," *NYT*, Nov. 28, 1886, 2.

3. "George F. Bristow," *AAJ*, (Nov. 10, 1877): 17–19. For problems with the claim about *Rip Van Winkle*, see Steven Ledbetter, "Bristow, George Frederick," *NGDO*.

4. The most important scholarship to date on Bristow includes works by Delmer Dalzell Rogers, "Nineteenth-Century Music in New York City as Reflected in the Career of George Frederick Bristow," PhD diss., University of Michigan, 1967; and Gregory Martin Fried, "A Study of the Orchestral Music of George Frederick Bristow," DMA diss., University of Texas, 1989. The most complete worklists of Bristow's compositions are Rogers's Appendix A to his dissertation (188–98) and his worklist in the article on Bristow in *AGII*. Current published editions of Bristow's works include those edited by Steven Ledbetter, *Rip Van Winkle: Grand Romantic Opera in Three Acts* (New York: Da Capo, 1991); David Griggs-Janower, *The Oratorio of Daniel* (Middleton, WI: A-R Editions, 1999); and Katherine K. Preston, *Bristow's Symphony No. 2 ("Jullien"): A Critical Edition*, Music of the United States of America series, vol. 23 (Middleton, WI: A-R Editions, 2011). Scholars who have written about specific compositions (or created unpublished editions of works) include Karl Erwin Gombert, "*Leonora* by William Henry Fry and *Rip Van Winkle* by George Frederick Bristow: Examples of Mid-Nineteenth-Century American Opera," DMA diss., Ball State University, 1977; Robert J. E. Hopkins, "String Chamber Music Performance in New York City, 1842–52: The Social and Cultural Context of Representative Works by George Frederick Bristow," DMA diss., University of Illinois, 2014; Brian Keith Bailey, "George Bristow's Mass in C for Choir and Orchestra (1885): Critical Edition and Commentary," DMA diss., University of Iowa, 2016; Timothy J. Cloeter, "A Performance Edition of the

Fourth Movement of the *Niagara Symphony*, Op. 62, by George Frederick Bristow (1825–1898)," DMA diss., University of Arizona, 2016; and Brandon Moss, "George F. Bristow's *Praise to God*: An Analysis and Historical Commentary," DMA diss., Ohio State University, forthcoming 2020. Other scholarship on specific aspects of Bristow's life (including contemporary commentary) is cited throughout the book.

### CHAPTER 1. *"The Life of a Musician"*

1. Genealogical information about the Bristows is from "William Richard Bristow, American Musician," an unpublished typescript by Carol Elaine Gohari (1943–2012) and from notes in Ms. Gohari's files. As a collateral descendant of George Bristow, Gohari conducted a great deal of research on the family. My sincere thanks to Jalal Gohari, who generously gave to me some of his wife's files (hereafter referred to as the Gohari Collection) after her premature death. Victor Yellin suggests that Bristow might have been born in England, but Gohari disproved that assertion. See Yellin, "Bristow's Divorce," *American Music* 12, no. 3 (Fall 1994): 253n13; Gohari, "George Frederick Bristow: Incidental Gleanings," *Sonneck Society for American Music Bulletin* 25 (Summer 1999): 39; *U.S. Census Mortality Schedules, 1850–1885* (via www.ancestry.com); and *Smith's Brooklyn Directory*, 1878–1883.

2. Rogers, 58–66; Lawrence I: 106n, 302n; George Frederick Bristow, "The Life of a Musician: His Troubles & Trials &c," manuscript (Bristow Collection, Additions), 1 (hereafter, Bristow, "Life"). Internal evidence suggests that this undated manuscript was written in 1867 or 1868, when the composer was in his early forties. This document was discovered by David Keilar, a graduate student working with Victor Yellin in the 1970s. Curtis confirms the elder Bristow's compositional activity. See G. H. Curtis, "George Frederick Bristow," *Music* 3 (1893): 549.

3. Bristow, "Life," 1.

4. Gohari, "W. R. Bristow," 15; Gohari, "Gleanings," 37.

5. The family lived variously at 220 Houston St. (1834), 197 Bowery (1835), and on Division Street (1839). *Longworth's American Almanac, New York Register and City Directory* (New York: T. Longworth, 1816– ), 1834–1835, 1835–1836, 1839.

6. J. Travis Quigg, *AM* I: 7; Bristow, "Life," 4–6. Insight into William Bristow's ambitions for his son is suggested by the young composer's name. In "Life" (1), Bristow is a member of "the Apollo family," and his name is "Handel, Haydn, Mozart, Beethoven Apollo."

7. Bristow, "Life," 8. Bristow's take on his forced employment as a child is insightful, for even thirty years later, the composer's resentment toward his father is apparent. He comments at one point (6–8) that he "felt himself more of a Slave than anything else."

8. Bristow notes in "Life" (7) that both he and his father lost their jobs only weeks before their engagement at the Olympic. They worked at two different theaters, one of which burned down, the other closed. According to what Bristow told Quigg (*AM* I: 7), he was working at the National when that theater burned (September 1839). He claims ("Life," 8) that he was twelve when he started to work at the Olympic, but he was thirteen. Rogers (60–61) states that Bristow worked at the Olympic until 1843.

9. Bristow, "Life," 9–10. William Musgrif is frequently mentioned as one of Bristow's teachers. He was sufficiently accomplished as a cellist to perform in the New York premiere

of Hummel's "Military" Septet in March 1843 (Lawrence I: 221). According to Norman Schweikert (a retired French horn player whose avocation is historical research), Musgrif was a member of the Philharmonic Society from 1842 to 1849, although he apparently did not play during the 1848–1849 season. His first name (as well as the spelling "Musgrif") is from the New York city directories for 1842 and 1843. Email communication with Mr. Schweikert, June 30, 2007; my thanks to him. Bristow, "Life," 13–14.

10. Bristow, "Life," 9–17; quotation is from 14–15. Bristow's autobiographical essay is the best source of information about Musgrif's important role in his musical education. Bristow identifies his mentor as the cellist in the Olympic Theatre orchestra during his first several years there.

11. Bristow, "Life"; quotations from 6, 7, 20–21.

12. Bristow, "Life," 21–23; Andrew Clarke, "Loder & Sons, Bath: A Band of Musicians," in *Musicians of Bath and Beyond: Edward Loder (1809–1865) and His Family*, ed. Nicholas Temperley (Woodbridge, UK: Boydell Press, 2016), 97–98.

13. Four of the seven instrumentalists at the Olympic are included in Howard Shanet's list of possible Philharmonic members for the first season: Henry Marks (violin), William Musgrif (cello), John Kyle (flute), and George Loder (double bass). The only musicians of the theater ensemble who were not members of the Philharmonic Society were Ayliffe (violin) and the two Bristows. See George C. D. Odell, *Annals of the New York Stage*, 15 vols. (New York: Columbia University Press, 1927–1949), IV: 650–51; Howard Shanet, *Philharmonic: A History of New York's Orchestra* (New York: Doubleday, 1975), 489–91; and Bristow, "Life," 22.

14. Bristow, "Life," 21–22. Bristow's name appeared in the society's Second Annual Report as a member of the ensemble in 1843–1844. According to Shanet (490–91), the same source indicates that Bristow and eight others had been asked to join the society *during* its second season, so either Bristow misremembered or the invitation from Loder was informal. See also Henry Edward Krehbiel, *The Philharmonic Society of New York: A Memorial* (New York: Novello, Ewer and Co., 1892), reprinted in Howard Shanet, ed., *Early Histories of the New York Philharmonic* (New York: Da Capo, 1979), 41. For an enlightening discussion of the conflicting information about charter members of the Philharmonic Society, see Shanet, 427n51.

15. Bristow, "Life," 24–28.

16. Bristow, "Life," 28. Bristow's name appears on the roster of musicians for the second season. William Bristow was apparently never a member of the orchestra. See Shanet, 490–91.

17. "New York Philharmonic Society," *MB*, June 15, 1850, 362; Bristow, "Life," 28, 22.

18. Lawrence I: 168, 409. According to Krehbiel (141) and H. Earle Johnson, *First Performances in America to 1900* (Detroit: Information Coordinators, 1979), 91, Bristow conducted the premiere performance of his Concert Overture. According to the program from January 9, 1847, however, H. C. Timm conducted the entire concert. See New York Philharmonic Society Archives, https://archives.nyphil.org. The Hummel concerto performance was on May 27, 1847; Bristow later played two movements of the work with the Philharmonic Society (March 1, 1851). See Lawrence I: 486, and Krehbiel, 106; Rogers (75) has an incorrect date for the concerto. "*Eleutheria* Grand Cantata," *NYH*, April 9, 1849, [3].

19. Bristow, "Life," 30–31.

20. Bristow, "Life," 31–32, 35–36, 41.

21. Bristow, "Life," 33–34; Quigg, *AM* I: 7; Rogers, 67–70. For Meyrer's work with the Philharmonic Society, see Shanet, 91 and 491. Bull was in New York intermittently from November 1843 through November 1845; see Lawrence I (index listing on p. 654). For Timm, see Shanet, 4, 91. About Macfarren, see Henry C. Banister, *George Alexander Macfarren: His Life, Works, and Influence* (London: George Bell and Sons, 1891), 171–72, 182; and Katherine K. Preston, "American Orchestral Music," introductory monograph to *Bristow's Symphony No. 2*, xviii, fn9.

22. Lawrence I: 282, 409, 482, 414, 404; "Theatrical and Musical," April 26, 1849, [3], and "Mrs Emma Gillingham Bostwick's Concert," June 16, 1849, [3], both in *NYH*; Lawrence I: 610.

23. Katherine K. Preston, "Art Music from 1800 to 1860," in *Cambridge History of American Music*, ed. David Nicholls, 188–213 (London: Cambridge University Press, 1998), and *Opera on the Road: Traveling Opera Troupes in the United States, 1825–1860* (Urbana: University of Illinois Press, 1993) (hereafter, *OoR*), 141–48. See also R. Allen Lott, "Bernard Ullman: Nineteenth-Century American Impresario," in *A Celebration of American Music: Words and Music in Honor of H. Wiley Hitchcock*, ed. Richard Crawford, R. Allen Lott, and Carol J. Oja, 174–91 (Ann Arbor: University of Michigan Press, 1990); and Ruth Henderson, "A Confluence of Moravian Impresarios: Max Maretzek, the Strakosches, and the Graus," in *European Music and Musicians in New York City*, ed. John Graziano, 235–52 (New York: University of Rochester Press, 2006).

24. Frédéric Louis Ritter, *Music in America* (New York: Charles Scribner's Sons, 1895, rev. ed.), 264. Information about instrumentalists who traveled with itinerant opera companies is notoriously difficult to find. In general, however, English opera companies during the 1840s tended to perform in conjunction with the house orchestras of the theaters in which they appeared. Italian companies sometimes traveled either with an orchestra or with a core group of instrumentalists to play with local musicians. One useful contemporary account is that of Thomas Ryan, *Recollections of an Old Musician* (New York: Dutton, 1899), 57.

25. For more information about these ensembles, their activities, and their immediate impact on American musical culture, see my "American Orchestral Music," xxxi–xxxv. For the Germanians, see Nancy Newman, *Good Music for a Free People: The Germania Musical Society in Nineteenth-Century America* (Rochester, NY: University Press, 2010).

26. It was not uncommon for singers who elected to settle in the United States to have spouses, other family members, and friends who were trained instrumental musicians, who also remained in the States or traveled from Europe to join the singer who elected to stay. Immigration by musicians of any kind, then, tended to increase the population of trained singers and instrumentalists in America. Excellent examples are the Patti/Barili families. See Elizabeth Forbes, "Patti," *GMO*, and N. Lee Orr, *Alfredo Barili and the Rise of Classical Music in Atlanta* (Atlanta: Scholars Press, 1996).

27. Preston, "Art Music."

28. Preston, "Art Music." SA entries on the various cities in *GMO* and Michael Broyles, *"Music of the Highest Class": Elitism and Populism in Antebellum Boston* (New Haven, CT: Yale University Press, 1992), 236, 261.

29. "Personal," *BDE*, Feb. 13, 1873, 4.

30. Quigg, *AM* IV: 8. Bristow reports that Pirsson lived on Mercer Street, just north of Broadway and West Houston; according to city directories, he lived there from 1845 to 1847.

31. Lawrence I: 404; Vera Brodsky Lawrence, *Strong on Music*, vol. 2. *Reverberations 1850–1856* (hereafter, Lawrence II) (Chicago: University Press, 1995), 105, 182. The best source on Bristow's activities in the realm of chamber music is Hopkins, 55, 102, 106–110, 123–25, 130–31, and 176–79.

32. Lawrence I: 409; Lawrence II: 105, 424.

33. See also Lawrence I: 504 (Kalliwoda); and Lawrence II: 15, 115 (Maurer), 146–47 (Hummel).

34. Jean W. Thomas claims that Bristow "accompanied singers Jenny Lind and Marietta Alboni on their American tours," and many others have repeated this erroneous information. See Thomas, "Bristow, George Frederick," *ANB*. For correction, see Preston, "American Orchestral Music," xx, n18.

35. William Treat Upton, *William Henry Fry: American Journalist and Composer-Critic* (New York: Da Capo, 1974). 122; Rogers, 104; Lawrence II: 145, 380, 360, 622–31. For the Jullien visit, see Katherine K, Preston, "'A Concentration of Talent on Our Musical Horizon': The 1853–54 American Tour by Jullien's Extraordinary Orchestra," in *American Orchestras in the 19th Century*, ed. John Spitzer, 319–47 (Chicago: University of Chicago Press, 2012).

36. Bristow, "Life," 14–15; "Isle of Sheppy Waltzes" (New York: Firth and Hall, 1840). A copy in the Library of Congress has on its cover "Composed by George F. Bristow, aged 14 years."

37. The "Rum Seller" is in the Lester S. Levy Sheet Music Collection, Johns Hopkins University. William Treat Upton, *Art-Song in America: A Study in the Development of American Music* (Boston: Oliver Ditson, 1930), 43–35.

38. Thanks to Candace Bailey for sharing a copy of this sheet music with me.

39. For information on Bristow's chamber compositions, see Rogers, 80–81, 143–49, 160–61, 169–70. Hopkins created a scholarly edition of Quartette No. 1, but otherwise there are neither publications nor commercial recordings of any of these works.

40. The Cremona Quartet performed the second quartet at Queensborough Community College on June 10, 1979, and a quartet of instrumentalists from the New York Philharmonic performed it at the Graduate Center, City University of New York, on December 2, 2002. See press release dated May 29, 1979, in the Bristow Collection, Additions; the program is in https://archives.nyphil.org. There is a nonprofessional recording from the Cremona Quartet performance. My thanks to John Graziano for sharing a copy of this recording.

41. Bethany Goldberg, "Curtis, George Henry" *AGII*; reviews from *Mirror*, April 13, 1849, 13, and *Albion*, April 14, 1849, 176; both cited in Lawrence I: 599.

42. "Eleutheria Grand Cantata," April 9, 1849, *NYH*, [3]; Advertisement, *BDE*, Feb. 18, 1850, 2.

43. *BDE*, Feb. 22, 1850, 3, quoted in Thurston Dox, *American Oratorios and Cantatas: A Catalog of Works Written in the United States from Colonial Times to 1985*, 2 vols. (Metuchen, NJ: Scarecrow Press, 1986), I: 421.

44. The dates were February 21, 1850, and April 25, 1851. "By Particular Desire," April 20, 1849, *NYH*, [3]; "City Items," April 26, 1851, *NYDTrib*, 9.

45. Rogers refers to the work as the Overture in E-flat, but the Philharmonic program (Jan. 9, 1847, https://archives.nyphil.org) has it titled Concert Overture. Bristow's holograph in the NYPL has no title. See Rogers, 147, and Lawrence I: 130. Rogers's date (189) for the overture's premiere (March 1, 1853) is incorrect.

46. "The Philharmonic," letter dated March 9, 1854, from H. C. Timm, *MW*, March 18, 1854, 121–22; Rogers, 76.

47. Rogers, 147.

48. *Albion*, Jan. 16, 1846, 35–36; *Mirror*, Jan. 13, 1847, quoted in Lawrence I: 424.

49. *C&E*, Jan. 16, 1847, quoted in Lawrence I: 424.

50. Concert program, https://archives.nyphil.org. Lawrence suggests that this lack of comment is "indicative of the current American attitude towards native musicians," i.e., that they were basically ignored. Lawrence I: 423.

51. Eisfeld lived in New York from 1848 to 1866. Howard Shanet and Bethany Goldberg, "Theodor Eisfeld," *GMO*.

52. A holograph full score, a reorchestrated Minuet, and manuscript partial score (for piano) are in the Bristow Collection. See also Rogers, 147–48, and Lawrence II: 130–32. Rogers's (189) premiere date (Feb. 8, 1853) is erroneous. See *MB*, June 15, 1850, 362.

53. Douglas Shadle, *Orchestrating the Nation: The Nineteenth-Century American Symphonic Enterprise* (New York: Oxford University Press, 2016), 74–75.

54. "Domestic Compositions," *SMT*, June 1, 1850, 422. According to Lawrence, Henry Watson advised "homegrown composers" to study foreign models and write accordingly. Lawrence I: 598–99. Other critics, as we shall see, gave similar advice. I deal with this issue in "American Orchestral Music," esp. xlvi–lxi and later. Shadle, 77.

55. Part of the *Staats-Zeitung* review was published in translation in "Music," *NYDTrib*, Feb. 12, 1853, 4; "The Eleventh and Final Lecture," *NYDTrib*, Feb. 11, 1853, 5. Thayer's identity is from Lawrence II: 253n and 384n.

56. *MB*, June 15, 1850, 362, and "Symphony in E-flat Major," *MB*, July 1, 1850, 377. Crouch's identity as the *MB* critic is from Lawrence II: 4n and 15. See also Bruce Carr, "Crouch, Frederick Nicholls," *GMO*, and John Warrack, "Crouch, Frederick Nicholls (1808—1896)," *ODNB*.

57. See "Band Music Then and Now," *NYT*, June 29, 1879, 10. See also Cipolla, "Dodworth," *GMO*. Shanet (423–24n42), however, points out that the memories of the founding members were frequently both faulty and shaded by subsequent events.

58. *Constitution and By-laws of the Philharmonic Society of New York. Adopted April 1843* (New York: Printed by S. W. Benedict and Co., 1843). Bylaw 7 is on page 14. Another copy of the constitution and bylaws, "containing all the amendments to January 1847," was published in 1847; bylaw 7 is still present. See https://archives.nyphil.org.

59. There were no additional American orchestral compositions performed in subscription concerts until March 1856, with the premiere performance of Bristow's Symphony No. 2. A serenade by William Mason was performed by a quartet in March 1853, and several solo works (concertos) by Europeans living in New York (Eisfeld, William Wallace, and the Mol-

lenhauer brothers) were presented during 1854 and 1855. See programs in https://archives .nyphil.org.

60. "To the President . . . of the Philharmonic Society," *NYH*, Dec. 16, 1848, [2], letter dated Dec. 14, 1848. My citation for this letter in "American Orchestral Music" (xlix) is incorrect.

61. *MB*, Nov. 15, 1849, 130. The author of this commentary identifies himself as an American (so he was not Crouch). Lawrence describes the 1853 editor (and presumably critic) of the *MB* as "a frustratingly anonymous 'gentleman of high literary and musical accomplishments.'" Lawrence I: 572.

62. "Musical Season Over," *SMT*, May 25, 1850, 410–11. For repertoire, see https://archives .nyphil.org.

63. See "Second Letter from Mr. Bristow," *MW&T*, April 1, 1854, 148–53. I deal with this issue in more detail in chapter 2 and in "American Orchestral Music," esp. lxii.

## INTERLUDE A. *Pedagogy I: Private Teaching*

1. Bristow, "Life," 60.
2. *Mirror*, Sept. 1, 1846, quoted in Lawrence I: 372.
3. Lawrence I: 494. About the AMI, see Lawrence I: 372, 492–94, 531–35.
4. Bristow, "Life," 41.
5. Ibid., 34–35. As mentioned in chapter 1, he also had an annual stipend of $125 as a church organist (roughly $4,350 in 2019 purchasing power).
6. Ibid., 35; *Doggett's New-York City Street Directory* (New York: John Doggett, 1846–1847). When this move occurred is unknown, but according to notes in the Gohari Collection, William Bristow purchased land in Bushwick in September 1845. Bristow told Travis Quigg (*AM* IV: 8) that in the mid-1840s he had lived "a short distance" from 16 Mercer Street (James Pirsson's residence from 1845 to 1847). According to the 1850 census (via www.ancestry.com), however, his official abode was in Brooklyn with his parents and siblings Angelina, Sarah, Charlotte, Mary, Caroline, William, and Edward. The Bristows disappear from the city directories of Manhattan and Brooklyn from 1848 to 1854. In the mid-1850s George shows up in the *New York City Directory for 1854–55* (New York: Charles R. Rode); William resurfaces as a Brooklyn resident in *Smith's Brooklyn Directory for the Year Ending May 1, 1856* (Brooklyn, 1856).
7. Bristow, "Life," 39.
8. Ibid., 38–39.
9. Ibid., 39–40, 52, 51, 53.
10. Ibid., 44–45.
11. *Trow's New York City Directory* (NY: J. F. Trow, 1854–1855).
12. Quotations from Bristow, "Life," 45–46. The other nocturnes are "La Pensée," op. 9; "La Belle de la Joi," op. 11; "Innocence," op. 14; and "La belle nuit," op. 20. Only "Blue Bell," op. 27, falls outside the 1850–1852 date range. "La Serenade Nocturne," op. 8, is for orchestra.
13. Rogers, 137.
14. Ibid., 90, 130, 193. According to Rogers, a copy of this imprint is in the collection at the Sibley Library at Eastman.

15. George F. Bristow, preface to *George F. Bristow's New and Improved Method for the Reed or Cabinet Organ* (New York: R. A. Saalfield, 1887). A copy is in the Bristow Collection.

16. The collection *Bristow's Two-Part Vocal Exercises* (op. 75) (New York: J. Van Loan, 1890) is labeled "Volume 2," but no "Volume 1" is known to exist.

## CHAPTER 2. *Fry and Willis*

1. The description is from an undated Mathew Brady photograph of the *Tribune* editorial staff (Division of Prints and Photographs, LC). Brady's notes identify Fry. Journalist Beman Brockway, who worked at the *Tribune* from 1853 to 1854, also identifies the May 1854 editorial staff, and all but one of those individuals are in the Brady portrait. Brockway, *Fifty Years in Journalism* (Watertown, NY: Daily Times Printing and Publishing Co., 1891), 141. Information about Brockway is from Catherine C. Mitchell, ed., *Margaret Fuller's New York Journalism* (Knoxville: University of Tennessee Press, 1995), 11. The *Tribune* was known as the *Daily Tribune* from 1842 to 1866.

2. Brockway, 172, 31; Advertisement, Nov. 29, 1852, 5, and "Amusements," Feb. 8, 1853, 5, both in *NYDTrib*. For Fry's lecture series, see Lawrence II: 254–60, 380–89.

3. Advertisement, *NYDTrib*, Nov. 29, 1852, 1; Upton, 121–22, 107; Rogers, 104; "Amusements," *NYT*, Nov. 29, 1852, 5; Lawrence II: 254–60, 380.

4. Rogers, 92; Lawrence II: 229n.

5. Upton, 51.

6. "The Eleventh and Final Lecture," *NYDTrib*, Feb. 11, 1853. 5.

7. Lawrence II: 388.

8. *Illustrated London News*, Nov. 9, 1850; quoted in Adam Carse, *The Life of Jullien* (Cambridge, UK: Heffer, 1949), 66.

9. See Preston, "'Concentration of Talent'"; "American Orchestral Music," especially parts 4–5; and "Encouragement from an Unexpected Source: Louis Antoine Jullien, Mid-Century American Composers, and George Frederick Bristow's *Jullien Symphony*," *Nineteenth-Century Music Review* vi: 1 (2009): 65–87.

10. Lawrence II: 368; Rogers, 117.

11. "Amusements," *NYT*, Dec. 29, 1853, 5; "George F. Bristow," *Brainard's*, Nov. 1877, reprinted in E. Douglas Bomberger, ed., *Brainard's Biographies of American Musicians* (Westport, CT: Greenwood, 1999), 46. The symphony was never identified in Jullien's programs by its nickname, so its subtitle and programmatic implications were not known to the public.

12. There is a holograph score.

13. For an in-depth examination of the symphony, see my "American Orchestral Music," part 7.

14. No title, *NYDTrib*, Dec. 31, 1853, 5. Fry also described Bristow's musical forms as "strictly classic" in "Rejoinder from Mr. Fry," *MW&T*, Feb. 18, 1854, 75.

15. Fried, 33; Willis, "The Philharmonic Society," *NYMW*, March 8, 1856, 110; "M. Jullien's Concerts," *The Times* (London), Dec. 11, 1854.

16. For information on brass in the New York soundscape, see Preston, "American Orchestral Music," esp. xcii, fn348. Bristow also benefited from the presence of Jullien's virtuoso trombonist William Winterbottom (1821–1889). For (limited) information on

Winterbottom, see Trevor Herbert, *The Trombone* (New Haven, CT: Yale University Press, 2006), 144–45, 154, 156; Shadle, 102.

17. *MW&T*, Jan. 7, 1854, 5

18. *NYDTrib*, Dec. 31, 1853. Autograph Letter Signed (hereafter ALS), Hill (London) to Bristow (New York), March 25, 1855, Bristow Collection, Additions. For the symphony's reception in the UK, its 1856 premiere performance, and a thorough critical examination of the work, see Preston, "American Orchestral Music" and chapter 3 in this book.

19. "Philharmonic Society," *MB*, May 1, 1850, 313–14; "Art National and Art Universal," *JFA*, May 1,1851, 50; Quigg, *AM* IV: 8.

20. Shadle, 83; Shanet, 109–110; Lawrence II: 229n.

21. The expression is from Lawrence II: 378. I also deal with the contretemps in some detail in "American Orchestral Music," esp. lxx–lxxx.

22. Gilbert Chase, *America's Music, From the Pilgrims to the Present*, rev. 3rd ed. (Urbana: Illinois Press, 1987), 313; Advertisement, *NYT*, Dec. 29, 1853.

23. "Musical News from Everywhere: New York," *MW&T*, Jan. 7, 1854, 5–6.

24. "A Letter from Mr. Fry," *MW&T*, Jan. 21, 1854, 29.

25. "Rejoinder from Mr. Fry," *MW&T*, Feb. 18, 1854, 74–76. For the various issues of *DJM* that include the reprints, see Lawrence II: 479–89, and my discussion in "American Orchestral Music," lxx–lxxx.

26. "Mr. Fry and His Critics," *DJM*, Feb. 4, 1854, 140–42 (quote from 141); *MW&T*, Feb. 18, 1854, 75.

27. "The Philharmonic Society. Letter from Mr. Bristow," *MW&T*, March 4, 1854, 100.

28. "William H. Fry," *DJM*, Feb. 25, 1854, 166–67.

29. "Reply," *MW&T*, March 4, 1854, 100.

30. Letters from the Philharmonic Society (or members of it), March 11, 1854, 109–110; March 18, 1854, 121–22; and March 25, 1854, 133, *MW & T*.

31. "Second Letter from Mr. Bristow," *MW & T*, April 1, 1854, 148–49.

32. Bristow's second and third letters: April 1, 1854, and "Letter from Mr. Bristow," April 22, 183–84, both in *MW&T*. Bristow missed five performances: the final concert of 1853–1854 (April 22), and four during 1854–1855. See https://archives.nyphil.org/programs. Rogers (87) erroneously states that he was absent only until the end of the 1853–1854 season.

33. See, for example, *The Knickerbocker*, xlii: 3 (March 1854), 316–17, and George William Curtis, "Editorial Notes—Music," *Putnam's Monthly Magazine of American Literature, Science, and Art* 3, no. 17 (May 1854): 564–65.

34. For information on Bristow's election to the board of directors, see Shanet, 112, and Board of Directors Meeting Minutes, Sept. 14,1853, https://archives.nyphil.org. *MW&T*, April 1, 1854.

35. The paraphrase from Hill is from *MW&T*, April 1, 1854. Hill accompanied Jullien's orchestra on its spring tours, which might also indicate his displeasure at the situation in New York. He did not, however, resign from the Philharmonic Society, for he performed in the concerts given in March and April 1854. Preston, "Concentration of Talent," 337, and https://archives.nyphil.org.

36. "The Operatic Ring," *AAJ*, Oct. 2, 1886, 386. See also Preston, "'A German for the Germans': Theodore Thomas as Musical Director of the American Opera Company,"

unpublished paper presented to the American Musicological Society (Nov. 13, 2015), (revised) the Society for American Music (March 10, 2016), *OfP*, 466–68.

37. Ritter, 273–74; Louis C. Elson, *American Music* (New York: Macmillan, 1904), 113; Chase, 308; Lawrence II: 484.

38. "Musical Matters," *NYDTrib*, Dec. 18, 1898, 10; Shadle, 88.

39. Quigg, *AM* IV: 7.

40. For further information on these performances, see "American Orchestral Music," xlvi. Jullien regularly misidentified the third movement as Andante, as did the Philharmonic Society in its 1856 program. Bristow's holograph score, however, clearly has this movement marked Adagio.

41. "Amusements," *NYT*, June 15, 1854, 5.

42. "M. Jullien's Farewell Benefit," *NYDTrib*, June 27, 1854, 4.

43. "The Farewell Benefit of Jullien at the Crystal Palace," *MR&CA*, July 6, 1854, 232–33.

44. "The Philharmonic Society," *MW&T*, March 18, 1854, 122.

45. *MW&T*, April 1, 1854, 153.

46. ALS, [Jullien] to Bristow, Dec. 14, 1854, Bristow Collection, Additions.

47. Letter from Justitia (Hopkins), *MW*, June 16, 1855, 74.

48. "Musical Correspondence, New York, Dec. 16," *DJM*, Dec. 20, 1856, 93; Shadle, 111.

49. "Musical Intelligence," *MW*, June 6, 1857, 344–45.

50. ALS, Hill to Bristow, March 25, 1855, Bristow Collection, Additions. The critic was W. J. Davison. Also see J. C. Hadden, rev. Anne Pimlott Baker, "Hill, Thomas Henry Weist, *ODNB*.

## CHAPTER 3. *The 1850s*

1. Bristow, "Life," 35

2. Ibid., 29.

3. Gohari, "Gleanings," 37, and Yellin, 252n13. Rogers (82) is incorrect about the date.

4. Population information from http://www.demographia.com/dm-nyc.htm *and* https://www1.nyc.gov/assets/planning/download/pdf/data-maps/nyc-population/historical-population/1790-2000_nyc_total_foreign_birth.pdf. Ira Rosenwaike, *Population History of New York City* (Syracuse University Press, 1972), 42.

5. "Amusements," Oct. 24, 1856, 7, and Oct. 23, 1857, 6, from *NYH*; Lawrence II: 753.

6. Vera Brodsky Lawrence, *Strong on Music*, vol. 3, *Repercussions. 1857–1862* (hereafter, Lawrence III) (Chicago: University of Chicago Press, 1999), 434.

7. N. Lee Orr, *Dudley Buck* (Urbana: University of Illinois Press, 2008), 25–26.

8. Ibid.; Stanley Boorman, Eleanor Selfridge-Field, and Donald Krummel, "Printing and Publishing of Music," (iv) 19th-Century Developments, *GMO*.

9. James Smith, Thomas Brawley, and N. Lee Orr, "Choral Music," *AGII*.

10. Rogers, 92. Bristow inexplicably resigned from his position in April 1856 and was replaced by Carl Bergmann, only to be reinstated the following September. See "City Items," *NYDTrib*, April 8, 1856, 7; Lawrence II: 145, 736–37; "The Harmonic Society," *NYMW*, Nov. 1, 1856, 554.

11. Rogers, 92; "Musical Intelligence," Sept. 28, 1854, 338, and "New-York Harmonic Society," Nov. 29, 1856, 372, both in *MR&G*.

12. Ritter, 298.

13. Ibid., 296–98; Rogers, 92–93.

14. Smith/Brawley/Orr, "Choral Music"; Rogers, 92–93. Repertoire information is from reviews and advertisements in New York City newspapers during this period. Hopkins's quote (writing as Timothy Trill) is from *NYDisp*, Jan. 5, 1861, as quoted by Lawrence III: 433–34.

15. Lawrence II: 393, 345; "Amusements," *NYT*, May 3, 1854, 5. Other information is from New York and Brooklyn newspapers.

16. Lawrence II: 494, 650. Rogers (102) reports that Bristow conducted some forty-five to fifty "known performances" with the Harmonic Society and other choral societies he led, in addition to at least that many benefit or special-events concerts for chorus, orchestra, or both.

17. "New-York Harmonic Society," *NYT*, Oct. 13, 1856, 6.

18. *MW*, July 1, 1852, 358; "Harmonic Society," *DJM*, Nov. 25, 1854, 62; "Oratorio of the Messiah," *NYT*, Dec. 25, 1858, 5.

19. "Amusements," *NYT*, Nov. 15, 1854, 4.

20. "Anniversary of the Battle of New-Orleans," *NYDTrib*, Jan. 9, 1856, 5; "Eighth of January: Anniversary of the Battle of New-Orleans," *NYT*, Jan. 9, 1856, 1.

21. Preston, *Opera on the Road* (hereafter, *OoR*), 265–67, 371n39; "English Opera at Niblo's," *NYDTrib*, May 24, 1855, 5.

22. Lawrence II: 622; Quigg, *AM* V: 7.

23. For the 1855–1856 tour of the Pyne and Harrison Company, see *OoR*, chapter 6. Reiff was born in May 1830; Quigg, *AM* V:7. It is interesting to speculate what a difference such an experience might have had on Bristow's life.

24. Lawrence II: 622; *MW*, Sept. 15, 1855, 229.

25. "The New Opera of *Rip van Winkle*," *NYDTrib*, Sept. 29, 1855, 6–7. Rogers (107) provides no sources for this information.

26. Wainwright was the son of Bishop Wainwright; see Interlude B. For an online copy of the original story, see "Rip van Winkle: A Posthumous Writing of Diedrich Knickerbocker," https://www.gutenberg.org/files/2048/2048-h/2048-h.htm#link2H_4_0008.

27. "Musical Correspondence," *DJM*, Oct. 6, 1855, 6; "Amusements," *NYT*, Sept. 29, 1855, 4; Ledbetter, vii–xi, description on ix.

28. Preston, *OoR*, 265; *NYDTrib*, Sept. 29, 1855; *DJM*, Oct. 6, 1855. There is a recording of the overture to the opera (see the Discography) but no professional recording of the opera itself.

29. *DJM*, Oct. 6, 1855; "Niblo's Garden—'Rip van Winkle,'" *NYH*, Oct. 2, 1855, 4; *NYT*, Sept. 29, 1855.

30. Ledbetter, ix; "The New Opera of Rip van Winkle," *NYDTrib*, Sept. 29, 1855, 6.

31. *NYH*, Oct. 2, 1855. The identity of the *Herald* critic during this period is from Lawrence II: 532.

32. *NYT*, Sept. 29, 1855; "Musical Chit Chat," *DJM*, Oct. 6, 1855, 7; *NYDTrib*, Sept. 29, 1855.

33. *NYH*, Oct. 2, 1855; *NYT*, Sept. 29, 1855.

34. "Rip van Winkle," *NYMW*, Oct. 13, 1855, 178–79; *NYT*, Sept. 29, 1855.

35. *DJM*, Oct. 6, 1855, 7; *NYMW*, Oct. 13, 1855; *NYT*, Sept. 29, 1855.

36. There is an excellent modern recording of both the *Winter's Tale* and *Rip Van Winkle* overtures (see the Discography for details). For more overture information, see my liner notes for the CD.

37. "The Drama," *Leslie's*, Feb. 23, 1856, 167; "Amusements," *NYT*, April 6, 1857, 3; "Mr. Bristow's Complimentary Concert," *NYEP*, March 8, 1859, n.p.

38. As noted in chapter 3, Bristow missed a total of five performances.

39. The peace offering idea is from Lawrence (II: 676), and it seems plausible. The society paid for the cost of copying parts. (Those used by Jullien's Orchestra presumably belonged to the conductor.) See Annual Report (1855–1856), financial records, and program in https://archives.nyphil.org.

40. Lawrence II: 676.

41. Trovator, "Musical Correspondence," *DJM*, March 8, 1856, 180; "N. Y. Philharmonic Society," *Leslie's*, March 15, 1856, 265.

42. As mentioned in chapter 2, the Philharmonic Society also incorrectly identified the third movement. "The Philharmonic Society," *NYMW*, March 8, 1856, 110.

43. "The Philharmonic Concert," *MR&G*, March 8, 1856, 68–69.

44. "Musical: The Philharmonic Society," *NYDTrib*, March 3, 1856, 3.

45. According to Lawrence (II: 577n), Girac became critic of the *Albion* in September 1855.

46. Gamma, "Music," *Albion*, March 8, 1856, 115.

47. Thurston Dox, "George Frederick Bristow and the New York Public Schools," *American Music* 9, no. 4 (1991): 339–52.

48. Recordings of this symphony are available in LP and digital formats. (See the Discography for details.) All of the recordings have the two inner movements inverted. There is some confusion about the sequence of movements in the holograph, as the final page of the first movement has "segue Andante," with "Andante" crossed out and "Scherzo" written in. But the public performances by the Philharmonic Societies of New York (1859) and Brooklyn (April 1, 1871), in which the composer participated, both followed the amended holograph. Programs in the Bristow Collection, Additions, and at https://archives.nyphil .org. There is no published score.

49. Thomson's *Seasons* is found in *The Cyclopedia of Practical Quotations*, ed. J. K. Hoyt (New York: Funk and Wagnalls, 1896); Collins's *Ode for Music* is in *A Cyclopedia of Poetical Quotations*, ed. H. G. Adams (London: Groombridge and Sons, 1881 (1st ed., 1853).

50. Fried, 55; Shadle, 130; correspondence from Trovator, *DJM*, April 2, 1859, 6. The identity of this critic is unknown (Lawrence III: 120n); "Music in New-York," *MR&G*, April 2, 1859, 99.

51. *MR&G*, April 2, 1859.

52. "Philharmonic Society," *MW*, April 2, 1858, 210; "Correspondence," *DJM*, April 2, 1859.

53. "From Our New York Musical Correspondent," *BFP*, March 30, 1859, [1]. Thanks to Douglas Shadle for this article.

54. Historians have assumed that the difference in reception represents a marked

improvement in compositional skill and style between the two works. That this is not the case is demonstrated by the modern recordings of both symphonies.

55. "Amusements," *NYT*, March 28, 1859, 4.

56. *BFP*, March 30, 1859; *MR&G*, April 2, 1859.

57. *MR&G*, April 2, 1859.

58. "Philharmonic Society," *MW*, April 2, 1858.

59. Lawrence III: 283–85. Quotation (by Lawrence) from *Sunday Press*, May 21, 1859; Rogers, 88–89, "Amusements," *NYDTrib*, May 16, 1859, 2; "Amusements," *NYT*, June 22, 1859, 7.

60. Rogers, 89; Lawrence III: 194n; Philharmonic Society, 1858 Annual Report, https://archives.nyphil.org.

61. "Amusements," *NYT*, Feb. 23, 1859, 2.

62. "Amusements," *NYT*, March 5, 1859, 3.

63. "Complimentary Concert to George F. Bristow," *Leslie's*, March 5, 1859, 216.

64. "Amusements," *NYT*, March 9, 1859, 4; *DJM*, March 12, 1859, 397.

65. ALS, Meignen (Philadelphia) to Bristow (New York), March 5, 1858, Bristow Collection, Additions; *Address of the Harmonia Sacred Music Society of Philadelphia, with its Constitution and By-Laws* (Philadelphia: Crissy and Markley, printer, 1852), https://archive.org/details/addon00harm/page/n11.

66. See *Laws of the General Assembly of the Commonwealth of Pennsylvania* (Harrisburg: A. Boyd Hamilton, State Printer, 1857), 296–97, https://babel.hathitrust.org/cgi/pt?id=uc1 .b3830857;view=1up;seq=352.

## INTERLUDE B. *Sacred Music*

1. Bristow, "Life," 54–55. He first mentions (34) a position "at a small church" in 1845 or 1846, for which he was paid $125 (approx. $4,350) per year. Lee Orr, however, has pointed out that some wealthier congregations paid quite well. Orr is also the source of information that May 1 was the traditional contract-signing date for churches. Email communication with Orr, May 1, 2018, and July 18, 2019.

2. Orr, *Buck*, 25–26.

3. Email message from Orr to the author, May 9, 2018. Orr's coverage of choral music developments in Victorian America (in his book *Dudley Buck*) is excellent and succinct.

4. Arthur Henry Messiter, *A History of the Choir and Music of Trinity Church, New York* (New York: Edwin S. Gorham, 1906), 321–24.

5. Ibid.; the Psalter was compiled by Henry Cutler, Trinity organist.

6. John Ogasapian and N. Lee Orr, *Music of the Gilded Age* (Westport, CT: Greenwood, 2007), 76.

7. See Rogers, 128, 131–32; and Preston, "American Orchestral Music," xxiii, xxv. More recent contributions are from Bailey, 40–45.

8. Bristow, "Life," 55; "Rev. Jonathan Mayhew Wainwright," https://www.findagrave .com/memorial/104271115/jonathan-mayhew-wainwright; "Choirs of New York and Brooklyn," *MB*, July 1, 1850, 376, confirms Bristow's position at St. John's. A previous

organist (Edward Hodges) left St. John's in 1846, which may have been when Bristow started there. L. M. Middleton/Nilanjani Banerji, "Hodges, Edward," *DNB*.

9. "Cathedral Organ," *Albany Journal*, Oct. 22, 1852; see also "Magnificent Cathedral Organ," *NYT*, Oct. 29, 1852, 6.

10. Rogers, 128; Henry Anstice, *History of St. George's Church in the City of New York* (New York: Harper & Bros., 1911), 196–97; "Musical Correspondence," *DJM*, Feb. 5, 1859, 359; Robert Bruce Mullin, "Tyng, Stephen Higginson," *ANB*.

11. "Church Music in New York," *DJM*, Feb. 23, 1861, 380; "The Feast of St. John's," *NYT*, Dec. 28, 1861, 4; "Organists and Singers in New York," *DJM*, May 14, 1864, 236–37.

12. Advertisement, *NYDH*, March 9, 1865, 7. The address was that of the Bristow and Hardenbrook piano store.

13. In 2019 the purchasing power of $2,500 (1865) would be roughly $40,000, $1,500 ($24,500), $500 ($8,000), and $200 ($3,200); Anstice, 196–97.

14. Bristow, "Life," 56, 60.

15. "Grand Organ Concert," Nov. 15, 1866, *NYH*, 8; "Amusements: Organ Exhibition and Concert," Dec. 4, 1866, *NYT*, 7.

16. Funeral information: Mortuary Notice, *NYH*, Dec. 15, 1898, [1]; information about these events is found in New York newspapers.

17. Bailey (40) first identified Zion Church as an employer. See also "Christmas at the Churches, Dec. 25, 1869, 3, and "Dawn of the Church," April 1, 1877, 6, both from the *NYH*; and "New York Church Choirs for '77–'78," *MTR*, iii: 12 (April 18, 1877), 205. "Easter Day," April 17, 1870, 8, and "The Christmas Festival," Dec. 24, 1876, 2, both from *NYT* (from Bailey). The June 18, 1876, issue of the *MTR* (58) notes that Bristow "still retains the leadership" at Zion. He left his position there at the end of April 1878. See "Trade Chat," *MTR*, iv: 4 (June 18, 1877), 76. For Holy Trinity Church: "Trinity Church, Harlem," July 10, 1871, 6, "Surrexit!," March 31, 1871, 5, and "Surrexit! Easter Sunday and Its Rejoicings," March 31, 1872, 5, all from the *NYH*.

18. "Music in the Churches," *NYT*, Dec. 25, 1878, 3, from Bailey, 40. For more information, see Bailey, 41n158, and http://holytrinityinwood.org/history/. "Christmas Music in the Churches," *AAJ*, Dec. 24, 1881, 170, confirms Bristow's position at Holy Trinity (Harlem) in 1881. According to the *Metropolitan Church and Choir Directory of New York and Brooklyn* (1888–1889) (New York: Metropolitan Printing and Publishing Company) (114), Bristow was still at the First Collegiate Reformed Church in in 1889. For the Universalist congregation—since 1867 known as the Fourth Universalist Society of New York—see Rogers (132) and Bailey, 41–42. "Death of Rev. Charles H. Eaton," *Gunton's Magazine*, xxii (May 1902), 462–63.

19. Bailey, 42. Rogers suggests that after 1891 he served as organist at St. Ignatius Church (certainly St. Ignatius of Antioch), but Bailey reports that there is no record in the church archives of Bristow's service there. For the Twenty-third St. Church, see *Metropolitan Church and Choir Directory* (1892–1893), 23; Curtis, 563–64.

20. "St. Mary's Church, Mott Haven," in *MTR*, vii: 9 (Dec. 28, 1878), 10; *NYH*, April 1, 1877.

21. *NYH*, March 31, 1872.

22. *NYH*, Dec. 25, 1869. Bristow was director of the Harlem Mendelsohn Union from 1871 to 1873.

23. "The Easter Holidays" *NYH*, April 9, 1860, [1], and "Church Music in New York," *DJM*, Feb. 23, 1861, 380.

24. *NYH*, July 10, 1871, April 6 and 1, 1877.

25. "Some New York Choir Lofts," *NYH*, Feb. 1, 1891, 24.

26. William Osborne, "Warren, Samuel P.," *AGII*, and David Crean, "Samuel P. Warren: Organist at Grace Church, New York," DMA diss., Juilliard, 2014. For Fairlamb, see Bomberger, *Brainard's*; for Mosenthal, see Waldo Selden Pratt, ed., *Grove's Dictionary of Music and Musicians: American Supplement* (New York: Macmillan, 1944).

27. *NYH*, March 31, 1872.

28. For Warren's transcription, see https://www.amazon.com/Overture-Euryanthe-Transcribed-Samuel-Warren/dp/B003EAP3QO.

29. "Easter Music," April 6, 1890, 20, and "Music for Christmas Day," Dec. 20, 1890, 3; both from the *NYT*.

30. The Easter service at St. Barnabas's P. E. Church in 1879, for example, included the composer's Te Deum in B-flat, probably from his *Morning Service*, op. 51 (1873), in B-flat. See "Easter Music," *BDE*, April 12, 1879, 1.

31. The Music Library at Yale University has a copy of this work, self-published in 1855; Rogers, 191.

32. The Te Deum was dedicated to G. Sidney Sampson, Esq. (New York: Richard A. Saalfield, 1888); see Rogers, 162.

33. There is a holograph score for this work.

**CHAPTER 4.** *The 1860s*

1. Yellin, 237.

2. Bristow, "Life," 63.

3. *Trow's Directory*, 1854–1855; Yellin, 252n17.

4. Gohari, "Gleanings," 38. The 1910 Federal Census records Nina's birth year as 1857. Rogers (83–84) erroneously identifies "Nina Bristow" as another name for Louise.

5. ALS, Good to Holder, New York, Feb. 11, 1861, Bristow Collection, Additions.

6. George Templeton Strong mentions Good in his diary; see Lawrence II: 446; Rogers, 97–98. See also Yellin, 233–36.

7. ALS, Bristow (Mt. Vernon) to Holder, Aug. 23, 1862, Bristow Collection, Additions. Yellin (249) discusses this letter in some detail but was unaware that Holder was a widow; Gohari ("Gleanings") also corrects this.

8. Yellin, 245.

9. ALS, Bristow (New York) to Holder, Jan. 6, 1864. A photocopy and transcription of this letter are in the Victor Yellin Papers, Special Collections in Performing Arts, University of Maryland. Location of the original is unknown. My thanks to Christina Gibson at the University of Maryland for sending me electronic copies of these documents.

10. Walter Tallmann Westervelt, compiler, *Genealogy of the Westervelt Family* (New York: T. Z. Wright, 1905); Gohari, "Gleanings," 38.

11. The first reference to Bristow's home in Morrisania is in *Trow's Directory*, 1865–1866; Louis V. Grogan, *The Coming of the New York and Harlem Railroad* (Pawling, NY: privately published, 1989), 55.

12. According to the 1870 US Census, the Bristow household included two daughters: Nina Louise, age thirteen, and Estelle, age two. In the 1880 census the older daughter is identified as Louise (age twenty-two), the younger is Estelle (age twelve). US Federal Census, 1870 and 1880, www.Ancestry.com. Rogers (83) erroneously gives 1871 as Estelle's birth year.

13. According to Howard Shanet (181), the Philharmonic Society performed only one public rehearsal per concert. Matthew Reichert, however, provides dates that indicate that there were three public rehearsals per concert in the 1870s. See Reichert, "Carl Bergmann in New York: Conducting Activity 1852–1876," PhD diss., City University of New York, 2011, Table 4.1 (154–57), 187, and Table 4.4 (188–91). Sarah Palermo, archives assistant at the New York Philharmonic, confirms Reichert's conclusions and notes that this did not change until at least 1881. Email communication with Ms. Palermo, May 2, 2019.

14. In the early years of the Philharmonic Society orchestra, instrumentalists are listed on the program by instrument and in alphabetical order. Starting with 1860–1861, they are no longer listed alphabetically, which suggests that they were listed by rank. Programs, Annual Reports (1858 and 1859), and Business Meeting Minutes, 1866–1882, https://archives.nyphil.org; "The Reason Still Unexplained," *AAJ*, April 7, 1867, 376.

15. Maurice Edwards, *How Music Grew in Brooklyn: A Biography of the Brooklyn Philharmonic Orchestra* (Lanham, MD: Scarecrow Press, 2006), 10. Also see programs for the Philharmonic Society of Brooklyn at http://levyarchive.bam.org.

16. "Editorial Items," *WAJ*, Feb. 1, 1868, 206; "Excursions," *NYH*, July 22, 1861, 6.

17. Program, https://archives.nyphil.org; "Patriotism and Music," May 9, 1861, 4, and "Musical and Dramatic Matters," May 27, 1861, 2, both in *NYH*; Lawrence III: 436; "Bristow's Patriotic Concert," *NYDTrib*, May 27, 1861, 3.

18. The events took place in October 1861, April 1862, December 1862, and January 1863 and 1864. Advertisements are from the *NYDTrib*, the *NYT*, and the *NYH*.

19. See, for example, "Amusements," March 12, 1864, *NYDTrib*, 1.

20. See *MiG*, June 15, 1864; Bristow Collection, Additions.

21. G.F.W. (George F. Whicher), "Wallace, William Ross," *DAB*; Lawrence III: 445.

22. https://www.battlefields.org/learn/articles/civil-war-facts. ALS, Bristow to Louise Holder, Aug. 23, 1852, Bristow Collection, Additions.

23. Programs, April 2, 1864, and Nov. 17, 1866, https://archives.nyphil.org. The 1864 concert predates the "premiere" performance cited by H. Earle Johnson (91) (Oct. 28, 1865) and that cited by Rogers (192) (Dec. 9, 1865).

24. A holograph transcription is all that exists.

25. "New York Philharmonic Society First Concert—25th Season," *AAJ*, Nov. 22, 1866, 67–68 (quote, 68); "Fourth Philharmonic Concert," *BDE*, Feb. 28, 1870, 3.

26. "Philharmonic," *BDE*, Feb. 24, 1870, 3; "Final Concert of the Teachers' Association," *AAJ*, July 18, 1885, 196–97, cited in Bailey, 30; "The Musicians' Convention," *NYT*, July 4, 1885; 5; "Music," *NYTrib*, Aug. 12, 1889, 5.

27. For more detail, see Katherine K. Preston, *Opera for the People: English-Language Opera and Women Managers in Late 19th-Century America* (New York: Oxford University Press, 2017) (hereafter, *OfP*), 36.

28. By the 1860s Bristow could travel into Manhattan from Morrisania on the New

York and Harlem Railroad, which by 1841 extended from city hall to Fordham (north of Morrisania). See E. Clarence Hyatt, *History of the New York and Harlem Railroad* (Mt. Kisco, NY, 1898). There were also numerous horse-drawn street cars that connected city hall to other parts of Lower Manhattan. For somewhat later, see Edwin Bolitho, *The Columbus Historical Guide and Map of New York City: From Official Records and the Latest Government Surveys* (New York: Real Estate Record and Builders' Guide, 1891).

29. "Grand Concert" by W. K. Bassford, *AAJ*, Jan. 5, 1867; *NY Clipper*, Jan. 12, 1867, 318 (from *MiG*).

30. The premiere was not on January 29, as reported by Lawrence III: 443. See "Amusements," *NYH*, Feb. 18, 1861, 7. The manuscript full score at the New York Public Library is labeled "Opus 31," but the work was published in 1860 as op. 33. Although the work is identified in Rogers's worklist as "Gloria Patri. Praise to God," all contemporary references identify it by the English title. Brandon Moss, email communications, June and July 2019.

31. Thanks to Brandon Moss for sharing a copy of the dedication page and Bristow's explanatory note from the oratorio publication (Boston: Ditson, 1860). Timothy Trill (pseud.), "Bristow's Oratorio 'Praise to God,'" *NYDisp*, quoted in *DJM*, March 2, 1861, 388–89.

32. "Bristow's New Oratorio" (reprinted from *Albion*), *DJM*, March 23, 1861, 411–12; "Music in New York: 'Praise to God,' Oratorio by G. F. Bristow," *MR&MW*, March 2, 1861, 51; email correspondence from Moss, July 5, 2019; "New Oratorio," *NYDTrib*, Feb. 26, 1861, 7.

33. "The Academy of Music," *BDE*, March 15, 1861, 3; "Praise to God," *WAJ*, Jan. 18, 1868, 182.

34. *NYDTrib*, Feb. 26, 1861; *DJM*, March 2, 1861.

35. *DJM*, March 23, 1861, and March 2, 1861; email communications with Moss, June 28 and July 5, 2019.

36. See Rogers, 100; Odell VII: 367, 372; uncited quotation from Lawrence III: 531–32. Bristow did, however, conduct the society's Christmas concert on December 25, 1863 ("Amusements," *NYT*, Dec. 20, 1863, 7).

37. For more information about the infighting and competition between these two societies, see Quigg, *AM* V: 7 and Lawrence III: 343–435, 532. Some sources state that the society disbanded in 1868, but Ritter conducted from 1864 to 1870 and James Pech during 1870–1871. See Odell VII: 693, "New York Harmonic Society," *NYTrib*, April 21, 1870, 7; "New York Harmonic Society," *NYH*, April 20, 1870, 5, and "New-York Harmonic Society," *NYTrib*, June 27, 1871, 5.

38. Quoted in Lawrence III: 532.

39. Quigg, *AM* VII: 5.

40. Ibid.; "Musical and Theatrical," *DFP*, Sept. 23, 1867, 3.

41. Lawrence II: 568, 651; Rogers, 101.

42. Rogers, 100–102. Quigg, *AM* VII: 5; for the 1867–1868 repertoire, see "Amusements," *NYTrib*, Dec. 4, 1867, 7.

43. "Complimentary Presentation to Mr. George F. Bristow, the Composer," *WAJ* vii: 10 (June 29, 1867), 157; "Musical and Theatrical Gossip," *NYH*, June 23, 1867, 5. A portrait of Bristow was donated to the National Portrait Gallery (Smithsonian Institution) by Mrs.

Louis T. (Marion) Edwards, niece of Bristow's granddaughter Violet Dearborn Latham. It is tentatively dated 1871 with no artist attribution. The American portraitist Benoni Irwin (1840–1896) was in New York City in 1867 (see advertisement, *NYH*, April 8, 1867, 12) and was probably the "B. Irwin" identified as the painter of Bristow's 1867 portrait.

44. "Complimentary Presentation to Mr. George F. Bristow, the Composer," *WAJ*, June 29, 1867, 152.

45. Obituary, *BDE*, Aug. 19, 1867, 2.

46. "The Week," Dec. 7, 1867, 104; "Amusements of the Week," Nov. 16, 1867, 56, both in *WAJ*. There is a modern recording of *Daniel*. See Discography for details.

47. Griggs-Janower, *Daniel*, x. Information about Hardenbrook is from Yellin, 235. The holograph full score is in the Bristow Collection.

48. Griggs-Janower, *Daniel*, xii.

49. "Moments Musical," *WAJ*, July 27, 1867, 218; "George F. Bristow's Oratorio, 'Daniel,'" *WAJ*, Jan. 4, 1868, 158.

50. For an in-depth analysis of the oratorio, see the introduction to Griggs-Janower's scholarly edition; his article "Rescued from the Fiery Furnace: George Frederick Bristow's *Oratorio of Daniel*," *Choral Journal* 38, no. 9 (April 1998), 9–21; and the insightful discussion in Howard Smither's *History of the Oratorio*, vol. 4. *The Oratorio in the Nineteenth and Twentieth Centuries* (Chapel Hill: University of North Carolina Press, 2000), 467–81. A published libretto exists that includes only those portions of Hardenbook's libretto that Bristow used; apparently it was available to the public at the work's premiere.

51. Smither, 4: 472.

52. Griggs-Janower, *Daniel*, xiii; Johnson, 323.

53. Griggs-Janower, "Fiery Furnace," 9–21, esp. 14–15.

54. Smither, 4: 476; Griggs-Janower, *Daniel*, xii. See also the articles in *WAJ* about his oratorios: "George F. Bristow's Oratorio," Jan. 4, 1868; "Intellectual Advancement of Music in America," Jan. 18, 1868, 182; and "Second Performance of Daniel," Feb. 8, 1868, 218.

55. For information on Parepa-Rosa, see Preston, *OfP*, chapter 2; untitled article, *DJM*, Jan. 4, 1868, 168; *WAJ*, Feb. 8, 1868.

56. "Music: Daniel," *NYEP*, Dec. 30, 1867; untitled, *DJM*, Jan. 4, 1868, 168; *NYEM*, Dec. 31, 1867, 3, quoted in Smither, 479; "George F. Bristow's Oratorio, 'Daniel,'" *WAJ*, Jan. 4, 1868, 158.

57. "Mr. Bristow's New Oratorio, 'Daniel,'" *NYT*, Feb. 3, 1868, 4, and "Second Performance of Daniel," *WAJ*, Feb. 8, 1868.

58. *DJM*, Jan. 4, 1868; and *WAJ*, Feb. 8, 1868. Bailey (48–49) discusses the influence of Mendelssohn, Handel, Haydn, and Beethoven on the oratorio. Griggs-Janower, *Daniel* (xii) suggests that Bristow's "putative model" was Mendelssohn's *Elijah*.

59. *WAJ*, Jan. 18, 1868.

60. *NYT*, Feb. 3, 1868; *WAJ*, Feb. 8, 1868.

61. Smither, 481; David P. DeVenney, *Varied Carols: A Survey of American Choral Literature* (Westport, CT: Greenwood Press, 1999), 38–39.

62. Dox, *American Oratorios*; see esp. 2: 921–31; Orr, "Cantata," *AGII*.

63. "Amusements," May 26, 1860, 7, *NYT*; "Amusements," Feb. 26, 1868, *NYT*, 7; "Amusements," *BDE*, April 23, 1870, 1.

INTERLUDE C. *Pedagogy II: Teaching in Schools*

1. The best source for information about Bristow's career as a public school teacher is Thurston Dox, "Public Schools."

2. Bristow is listed as a teacher in the *Valentine's Manual* starting in 1857 (at school No. 44), but 1855 notices in the *Times* assert that he was teaching music in Ward School No. 44 by at least spring 1855 (probably for the 1854–1855 school year). See "New-York City," July 7, 1855, 8, and "Educational: Fifth Ward School No. 44," May 22, 1855, 3, both in *NYT*. See also *Valentine's Manual* (*Manual of the Corporation of the City of New York*, 1854–1898), 1857: 257, https://catalog.hathitrust.org/Record/008607621.

3. Dox claims that Bristow never worked in more than eight schools at once but cites no sources. Dox, "Public Schools," 341. I have confirmed a connection with only six: ward schools Nos. 7, 10, 20, 42, 44, and 47. See *Valentine's Manual*. My thanks to John Graziano for some of this information.

4. Dox, "Public Schools," 340–41.

5. Quoted by Dox, "Public Schools," 340.

6. Thomas Boese, *Public Education in the City of New York: Its History, Condition, and Statistics* (New York: Harper & Bros., 1869), 89.

7. Diane Ravitch, *The Great School Wars: A History of the New York Public Schools* (1974; New York: Basic Books, 1988), 94–95; George Frederick Bristow, "Music in the Public Schools of New York," *The Ninth Annual Meeting of the Music Teachers National Association Official Report* (New York: Music Teachers National Association, 1885), 28.

8. Bristow, "Public Schools," 30. Grammar schools sometimes required admissions tests; most elementary-school-age children in New York attended primary schools. See Boese, 131–39.

9. Bristow, "Public Schools," 38; *NYEP*, March 15, 1869, quoted by Ravitch, 89. During the 1860s the city superintendent believed that primary-school classes should number between sixty and one hundred students. See Ravitch, 102–103.

10. Boese, 132.

11. Information about Bristow's teaching assignments (in the author's possession) is from *Valentine's Manual* and notices in city newspapers. Boese, 132.

12. Bristow, "Public Schools," 28.

13. Frederick Wertz, "A New Look at the Demographics of a 19th-Century Lower East Side Neighborhood," New York Genealogical and Biographical Society, https://www.newyorkfamilyhistory.org/blog/new-look-demographics-19th-century-lower-east-side-neighborhood, 3–4; Stanley Nadel, *Little Germany: Ethnicity, Religion, and Class in New York City, 1845–80* (Urbana: University of Illinois Press, 1990), 37–39; Edwin G. Burrows and Mike Wallace, *Gotham: A History of New York City to 1898* (New York: Oxford University Press, 1999), 745; Bristow, "Public Schools," 28.

14. Ronald H. Bayor and Timothy J. Meagher, *The New York Irish* (Baltimore: Johns Hopkins University Press, 1996), 552–53.

15. Bristow, "Public Schools," 30; Ravitch, 101.

16. Bristow, "Public Schools," 30–31.

17. "New-York City," *NYDT*, July 4, 1855, 8.

18. "Commencement Exercises of Ward School No. 42," *NYDTrib*, July 15, 1865, 6.

19. Bristow, "Public Schools," 29; "Fifth Ward School, No. 44," *NYT*, Sept. 11, 1855, 8; "Amusements," *NYH*, May 20, 1856, 7.

20. "General News," April 8, 1864, 4, and "The Metropolitan Fair," April 8, 1864, 8, both in *NYT*.

21. "Grand Juvenile Beethoven Festival," *NYT*, May 23, 1870, 7.

22. "Juvenile Beethoven Festival," *NYH*, June 17, 1870, 7.

23. *NYT*, May 23, 1870.

24. Dox, "Public Schools," 341. These names also appear repeatedly in yearly issues of *Valentine's Manual*. Nash is listed in J. Thomas Scharf, *History of Westchester County, N. Y.* (Philadelphia: L. E. Preston, 1886), 1: 600.

25. Dox, "Public Schools," 343; "Amusements," *NYH*, Dec. 9, 1856, 7.

26. "Twelfth Ward School Concert," *WWAJ*, Feb. 25, 1865, 266. This headline is probably an error and refers instead to a concert by the Twelfth *Street* ward school. The Twelfth Ward was mostly rural in 1866.

27. Dox, "Public Schools," 343–44.

28. A copy is in the Bristow Collection.

29. Dox, "Public Schools," 346.

30. Rogers, 136–37.

31. "Music in our Public Schools," *WAJ*, Sept. 11, 1875, 196–97, quoted in Dox, "Public Schools," 348.

32. "Grammar School No. 42," *NYH*, June 30, 1877, 6.

33. Dox, "Public Schools," 348–49; Bristow, "Public Schools," 37.

34. Dox, "Public Schools," 250.

35. Ravitch, 102.

36. Lawrence III: 195; https://Cooper.edu/about/history.

37. Advertisement, *NYDTrib*, April 23, 1862, 2; "Cooper Institute Commencement," May 25, 1862, 3, and "Amusements," Dec. 23, 1862, 7, both in *NYT*; Lawrence III: 536.

38. "Musical Squabble," June 27, 1866, 2; "Card from the Instructors of the National Conservatory," June 13, 1866, 7; Advertisement, Sept. 18, 1867, 9, all from *NYH*.

39. "Commencement of the Musical Season," *AAJ*, Sept. 6, 1866.

40. "Musical," Oct. 22, 1871, 8; "For Sale—The National Conservatory of Music," Aug. 17, 1873, 9; "Musical," Sept. 28, 1873, 10, all from *NYH*.

41. "Musical," *NYH*, April 28, 1874, 13; "A Card," *NYH*, Jan. 17, 1875, 16.

42. Advertisement, *NYH*, Oct. 3, 1875, 4.

43. "Musical," Sept. 5, 1880, 3, and "Musical, Nov. 11, 1883, 4, both in *NYH*; "The Grand Conservatory's Concert," *NYTrib*, June 23, 1898, 16.

44. "Musical," Nov. 19, 1882, 21, and "New-York College of Music," Dec. 8, 1878, 17, both in *NYH*.

45. Advertisements, Jan. 12, 1879, 16; Nov. 23, 1879, 20; and April 16, 1882, 27, all in *NYH*.

46. "Musical," Oct. 10, 1880, 13; Feb. 12, 1882, 4, both in *NYH*.

47. "In the World of Music," *NYT*, Dec. 18, 1898, 6.

1. "Musical and Dramatic Notes," *NYH*, Aug. 25, 1870, 5; "Amusements," *NYH*, Nov. 17, 1870, 9; "Amusements," *NYT*, Jan. 15, 1871, 7; "Amusements," *BDE*, Jan. 29, 1871, 1; "Amusements," *NYH*, Feb. 17, 1871, 2; "Amusements," *NYH*, March 12, 1871, 4; "Miss Nilsson in Oratorio," *NYT*, March 16, 1871, 4.

2. Odell IX: 208; Henry Edward Krehbiel, *Notes on the Cultivation of Choral Music and the Oratorio Society of New York* (New York: Edward Schuberth and Co., 1884), 51.

3. "New-York City," *NYTrib*, July 23, 1875, 8; "Amusements," Oct. 8 and 16, 1875 (pp. 7 and 9), both in *NYT*; "Oratorio at Steinway Hall," Oct. 21, 1875, 10, and "Amusements," Nov. 24, 1875, 2, both in *NYH*. The Centennial Choral Union's demise is reported in "Amusements," *NYT*, Dec. 29, 1875, 5.

4. "Amusements," *NYH*, Nov. 26, 1870, 10; "Music: Miss Nilsson in the Creation," *NYTrib*, March 16, 1871, 5; "Amusements," *NYT*, Oct. 25, 1871, 8.

5. "Plymouth Organ Concerts," March 17, 1871, May 3 and 4, 1871, 4, both from *BDE*.

6. "Musical and Dramatic," *Leslie's*, Jan. 7, 1871, 275; and "Amusements," *NYT*, Jan. 15, 1871, 7.

7. I discuss the repercussions of the financial crisis on the production of music more thoroughly in my *OfP* (154–63), but a chart of the financial receipts of the Philharmonic Society from 1867 to 1884 (Shanet, 61) clearly illustrates the effects of the Panic on concert life in New York.

8. "Fourth Philharmonic Concert," *BDE*, Feb. 28, 1870, 3. See "William Cadwallader Hudson," *The Writer*, January, 1892, 2–3.

9. For more on Richings, see chapter 2 in *OfP*.

10. Odell IX: 25.

11. "Mr. Bristow's Rip van Winkle," *NYTrib*, Nov. 11, 1870, 5. According to Brian Thompson, the Richings Company also performed *Rip Van Winkle* in Chicago and Philadelphia. See Thompson, "Henri Drayton, English Opera and Anglo-American Relations, 1850–1872," *Journal of the Royal Musical Association*, cxxxvi: 2 (2011): 247–303, p. 298.

12. "Musical: Mr. Bristow's Opera," *NYT*, Nov. 10, 1870, 5; "Musical and Dramatic," *Leslie's*, Nov. 26, 1870, 163.

13. "Musical and Dramatic," *Leslie's*, July 15, 1871, 295; Quigg, *AM* VI: 9.

14. Rogers, 180. I followed Rogers's lead in my introduction to the "Jullien" Symphony, but Bailey argues persuasively that the composition dates from earlier in the decade. Holograph vocal score of the ode and a copy of the 1880 publication (New York: Bigelow and Main) are at the Newberry Library in Chicago; holograph score of the overture, incomplete instrumental parts, and some vocal sketches are in the Bristow Collection, *NYPL*. See Rogers, 194; Preston, "American Orchestral Music," xxv; and Bailey, 139–40.

15. Other representative poems include "National Song," "Battle Hymn," "In Memoriam—Gettysburg," and "The American Union" (New York: E. O. Jenkins, printer, 1864). A piano/vocal version of Bristow's patriotic *Keep Step with the Music of Union* appeared in the 1865 *Centennial School Singer*, ed. William Oland Bourne and George H. Curtis (New York: Wm. A. Pond, 1865).

16. DeVenney, 37–38.

17. ALS, Bristow to Lee and Walker, Aug. 6, 1875; ALS, Lee and Walker to Simon Gratz Esq., Aug. 9, 1875; ALS, Bristow to Graft, Aug. 18, 1875; all in Simon Graft Papers, case 13, box 4. Musicians and Composers, Historical Society of Philadelphia. There are copies of these letters in the Gohari Collection.

18. Ezra Schabas, *Theodore Thomas: America's Conductor and Builder of Orchestras* (Urbana: University of Illinois Press, 1989), 71, 199. See also Shadle, 268.

19. "New York Musical Notes," *BU*, April 5, 1876.

20. DeVenney, 38.

21. "Up in Busy Harlem," *NYTrib*, May 6, 1890, 5; "Bristow's Great Republic," *NYH*, Feb. 22, 1891, 8; "A Teachers' Benefit Concert," *NYH*, May 7, 1892, 8. A program from this concert is in the Bristow Collection, Additions.

22. "Prejudice and Principle," *MTR*, May 24, 1879, 8; "Gilmore in Philadelphia," *NYH*, July 4, 1876, 8; "Steinway Hall—Musical Fund Concert," *NYH*, March 2, 1873, 5. Bristow and another pianist performed *The Great Republic: Allegory and Tableaux* in a benefit concert on December 13, 1871, at the Academy of Music; this may have been an early version of the work. "Amusements," *NYT*, Dec. 13, 1871, 7.

23. "Steinway Hall—Musical Fund Concert," *NYH*, March 2, 1873, 5; Curtis, 692.

24. "Local Miscellany," Jan. 30, 1876, 7, and "Amusements," Feb. 20, 1876, 11, both in *NYT*; "The Last Philharmonic Concert," *BDE*, May 11, 1879, 3.

25. "Prejudice and Principle," *MTR*, May 24, 1879, 8; "Excursions," July 1, 1881 [2] and Aug. 16, 1890 [1], both in *NYH*. Program from the August 27 performance is in the Manuscript Society Collection, NYPL. Microfilm *ZB561.

26. According to *Leslie's*, in March 1871 Bristow was "nearly finished" with the work, which had not yet been split into two parts. "Musical and Dramatic," *Leslie's*, March 11, 1871, 423.

27. The holograph full score of the *Arcadian* is extant; for *The Pioneer* only six manuscript vocal parts are extant (solo soprano and bass, parts for SATB chorus), in piano/vocal format.

28. Curtis, 563.

29. Rogers, 177.

30. Bristow was then director of the Harlem Mendelssohn Union but may have considered it insufficiently robust to tackle a work of this nature.

31. "Concerning Music," *BDE*, Oct. 4, 1872. George Macfarren told Bristow that Henri Herz, who paid him thirty dollars for his "Chevy Chase" overture, was "the only man in America who ever paid him for a composition." Quigg, *AM* I: 7.

32. "A New Club—The Arcadians," *NYT*, May 18, 1872, 5; "Amusements," *BDU*, Feb. 10, 1873; "Philharmonic," *BDE*, Jan. 14, 1873; "Arcadian Club," *NYH*, May 20, 1872, 5.

33. Johnson (92) erroneously credits Theodore Thomas with conducting both this performance and that by the Philharmonic Society of New York a year later.

34. Program, Feb. 14, 1874, https://archives.nyphil.org; Shadle, 174.

35. Shadle, 175. The Philharmonic Society performed Schumann's Symphony in 1861, 1866, and 1871.

36. Michael Pisani, "'I'm an Indian too': Creating Native American Identities in Nine-

teenth- and Early Twentieth-Century Music," *The Exotic in Western Music*, ed. Jonathan Bellman, 218–57 (Boston: Northeastern University Press, 1998), 242.

37. This symphony is available on LP. (See the Discography.)

38. "Progress of Instrumental Music in America," *NYH*, Nov. 10, 1872, 8.

39. "Philharmonic," *BDE*, Jan. 14, 1873; "Amusements: The Philharmonic Rehearsal," *BDU*, Jan. 23, 1873. Douglas Shadle (176n10) erroneously cites the *BDU* of January 16 for this quote.

40. "Philharmonic," *BDE*, Feb. 10, 1873; "Musical Correspondence," *DJM*, March 8, 1873, 399; "Philharmonic," *BDE*, Jan. 16, 1873.

41. *BDE*, Feb. 10, 1873; *DJM*, March 8, 1873; "Amusements," *BDU*, Feb. 10, 1873.

42. "Philharmonic," *BDE*, Feb. 18, 1874. Thanks to Douglas Shadle for sharing this and the other Brooklyn reviews with me. "Record of Amusements: Musical," *NYT*, Feb. 15, 1874, 5; "Philharmonic Rehearsal," *NYH*, Feb. 7, 1874, 7; "Music," *Appleton's*, March 7, 1874, 317.

43. "Music and the Drama," *NYTrib*, Feb. 16, 1874, 7; Shadle, 177.

44. Letter to the London *Musical Standard* dated May 9, *DJM*, June 27, 1874, 251.

45. "Record of Amusements. Musical: The Philharmonic Concert," *NYT*, April 25, 1880, 9.

46. James Dobes Reitzell, "Boise, Otis Bardwell," *AGII*. For Bassford and Pease, see Bomberger, *Brainard's Biographies*.

47. "Eleventh Peabody Concert—American Night," *Baltimore Sun*, March 15, 1875 [4].

48. "The Bristow Testimonial Concert," *NYTrib*, Dec. 16, 1875, 4.


**INTERLUDE D.** *Bristow as Businessman and Musical Authority*

1. "Musical Instruments: Piano-Fortes," *NYT*, April 10, 1854, 5. *Trow's City Directory*, 1854–1855; 1855–1856. Bristow's abode on Broome Street was across the street from where his family had lived in the mid-1840s.

2. Quigg, *AM* V: 7. At the end of the Pyne and Harrison Opera Company season in November 1855, the principals invited Bristow to continue as their conductor and accompany them on what would be a fabulously successful tour (1855–1856). Because of the recent failure of the piano business, Bristow decided that he had to remain in New York "to repair his shattered fortune," and recommended Anthony Reiff Jr, the son of his good friend Reiff Sr. It is interesting to speculate what a difference such an experience might have had on Bristow's life. I write about the tour in *OoR*.

3. Advertisements, *NYT*, Jan. 29, 1863, 7; and *NYTrib*, May 26, 1864, 3.

4. "Weber's New Piano-Forte Manufactury," *WAJ*, Aug. 24, 1867, 281–82.

5. "Miscellaneous," *NYH*, Sept. 21, 1867, 3; "Amusements," *NYT*, May 7, 1867, 7; "Distribution of Pianofortes," *AAJ*, May 18, 1867, 58; "Soiree and Distribution of Pianofortes," and "The Week," *WAJ*, Oct. 12, 1867, 382, and Dec. 7, 1867, 104.

6. Bristow, "Life," 60–61.

7. "The Centennial Exhibition, Philadelphia, PA," http://www.lcpimages.org/centennial (accessed Jan. 21, 2019); Cynthia Adams Hoover, "The Great Piano War of the 1870s," in *A Celebration of American Music: Words and Music in Honor of H. Wiley Hitchcock*, ed. Richard

Crawford, Allen Lott, and Carol J. Oja (Ann Arbor: University of Michigan Press, 1990), 136; "The Exhibition," *NYH*, July 16, 1876, 4.

8. Hoover, 133, 139.

9. Ibid., 142, Oliver Obituary, *Bay State Monthly* iii: 4 (Sept. 1885); Margaret Cranmer, "Schiedmayer," *GMO*; *NYH*, July 16, 1876; "The Piano War: Letter of George F. Bristow Defending Himself," *NYH*, July 19, 1876, 3.

10. "The Piano War," interview with Bristow, *NYT*, Oct. 27, 1876, 5. Hoover also provides a clear description of the judging process. Hoover, 141–42.

11. For accusations, see *NYH*, July 16, 1876; for denial, see "Explanation of Steinway & Sons," *NYH*, July 19, 1876, 3; for collusion, see "The William Steinway Diary, 1861–1896," entries for June 7, 8, 15, 16, 26, and later. See https://americanhistory.si.edu/steinwaydiary/diary.

12. "Piano Frauds and the Exhibition," *NYH*, July 16, 1876, 6; and "The Piano War," July 19, 1876.

13. "The Alleged Piano Frauds," *NYH*, July 19, 1876, 4. Articles in the *Times*, *Tribune*, *Herald*, and other newspapers kept the controversy alive as late as November and December 1877; lawsuits prolonged it even further.

**CHAPTER 6.** *The 1880s and 1890s*

1. The 1880 total was aided by the addition in 1874 of the Bronx (population in 1870: 37,000). http://www.demographia.com/dm-nyc.htm.

2. Mary Sue Morrow, "Somewhere between Beer and Wagner: The Cultural and Musical Impact of German Männerchöre in New York and New Orleans," in *Music and Culture in America, 1861–1918*, ed. Michael Saffle, 79–110 (New York: Routledge, 1998).

3. The number of performances for each ensemble is confirmed by "Mr. Damrosch's Projects," Oct. 9, 1889, 5, and "Amusements: Notes of the Stage," Oct. 6, 1889, 2, both in *NYT*.

4. "Live Musical Topics," *NYT*, April 27, 1890, 11.

5. For further information on the "Wagnerization" of the United States, see my *OfP*, especially chapters 3, the end of chapter 5 (389), and chapter 6. For Seidl's impact (and a somewhat different interpretation), see Joseph Horowitz, *Wagner Nights* (Berkeley: University of California Press, 1994), and *Moral Fire: Musical Portraits from America's Fin de Siècle* (Berkeley: University of California Press, 2013), especially chapters 2 and 3.

6. "Discussing Wagner: Members of the Nineteenth Century Club Listen to a Debate," *NYT*, Dec. 10, 1885, 5; and "Personal Mention," *Hartford (CT) Courant*, Nov. 16, 1885, 1.

7. See, in particular, chapter 6 in *OfP*.

8. Quigg, *AM* I: 7; "Bristow's New Choral Symphony, 'Niagara,'" *AAJ*, June 6, 1896, 130–31; "Mr. Bristow's Benefit," *NYT*, Feb 23, 1887, 4.

9. Curtis, 563–64.

10. "Instruction," April 11, 1880, 9, and "Amusements," April 13, 1890, 8, both in *NYH*.

11. "The Messiah," *NYT*, Jan. 7, 1890, 4.

12. "The Philharmonic Society Singers," *NYT*, Feb. 18, 1892, 9.

13. This does not take into consideration the several concerts he missed in 1854 and 1855.

14. "Correspondence—1870–1908 regarding Personnel, Artists, and Soloists" and Programs, March 11 and April 15, 1882, https://archives.nyphil.org. Orchestral musicians were paid a dividend at the end of the season—the balance left in the treasury divided by the number of performers. There are no annual reports for 1875–1883, so what Bristow might have been paid in 1882 is a guess. In 1875 his dividend was less than $40 (just under $1,000 in 2019 terms); in 1884 he would have been paid almost $190 (or around $5,100 in 2019). Rogers (131). erroneously states that Bristow resigned from the orchestra in 1879.

15. After 1866–1867 (when Thomas took over), the members of the orchestra are no longer named on programs of the Brooklyn orchestra. See http://levyarchive.BAM.org.

16. Douglas Bomberger, *"A Tidal Wave of Encouragement": American Composers' Concerts in the Gilded Age* (Westport, CT: Praeger Press, 2002), 145; description of purpose is from undated Prospectus, Clipping File, Manuscript Society, PAL/NYPL.

17. Rogers, 135–36; Public Programs, 1890–1891 to 1897–1898, Manuscript Society Collection.

18. The precise number of songs and piano works is difficult to determine, for additional sheet music imprints continue to surface in sheet music collections, copyright deposits, and so forth.

19. See the Discography.

20. Adrienne Fried Block, "Dvořák's Long Reach," in *Dvořák in America*, ed. John C. Tibbetts, 157–81 (Portland, OR: Amadeus Press, 1993); Shadle, 242–62; "Real Value of Negro Melodies," *NYH*, May 21, 1893, 28. Bomberger points out that Dvořák's pronouncement reflected established European views of nationalism. *"Tidal Wave,"* 170.

21. "Dvorak's Theory Not New" (letter from A. Thompson), and "Criticisms on Dvorak's Theory," *NYH*, June 4, 1893, 10.

22. For Phelps, see Shadle, 205–210.

23. Rogers (197–98) assigns op. 74 to an unknown song, "Remember Me," which he includes on a list of "unlocated titles accredited to Bristow."

24. The copyright date stamp is from Oliver Ditson. Apparently, however, it was never published.

25. For immediate reaction to Dvořák's pronouncement by Boston composers, see the *Boston Herald*, May 28, 1893. This is reprinted with commentary in Adrienne Fried Block's "Boston Talks Back to Dvořák," *I.S.A.M. Newsletter* xviii: 2 (May 1989): 10–11, 15 (available online at http://www.brooklyn.cuny.edu/web/aca_centers_hitchcock/NewsS89.pdf). For an intriguing reexamination of the Dvořák controversy that takes into consideration earlier attempts by American orchestral composers to use either "negro melodies" or inspiration from Native Americans, see Shadle, chapter 12 (242–62). Another criticism of the implied primacy of Dvořák's "discovery" is A. J. Goodrich, "Is There a Basis for American Music?" *AAJ*, Jan. 6, 1894, 260.

26. The copyright application for the revised libretto, dated September 13, 1882, is in the Bristow Collection, Additions. For Shannon, see *Munsey's Magazine*, Sept. 1893, 683.

27. Ledbetter, "Bristow," *NGDO*; "Notes," *BDE*, Feb. 20, 1887, 10; "Editorial Notes," *MH*, April 1881, 79.

28. "Notes of the Week," *NYT*, Sept. 21, 1890, 13. Steven Ledbetter (x) erroneously gives the date of the New York Banks Glee Club concert as December 11. A program from the concert is in the Bristow Collection, Additions. Reviews are in both the *NYH* and the

*NYTrib*, "Banks Glee Club Concert," Dec. 10, 1898, 12 and 2, respectively. The only modern performance of the opera was by the University of Illinois's American Music Group, Neely Bruce, director, on February 2, 1974. A program from this performance is in the Bristow Collection, Additions.

29. Rogers, 135; "World's Fair Music," *CIO*, Oct. 29, 1893, 25. Johnson, 91; a program from the 1894 concert is in Bristow Collection, Additions. There is a partial transcription of the overture for piano (dated 1886).

30. The best source of information on Bristow's mass is Bailey.

31. "Daniel," *WAJ*, Jan. 4, 1868, 158; "Intellectual Advancement of Music in America," *WAJ*, Jan. 18, 1868, 182.

32. "Musical and Dramatic Notes," *NYH*, Jan. 17, 1874, 3; *Musical Items*, Sept. 1884, quoted in Rogers, 194.

33. "Death of a Well-Known Musician," *BDE*, Aug. 19, 1867, 2.

34. Paine: *Mass in D* (piano-vocal score) (New York: Beer and Schirmer, 1866). Also see David P. DeVenney, "A Conductor's Study of the 'Mass in D' by John Knowles Paine," DMA diss, University of Cincinnati, 1989, 11, 12–13; for Dossert, see Bailey, x, n3.

35. Bailey, x; Upton, 171, 253. About Whiting, see William Osborne, "Whiting, George E.," *GMO*; John Tasker Howard, "Whiting," *DAB*; and Bailey, x, n3.

36. Bailey, 58–59. The girls of the school (seven to seventeen years old) performed "Come Let Us Sing unto the Lord," an adaptation of the "celebrated and difficult Cannon [*sic*]" from the mass. See "Commencement of Ward School No. 42," *NYDTrib*, July 15, 1865, 6; Advertisement, *WAJ*, May 23, 1866, 79. For the excavation of much of the very useful information in this paragraph I am indebted to Bailey; see 55–59.

37. For a thorough discussion of influences on the Mass, see Bailey, 58.

38. Bailey, 58–59, 60–63; see also his examination of Beethoven's influence on the Mass, 60–80.

39. Bailey, 85.

40. The world premiere of this work was scheduled for March 13, 2020, in Cleveland, Ohio, by Choral Arts Cleveland (with organ accompaniment) and conducted by Prof. Brian Bailey. Because of the coronavirus pandemic, this performance was postponed to a later date that, by press time, had not been announced. Email correspondence with Bailey, March 7, 12, 31 and April 13, 2020; Bailey, 41.

41. For a discussion of this performance, see Bailey, 93–94. The orchestral accompaniment to the Benedictus has a solo line for cello, which, in the transcription for organ, is indicated by the suggestion of a gamba stop (89). Bailey suggests that a small group of string players might have accompanied the Benedictus; there are individual string parts for the movement in the Bristow Collection at the NYPL. The orchestration of the Benedictus would make viable a performance without winds or brass. Email from Bailey, June 6, 2019.

42. This two-part structure is indicated on the program for the premiere performance, April 11, 1898, Bristow Collection, Additions.

43. "Bristow's New Choral Symphony, 'Niagara,'" *AAJ*, April 2, 1898, 402–403, Bristow Collection, Additions.

44. Cloeter, 36–37; Fried, 87; Shadle, 258.

45. *AAJ*, April 2, 1898. For more information on Lord, see Cloeter, 149–50; for further analysis of the text, see 150.

46. For some of this discussion I rely on the observations of Denise Von Glahn, *The Sounds of Place: Music and the American Cultural Landscape* (Boston: Northeastern University Press, 2004), 53.

47. The best analysis of the *Niagara* (especially the fourth movement) is Cloeter's dissertation. See *AAJ*, April 2, 1898. Thoms erroneously describes the brass quartet as comprised of trombones and tuba, perhaps confusing this with Bristow's use of those instruments in Part 2, No. 5; Cloeter (126) corrects this.

48. *AAJ*, April 2, 1898.

49. The British Library has copies of "Long, Long Ago"; the earliest date is 1835 (?). Digital copies of American imprints are in the Levy Collection at Johns Hopkins University. "Near the Lake" is an arrangement by Charles Edward Horn (New York: Hewitt and Jacques, 1839). Thoms identifies this tune in his April 1, 1898, description of the symphony.

50. For a close analysis of the cyclic reuse of material, see Cloeter, 120–26. He also points outs that the printed program includes some errors about the fourth movement; see 33–34.

51. Von Glahn, 60. Lake St. Claire, while part of the Great Lakes system, is a much smaller body of water located between lakes Huron and Erie. Missing from the list, of course, is Lake Ontario.

52. Cloeter, 30.

53. Minutes, March 24 and Jan. 7, 1898, Manuscript Society of New York Collection. Minutes (1896–1912).

54. Rogers, 135; Cloeter, 32; Minutes, Jan. 7 and March 3, 1898, Manuscript Society of New York. Thoms repeated this call for support in "Bristow's Choral Symphony in Rehearsal," *AAJ*, April 2, 1898, 403.

55. Horowitz, *Wagner Nights*, 249–50; Cloeter, 29.

56. Von Glahn concluded that the concert did not occur. But there is a short report of the performance (not a review) in the *New York World*, April 12, 1898, 8, that confirms that it took place. Von Glahn, 58–59. Thanks to Douglas Shadle for a copy of this notice.

57. Manuscript Society Minutes, May 9, 1898.

58. Shadle, 258; "George Frederick Bristow," *Choir Leader* v: 10 (Dec. 1898): 1–2

59. "Bristow's New Choral Symphony," *AAJ*, June 6, 1896, and April 2, 1898.

60. "Bristow's Last Work: The 'Niagara' Choral Symphony," *AAJ*, Jan. 7, 1899, 210–11.

## Conclusion

1. John C. Freund, "The Passing Show," *MA*, i: 12 (Dec. 24, 1898), 5.

2. ALS, Bristow to Estelle Bristow Dearborn, Bristow Collection, Additions.

3. George Bristow Dearborn (1897–1952) was born in November 1897. His dates are from various historical records (1910 Federal Census; New York State Birth Certificate, etc.) available via www.ancestry.com and in the Gohari Collection. He was the first child of Estelle Viola and William Dearborn, who were married in 1895; his younger sister was

named Violet (ca. 1901–1976). See Church Records (St. Mark's, Jersey City), Episcopal Diocese of Newark, and 1905 New York Census, available via www.ancestry.com.

4. The cause of death was general arteriosclerosis. Death certificate, Bristow Collection, Additions.

5. Program is in Bristow Collection, Additions.

6. Unidentified obituary, Dec. 18, 1898, in Bristow Collection, Additions.

7. William Thoms, "Death of George F. Bristow, American Composer," *AAJ*, Dec. 17, 1898, 162–63; "George F. Bristow," *Music*, Feb. 1899, 471; William James Henderson, "In the World of Music," *NYT*, Dec. 18, 1898, 6; Freund, "Passing Show"; Henderson, "World of Music." The Department of Education of the City of New York acknowledged this service by naming a street and an elementary school (PS 134, on 1330 Bristow Street in the Bronx) in his honor. Attempts to discover any additional information about the naming of the school proved fruitless.

8. Freund, "Passing Show"; "Bristow," *Music*; F. O. Jones, A *Handbook of American Music and Musicians* (New York: Da Capo Press, 1971; originally published 1886).

9. Henderson, "World of Music"; Thoms, "Death of Bristow"; "George Frederick Bristow," *Choir Leader* v: 10 (Dec. 1898); Jones.

10. "New York Banks Glee Club: A Bristow in Memoriam," *AAJ*, Feb. 18, 1899, and ALS, S. N. Penfield to Mrs. G. F. Bristow, Dec. 18, 1898, both in Bristow Collection, Additions. Penfield was also former president of the MTNA and an early member (and officer) of the Manuscript Society.

11. "George F. Bristow" (obituary), *Music* (1899), 471–73 (quote on 473).

# DISCOGRAPHY

*Orchestral Music*

### SYMPHONY NO. 2 ("JULLIEN" SYMPHONY)

*Symphony No. 2 in D Minor, op. 24 ("Jullien")* (1853). Royal Philharmonic Orchestra, Karl Krueger, conductor. Society for the Preservation of American Music, MIA 143 [1969] (LP)

*George Frederick Bristow, Symphony No. 2 ("Jullien")*, plus *Overture to Rip Van Winkle* and *Winter's Tale Overture*. Royal Northern Sinfonia Orchestra, Rebecca Miller, conductor. New World Records, 80768-2 (CD)

### SYMPHONY NO. 3 IN F-SHARP MINOR, OP. 26

*Symphony No. 3 in F-sharp Minor, op. 26* (1858), Royal Philharmonic Orchestra, Karl Krueger, conductor. Society for the Preservation of American Music, MIA 144 [1969] (LP)

*Symphony No. 3: Nocturne* and *Scherzo*. Royal Philharmonic Orchestra, Karl Krueger, conductor. Society for the Preservation of American Music, MIA 129 [1966] (LP); misidentified as Bristow's "Symphony No. 6"

*Symphony in F-sharp Minor, op. 26*. Detroit Symphony Orchestra, Neeme Järvi, conductor. Chandos 9169 (1993) (CD)

### SYMPHONY NO. 4 ("ARCADIAN")

*Arcadian Symphony: The Pioneer, op. 49 (1872)*. Royal Philharmonic Orchestra, Karl Krueger, conductor. Society for the Preservation of American Music, MIA 135 (1967) (LP). This recording is also available on YouTube.

### OVERTURES

*Rip Van Winkle Overture*. See *George Frederick Bristow, Symphony No. 2 ("Jullien")*. New World Records, 80768-2 (CD)

*Winter's Tale Overture*. See *George Frederick Bristow, Symphony No. 2 ("Jullien")*. New World Records, 80768-2 (CD)

*Vocal Music*

*The Oratorio of Daniel, op. 42* (1868). Albany Pro Musica and Catskill Choral Society. Albany, NY: Albany Pro Musica. APM-97-2, 1997 (CD)

"Praise to God" and "We Praise Thee." *Nineteenth-Century American Sacred Music: From Fuguing Tune to Oratorio.* Folkways FTS 32381 (LP) and Smithsonian Folkways F-32381 (CD)

*Keyboard Music*

"Andante et Polonaise," op. 18. *Piano Music in America, Volume 1: 19th Century Concert & Parlor Music.* Neely Bruce, piano. SVB 5302 (LP).

"Dream land." *The Wind Demon, and Other 19th-Century Piano Music.* Ivan Davis, piano. New World Records 80257-2 (CD)

Six Pieces for the Organ, op. 45: No. 1 (F Major), No. 4 (G Minor), No. 6 (C Major). *Anthology of American Organ Music*, vol. 2, *The Nineteenth Century.* Janice Beck, organ. Musical Heritage Society ORA-263 (LP)

*Chamber Music*

Quartet No. 2, op. 2. There is only a nonprofessional recording of this quartet, by the Cremona Quartet, which performed the work at Queensborough Community College in 1979. I was given a copy by one of the members of the ensemble.

# SELECTED BIBLIOGRAPHY

*Databases Consulted*

Ancestry.com. https://www.ancestry.com

Brooklyn Newsstand (Brooklyn Public Library). https://bklyn.newspapers.com/#

Centennial Exhibition. http://www.lcpimages.org/centennial

Commonwealth of Pennsylvania. https://babel.hathitrust.org/cgi/pt?id=uc1.b3830857;
   view=1up;seq=352

Cooper Institute. https://Cooper.edu/about/history

Harmonia Sacred Music Society of Philadelphia. https://archive.org/details/addon100harm/
   page/n1

*Lester S. Levy Sheet Music Collection, Johns Hopkins University.* https://levysheetmusic.mse
   .jhu.edu

*Music in Gotham.* https://www.musicingotham.org

Music Teachers National Association (MTNA) (via Hathitrust). https://babel.hathitrust
   .org/cgi/pt?id=nyp.33433082279120;view=1up;seq=1

New York City population sites: http://www.demographia.com/dm-nyc.htm; https://www1
   .nyc.gov/assets/planning/download/pdf/data-maps/nyc-population/historical
   -population/1790-2000_nyc_total_foreign_birth.pdf

New York Philharmonic Society. https://archives.nyphil.org

Philharmonic Society of Brooklyn: Brooklyn Academy of Music. http://levyarchive.bam.org

Steinway Diaries. https://americanhistory.si.edu/steinwaydiary/diary

*City Directories*

*Doggett's New York City Directory.* New York: John Doggett, 1846–1847.

*Longworth's American Almanac, New-York Register and City Directory.* New York: T. Longworth, 1816–1847.

*New York City Directory for 1854–55.* New York: Charles R Rode.

*Smith's Brooklyn Directory* (1856–1883). https://archive.org/details/brooklynpubliclibrary
   ?&sort=date&page=2.

*Spooner's Brooklyn Directory.* https://catalog.hathitrust.org/Record/100216278.

188

*Trow's New York City Directories.* https://digitalcollections.nypl.org/collections/new-york
-city-directories#/?tab=about.

*Valentine's Manual (Manual of the Corporation of the City of New York, 1854–1898).* https://archive
.org/stream/manualofcorporat1864newy#page/286/mode/2up. Also https://catalog
.hathitrust.org/Record/008607621.

*Primary and Secondary Sources*

Anstice, Henry. *History of St. George's Church in the City of New York.* New York: Harper &
Brothers, 1911.

Bailey, Brian Keith. "George Bristow's *Mass in C* for Choir and Orchestra (1885): Critical
Edition and Commentary." DMA diss., University of Iowa, 2016.

Boese, Thomas. *Public Education in the City of New York: Its History, Condition, and Statistics.*
New York: Harper & Brothers, 1869.

Bomberger, E. Douglas, ed. *Brainard's Biographies of American Musicians.* Westport, CT:
Greenwood, 1999.

———. *"A Tidal Wave of Encouragement": American Composers' Concerts in the Gilded Age.*
Westport, CT: Praeger, 2002.

Bristow, George F. "The Life of a Musician. His Troubles & Trials &c." Manuscript [1867?].
Bristow Collection, Additions, New York Public Library.

———. "Music in the Public Schools of New York." *The Ninth Annual Meeting of the Music
Teachers National Association Official Report.* New York: Music Teachers National Association, 1885.

Chase, Gilbert. *America's Music: From the Pilgrims to the Present,* rev. 3rd ed. Urbana: University of Illinois Press, 1987.

Cloeter, Timothy J. "A Performance Edition of the Fourth Movement of the *Niagara Symphony,* Op. 62, by George Frederick Bristow (1825–1898)." DMA diss., University of
Arizona, 2016.

Curtis, G. H. "George Frederick Bristow." *Music* 3 (1893): 547–64.

DeVenney, David P. *Varied Carols: A Survey of American Choral Literature.* Westport, CT:
Greenwood, 1999.

Dox, Thurston. *American Oratorios and Cantatas: A Catalog of Works Written in the United
States from Colonial Times to 1985.* 2 vols. Metuchen, NJ: Scarecrow Press, 1986.

———. "George Frederick Bristow and the New York Public Schools." *American Music* 9,
no. 4 (1991): 339–52.

Fried, Gregory Martin. "A Study of the Orchestral Music of George Frederick Bristow."
DMA diss., University of Texas, 1989.

Gohari, Carol Elaine. "George Frederick Bristow: Incidental Gleanings." *Sonneck Society
for American Music Bulletin* 25 (Summer 1999): 37–39.

Griggs-Janower, David. *The Oratorio of Daniel.* Madison, WI: A-R Editions, 1999.

———. "Rescued from the Fiery Furnace: George Frederick Bristow's *Oratorio of Daniel.*"
*Choral Journal* 38, no. 9 (April 1998): 9–21.

Hoover, Cynthia Adams. "The Great Piano War of the 1870s." In *A Celebration of American Music: Words and Music in Honor of H. Wiley Hitchcock,* edited by Richard Crawford,
R. Allen Lott, and Carol J. Oja, 132–53. Ann Arbor: University of Michigan Press, 1990.

Hopkins, Robert J. E. "String Chamber Music Performance in New York City, 1842–52: The Social and Cultural Context of Representative Works by George Frederick Bristow." DMA diss., University of Illinois, 2014.

Horowitz, Joseph. *Wagner Nights*. Berkeley: University of California Press, 1994.

Johnson, H. Earle. *First Performances in America to 1900: Works with Orchestra*. Detroit: Published for the College Music Society by Information Coordinators, 1979.

Jones, F. O. *A Handbook of American Music and Musicians*. New York: Da Capo Press, 1971; originally published 1886.

Krehbiel, Henry Edward. *The Philharmonic Society of New York: A Memorial*. New York: Novello, Ewer & Co., 1892; reprinted in *Early Histories of the New York Philharmonic*, ed. Howard Shanet. New York: Da Capo Press, 1979.

Lawrence, Vera Brodsky. *Strong on Music: The New York Music Scene in the Days of George Templeton Strong*. Vol. 1. *Resonances: 1836–1850*. New York: Oxford University Press, 1988.

———. *Strong on Music*. Vol. 2. *Reverberations: 1850–1856*. Chicago: University of Chicago Press, 1995.

———. *Strong on Music*. Vol. 3. *Repercussions: 1857–1862*. Chicago: University of Chicago Press, 1999.

Ledbetter, Steven, ed. *Rip Van Winkle: Grand Romantic Opera in Three Acts*. New York: Da Capo Press, 1991.

Messiter, Arthur Henry, *A History of the Choir and Music of Trinity Church, New York*. New York: Edwin S. Gorham, 1906.

Moss, Brandon. "George F. Bristow's *Praise to God*: An Analysis and Historical Commentary." DMA diss., Ohio State University, forthcoming 2020.

Odell, George C. D. *Annals of the New York Stage*. 15 vols. New York: Columbia University Press, 1927–1949.

Orr, N. Lee. *Dudley Buck*. Urbana: University of Illinois Press, 2008.

———. "The United States." In *Nineteenth-Century Choral Music*, edited by Donna M. Di Grazia, 475–99. New York: Routledge, 2013.

Pratt, Waldo Selden, ed. *Grove's Dictionary of Music and Musicians: American Supplement*. New York: Macmillan, 1944.

Preston, Katherine K. "American Orchestral Music at the Middle of the Nineteenth Century. Louis Antoine Jullien and George Bristow's Jullien Symphony." Introductory monograph to *Bristow's Symphony No. 2 ("Jullien"): A Critical Edition*, in *Music of the United States of America*. Vol. 23. Middleton, WI: A-R Editions, 2011.

———. "Art Music from 1800 to 1860." In *Cambridge History of American Music*, edited by David Nicholls, 188–213. London: Cambridge University Press, 1998.

———. "'A Concentration of Talent on Our Musical Horizon': The 1853–54 American Tour by Jullien's Extraordinary Orchestra." In *American Orchestras in the 19th Century*, edited by John Spitzer, 319–47. Chicago: University of Chicago Press, 2012.

———. "Encouragement from an Unexpected Source: Louis Antoine Jullien, Mid-Century American Composers, and George Frederick Bristow's *Jullien Symphony*." *Nineteenth-Century Music Review* 6, no. 1 (2009): 65–87.

———. *Opera for the People: English-Language Opera and Women Managers in Late 19th-Century America*. New York: Oxford University Press, 2017.

————. *Opera on the Road: Traveling Opera Troupes in the United States, 1825–1860.* Urbana: University of Illinois Press, 1993.

Quigg, J. Travis. Series of interviews with Bristow in *American Musician*, Sept.–Dec. 1888. (See Abbreviations table in Notes).

Ravitch, Diane. *The Great School Wars: A History of the New York Public Schools, 1805–1973.* New York: Basic Books, 1988.

Ritter, Frédéric Louis. *Music in America.* New York: Charles Scribner's Sons, 1895; revised edition.

Rogers, Delmer Dalzell. "Nineteenth-Century Music in New York City as Reflected in the Career of George Frederick Bristow." PhD diss., University of Michigan, 1967.

Scharf, J. Thomas. *History of Westchester County, New York, Including Morrisania, Kings Bridge, and West Farms, Which Have Been Annexed to New York City.* Philadelphia: L. E. Preston, 1886.

Shadle, Douglas. *Orchestrating the Nation: The Nineteenth-Century American Symphonic Enterprise.* New York: Oxford University Press, 2016.

Shanet, Howard. *Philharmonic: A History of New York's Orchestra.* New York: Doubleday, 1975.

Smither, Howard E. *History of the Oratorio.* Vol. 4. *The Oratorio in the Nineteenth and Twentieth Centuries.* Chapel Hill: University of North Carolina Press, 2000.

Upton, William Treat. *William Henry Fry: American Journalist and Composer-Critic.* New York: Da Capo Press, 1974; originally published 1954.

Von Glahn, Denise. *The Sounds of Place: Music and the American Cultural Landscape.* Boston: Northeastern University Press, 2004.

Yellin, Victor Fell. "Bristow's Divorce." *American Music* 12, no. 3 (1994): 229–54.

# INDEX

146–49; *Niagara Symphony*, 135, 146, 147, 148–49; *Seventh Regiment March*, 135

Mapleson, James, 133

Mapleson's Her Majesty's Italian Opera Company (1885–1886), 133

Maretzek, Max, 9, 26, 48

Maretzek Italian Opera Company, 26

Marks, Henry, 159n13

Marschner, Heinrich August, 18

Mason, Lowell, 67, 96

Mason, William, 10, 64. 101, 125; *Serenade*, 162n59

Maurer, Ludwig: *Concertante for Four Violins and Orchestra*, 12

Meiggs, Henry, 21, 106

Meignen, Leopold, 64–65; Double Quartett (vocal) dedicated to Bristow, 65

Mendelssohn, Felix, 16, 17, 28, 39, 58, 73, 90; *Athalie* (cantata), 87, 94; *Elijah* (oratorio), 48, 50, 91, 92, 108, 174n58; influence on Bristow, 16, 29–31, 55–56, 57, 61–63, 86, 90–92, 143, 174n58; *Lobgesang*, 50; *Psalm 42*, 87; *St. Paul* (oratorio), 87

Mendelssohn Glee Club, 131

Mendelssohn Society, 132

Mendelssohn Union, 50, 72, 81, 94, 108; Bristow as director, 50, 87; founded by Morgan and Timm; merge with Harmonic Society, 86; performance of *Daniel*, 87, 89–93; repertory, 87, 94

Mercadante, Saverio, 82; *Il Bravo*, 123

Metropolitan Hall, 27, 51

Metropolitan Musical Society (chorus), 48, 63, 132

Metropolitan Opera Company (1884–1885, 1885–1886), 132, 133

Metropolitan Opera House, 130, 131, 132

Meyerbeer, Giacomo: *Les Huguenots* overture, 73

Meyrer, C. W., 8, 160n21

Mills, Sebastian Bach, 81, 125

Mollenhauer, Edward, 105, 126; concertos, 162n59

Mollenhauer's Conservatory of Music, 126

Moore, Thomas: "'Tis the Last Rose of Summer," 109

Morgan, George Washbourne, 86, 87, 125, 141; "America," arranged for organ, 123

Morgan, John Paul, 91

Morrisania Mendelssohn Union. *See* Harlem (Morrisania) Mendelssohn Union

Mosenthal, Robert: *Gloria*, 73

Mozart, Wolfgang Amadeus, 11, 17, 28, 50, 58, 158n6; influence on Bristow, 31, 56–57, 141; *Second Mass* "Gloria," 99; Symphony No. 39, 16

Mozart Hall, 48

Müller, Wenzel: *Twelfth Mass*, 141, 142

Music Hall, 114

Music Teachers National Association (MTNA), 84, 96, 151, 184n10

Musical Fund Society (New York), 63, 114; Bristow as officer, 58

Musgriff (Musgrif), William (Bristow teacher), 4–5, 6, 158n9, 159n10, 159n13

music schools and conservatories, NY, 103–6. *See also* American Musical Institute (1847); Brooklyn Female Academy; Cooper Union for the Advancement of Science and Art; Grand Conservatory of Music; Mollenhauer's Conservatory of Music; National Conservatory, New York College of Music; New York Conservatory

musical battle (1854: Bristow, Fry, Willis, and Dwight), 32–39, *34*, 165n30

Musical Fund Society (New York), 63, 114

Musical Fund Society (Philadelphia), 64, 114

**KATHERINE K. PRESTON** is a professor emerita of music at the College of William & Mary. Her six previous books and many edited volumes include *Opera for the People: English-Language Opera and Women Managers in Late Nineteenth-Century America* and *Opera on the Road: Traveling Opera Troupes in the United States, 1825–1860*.

The University of Illinois Press
is a founding member of the
Association of University Presses.

_____

University of Illinois Press
1325 South Oak Street
Champaign, IL 61820-6903
www.press.uillinois.edu